So You Can See In The Dark
and other indian essays

So You Can See In The Dark

and other indian essays

CLAUDIA HYLES

[signature: Claudia Hyles]

AUSTRALIAN SCHOLARLY

For Oscar, Maitland, Coco and Harry

© Claudia Hyles 2016

First published 2016 by Australian Scholarly Publishing Ltd
7 Lt Lothian St Nth, North Melbourne, Vic 3051
Tel: 03 9329 6963 / Fax: 03 9329 5452
enquiry@scholarly.info / www.scholarly.info

ISBN 978-1-925588-00-2

ALL RIGHTS RESERVED

Cover: Punjab, India or Pakistan. Ceremonial cover or woman's head covering mid-20th century. Cotton fabric, cotton yarns, silk floss; hand stitching, surface darning stitch and blanket-stitch, 223.0 h x 134.5 w cm. National Gallery of Australia, Canberra. Gift of Claudia Hyles 2006

Acknowledgements

Kind thanks to Anil Bhattacharji, Philip Flood AO, Emily Gibbs, Harry Gibbs, James Hyles, Brigid Keenan, Peter Rose, Penny Tideman, Rev. Robert Willson and the late Robyn Beeche

Contents

Paradise Gardens   1

So You Can See In The Dark   41

A Big Tamasha: Free Speech and Sectarian Tensions at the Jaipur Festival 2012   59

The Kumbh Mela   68

Cautionary Tales and Ripping Yarns   122

Being Carsick   185

From Greenland's Icy Mountains   201

Birds and Cosmic Eggs   236

Gone for Shopping   257

Krishna! Krishna!   291

Bibliography   319

About the Author   323

Paradise Gardens

MOST OF MY JOURNEYS TO INDIA end in the middle of the night at the Indira Gandhi International Airport at New Delhi. The next day always seems to dawn far too soon. Depending on whether I've slept or not I set off for a very early morning walk or else wait until after breakfast to stroll in the sunshine in the Lodi Gardens, a green haven covering 90 acres in south Delhi. Sometimes I stay in a slightly eccentric guesthouse located just a block away from the gardens, close to Safdarjang's Tomb. It is a great place, close to a remarkably uncrowded and unintimidating Post Office across Lodi Road which bounds the southern edge of the gardens, within easy walking distance of three good markets and near two Metro Stops which offer quick and easy access to just about anywhere in the city. Just don't exit on the wrong side at the Jorbagh Station though. What a nuisance that is, necessitating paying another fare just to walk through the station to the correct side of an otherwise completely uncrossable road.

The gardens enclose expanses of lawn, massive trees, dense shrubby thickets and a collection of beautiful monuments and tombs, some 500 years old. On weekends and holidays family groups picnic and children run about in a happily plastic-bag-free zone. Every morning it buzzes with joggers and walkers—some with dogs on leads, yoga and laughing clubs and groups of elderly men enjoying tea together. Once while walking with a friend, a young man pounded by on the jogger's track. 'Oh that's Aatish Taseer' she said. 'I've just reviewed his book' I said so she called him back and introduced us. It is the place to see who is back in town and as in one of Kushwant Singh's novels, to discover by absence, who has left for a heavenly abode. Sometimes the dewy lawns look too damp for the yoga practitioners but they seem unworried and often meet in the rose garden. Later in the day, as in all Indian public gardens, courting couples find secluded spots to sit and spoon, private space is hard to find.

The garden is full of birds which can be identified from picture-boards showing the resident species. Pigeons used to be fed messily on the stone parapets of the Athpula Bridge. Now it is prohibited and the area is beautifully clean with no bird-food or guano in sight. The pretty bridge whose name means eight-piered, spans the remains of a watercourse once connected to the Yamuna River but now sourced by a man-made reservoir. Some consider that 1968 addition unfortunate but it gives the lovely Athpula something to span. It was built by a nobleman, Nawab Bahadur, during the reign of the Mughul Emperor Akbar. A gateway and two small mosques in the gardens also date to the Mughul era, younger than the other monuments.

Mohammad Shah's 15th century tomb is the oldest of the ten structures and has recently been conserved and restored. The Sayyids established their Delhi sultanate after the collapse of the Tughlaqs. Mohammad Shah, third in the Sayyid dynasty, ruled from 1434 until 1444 and his octagonal tomb was built by his son, Alauddin Alam Shah. Eight, the paradisiacal number for Muslims, accounts for many octagonal tombs, the journey to the hereafter getting off to a good start. Mohammad Shah's sepulchre is unusually not encompassed by walls. It is located on a hillock surrounded by a wide green lawn and a line of royal palms, their uniform smooth grey trunks like pillars. Paradise gardens should contain palm trees but it is unlikely that the writers of the Qur'an had ever seen such palms as these stately Cuban natives which were planted in 1968.

The garden site is undulating with banks dense with trees screening one area from the next. Walks along the paths bring surprise vistas, mysterious tunnels of bamboo and sheltering shrubs. Flower beds where the sun reaches them, are full of blooms, exotic and indigenous. In season, gardenias the size of small saucers scent the air close to two neighbouring buildings named for their appearance, the Bada Gumbad or Big Dome and the Sheesh Gumbad or Glass Dome. They date to the Lodi Dynasty which succeeded the Sayyid in 1451. The Lodi's re-established the Delhi Sultanate which lasted seventy-five years until it fell to the Mughuls under Babur.

There are no graves within the Bada Gumbad which may have been a gateway. Facing it, the dome of the Sheesh Gumbad has remnants of the turquoise and cobalt-blue glazed tiles which once covered it. It contains several graves of unknown but surely eminent people from the time of Sikander Lodi.

Sikander, the second and most important of the Lodi's, lies in another octagonal tomb in the gardens' north-western corner, on a hill overlooking the duck pond. He was said to be an almost ideal ruler although ruthless on military campaigns. When not fighting, the brave and handsome king was described as charitable and just. Hindus were not writing the history books however and those who were, didn't mind countenancing his severe repression of non-Muslims. Entry to the tomb which contains his single grave, is through an elaborate gateway in high fortress-like walls. It is the earliest surviving enclosed garden tomb, similar though less elaborate to that of Mohammad Shah at the other end of the gardens. The shaded grassy garden enclosure surrounding the central tomb is green and peaceful.

The gardens were not always so charming. The current incarnation was designed as a setting for the scattering of old monuments when construction of Lutyens' new British Indian capital was nearing completion in 1931. South Delhi had been little affected by the grand design and the village of Khairpur was located in the centre of today's park in a scrubby, broken landscape. An old photograph shows the sentinel Bada Gumbad and Sheesh Gumbad at each end of a settlement of low huts. The villagers were resettled and a garden established with mainly native trees in a fairly unstructured landscape. Called The Lady Willingdon Park, it was inaugurated on 9 April 1936.

Lady Willingdon was the Viceroy's wife and a very determined person, described as 'pushful', autocratic, vulgar and imperious. Her meddlesome 'improvements' to his designs enraged Lutyens in both the vast interiors of the Viceroy's House and in its Mughul Garden. She cut down his shady eucalyptus trees, replacing them with unsuitable stiff cypresses and moved splendid stone elephants from the forecourt screen of the building to be placed like bits of random ornament in the garden, reducing them to garden gnome status. She was mad about the colour mauve and left a trail of it all over India—Lutyens called her 'the mauvey sujet'. I'm sure she was the model for Lady Montdore in Nancy Mitford's *Love in a Cold Climate* who shared the passion for mauve. The actors who played Lord and Lady Montdore In the 1980 television series even looked like the Willingdon's. Happily for Lutyens, Lord Linlithgow who succeeded Willingdon as Viceroy, invited him to undo the damage perpetrated by his nemesis. His plans were restored, the cypresses removed and the elephants returned to their original dignified place.

Inscribed on a gatepost at the north-western entrance to the gardens, close to Sikandar Lodi's tomb, Lady Willingdon's name remains, but in Post-Independence 1968 the gardens were formally and more appropriately renamed and redesigned by Joseph Stein, an American architect who spent forty years of his professional life in India. Before starting the park project he had been involved in designing many of the interesting new buildings nearby. The Indian International Centre was first and a consideration for its location had been the proximity to the gardens. Stein loved their soft quality of light, such a contrast to the 'harsh dust-laden atmosphere of the Delhi summer', the luminous patterns of soft green, the long shadows across the garden vistas and the contrast to the rugged stone walls of the tombs and the distinctive silhouettes of their domes. The repetitive shell structures he designed as eaves, roofs and shelters related to the domes and old walls provided a reference for modern textures.

The Indian International Centre was built between 1959 and 1962 as a conference and resource facility funded by the Rockefeller Foundation to promote international understanding and friendship. The Centre was intended as a modern extension to the gardens with a varying sequence of indoor and outdoor spaces, a feature of all Stein's Delhi works. His self-contained designs were never meant to impose. New gardens were conceived as a layer in an overall sequence, peeping in here, making more definite statements there, always part of the whole. Many traditional Indian buildings were planned around courtyards and Stein's designs were a sympathetic continuation. Interiors spread into out-door areas with the same wall and floor finishes.

Now I've learned more about Stein, I am delighted to think that my flat in Canberra is a bit Steinesque. Tiles start inside and continue onto the veranda, the walls are roughcast in and out and my doors open almost from floor to ceiling like some of Stein's early California houses. I have had little experience in making decisions about house design, living for many years in idiosyncratic rented accommodation overseas or unalterable houses at home. It would have been fun to renovate an old house but they don't exist in Canberra and I don't think I have the talent. I am in awe of friends who can plan a brand new house or have the vision to change awful into wonderful. I'm better at camouflage and endurance. Some of our rented houses had frightful features like a huge painting of stampeding elephants and an appalling bar in Nairobi; plush velvet upholstery like the pelts of lions and tigers in Port-of-Spain; an exploding stove, no fans, hot water service or security bars in Port Moresby; freezing temperatures and a Hiawatha wallpaper mural in Norfolk and no bathroom or kitchen in Tra Vinh.

In autumn last year as I walked down the drive of the Indian International Centre, several gorgeous pink floss-silk trees were in flower, marigolds bloomed in regiments of pots and the lawns were perfectly mown. An early visit more than twenty years ago was on a hazy winter afternoon, for tea with Jasleen Dhamija. As we sat down in cane chairs on the veranda she greeted a man at the next table who was Gandhiji's grandson. We went for a saunter in the gardens after tea and I was captivated—the tombs mistily looming in the weak winter sunshine were straight from a picture-book.

I have been back to the IIC many times. Once was to attend *New Horizons*, an interesting cultural conference arranged by the Australian High Commission in 1996. I attended sessions connected with the performing arts as I was then a board member of the Padma Menon Dance Company, a brave and innovative group. My friend Shama Chowhury was a speaker in a literature session along with David Malouf and other luminaries. I had just given Shama a copy of Malouf's *Remembering Babylon* which was a piece of good timing. The main sessions of the conference were held in the IIC's auditorium which has an interesting ceiling of pre-cast concrete lattice shells.

The performing arts sub-group migrated across a laneway to a seminar room in the Stein-designed UNICEF offices in Lodi Estate. Two short performances were staged with an unintended third by the Indian section of the audience. A group of men from Orissa had given a mesmerising presentation of their art, a silent balletic kind of gymnastics, strange but compelling. Then a young woman danced a solo piece of Kathakali. This stylised classical dance drama from Kerala is always performed by men who take even the female parts. It was extremely interesting to the foreigners and the dancer was professional and polished. At the conclusion however, both she and the gymnasts were pilloried by the Indians, verbally attacked in a very nasty way. So unpleasant, it became embarrassing until a huge young man, a member of Circus Oz, spoke up. He was wearing loose Indian clothes and looked a bit like Lord Siva with long dreadlocks swept up in a cone on the top of his head. Very politely he told them to drop it which they did with bad grace. The Indian chair had constantly talked over the top of Barry Kosky, the Australian chair, to the point where Barry lapsed into silence. The display was disgraceful but revealing. Life is competitive in India and Indian critics can be vicious.

I've been back to the IIC for other less controversial talks and performances but once, with Victoria and Alex to see Al Gore's film *An Inconvenient Truth* was very sad. Poor little Alex was about 14 and wept for days for the plight of the polar bears.

Extra accommodation at the IIC Annexe, charmingly pronounced Annexie, just down the road from the main buildings, is comfortable but not luxurious, hard beds and brown blankets. The dining room in the main building has a good view through the gardens, the height of all the Lodi Estate buildings is kept below the base of the domes of the Bada Gumbad and Sheesh Gumbad. Stein related his buildings to the landscape in an elemental way and with an understanding that embodied his clients' humanitarian, cultural and environmental aims. He and they arrived in post-Independent India at virtually the same time, when the vision of the brand new nation was at its optimistic and idealistic peak. Despite its extraordinarily rich and ancient history, India presented a brand new page.

Other famous architects driven by humanitarian and environmental passions appeared at the same time elsewhere in the country, for instance Le Corbusier in Chandigarh. Stein would later work with Balakrishna Doshi, Le Corbusier's supervisor in India. The atmosphere was exciting and Stein said it was like being in the 'United States when Jefferson was alive'. His ideas of social responsibility had been honed in the USA where he worked on low-cost housing in California's worsening depression in the late 1930s. He understood the need for human dignity and his work was a cooperation between architecture and nature. He also believed that India offered a 'great possibility of beauty with simplicity ... a rare and little understood thing in the world today'. As an expatriate he was at one remove, having the ability to be detached but at the same time involved, retaining his own identity while absorbing local elements, becoming what today we call a global person.

Oasis is a word that pops up often in India. It is real enough in desert areas of Rajasthan where sheer wealth and introduced water have changed some inhospitable landscapes into places of beauty and refuge. Similarly Stein's vision created oases in increasingly industrialised urban deserts, to refresh the spirit in a tranquil asylum after the madness of the city. His new urban architecture respected remnants of the past without disturbing the environment and each new project in the Lodi Estate referred to the last, complementing, relating and turning towards the nurturing Lodi Gardens. In a secluded section his glasshouse in turn nurtures new plants. The Lodi Estate is attractive and interesting, gently inviting investigation and a journey of Stein exploration can start by walking down a lane named after him.

One of his earliest Delhi designs was the Australian High Commission Residence commissioned in 1955. One of his few private houses in India, it is a simple and beautiful modern building in harmony with lush green gardens designed to attract birds. Peacocks pay regular visits. It is located on Shantipath which means path of peace, one of the main arteries in the Diplomatic Enclave of Chanakyapuri. The garden face of the house is a modern reference to Mughul architecture with an arched colonnade of slim columns and a flat bridge spanning a shallow pool leading to the lawn. Evening parties are often held here when thousands of tiny lights in the trees create a magical scene. Stein developed the use of the traditional north Indian *jali* or pierced stone screen as a feature in his buildings. In old palaces and forts, guides say that *jalis* allowed the ladies to watch proceedings without being observed. In the hands of Stein they afford the same privacy but also dramatically filter light and heat, and by substituting for a solid wall, give lightness and sense of freedom. Used unselfconsciously they look perfect. When Margaret and Peter Varghese were the residents of this lovely building, they kindly asked me to stay with them. It was a comfortable and happy time.

One of Stein's last designs, the India Habitat Centre, is quite a contrast. On the busy and noisy intersection of Lodi Road and Max Mueller Marg, it was built between 1986 and 1992, tall, square and imposing. Inside, the square is slashed by open space and softened with diffused green light. It is occupied by organisations sharing a common concern for habitat—housing and building research, science and the environment, rural technology, population and urban affairs, energy and resources—the physical factors that affect our existence. The aim was to develop an integrated environment where issues facing one or more member institutions could be easily discussed and solutions found. As icing on the cake, within the Centre's tall walls there are galleries, restaurants and cafes. Excellent events are held in lecture theatres and there is comfortable accommodation for members. It is another oasis and because it is Stein's design, gardens are important, in courtyards, access routes, in the ubiquitous Indian clusters of pots and as an update of ancient hanging gardens, swathes and fringes of green are suspended from great heights.

Char means four, *bagh* means garden and the *charbagh* or fourfold garden although Persian in origin, is the landscape design associated with the Mughul Empire. The Mughuls came from Central Asia, modern-day Uzbekistan, and established a powerful and fascinating empire in South Asia. Their extraordinary legacy includes some of the most remarkable monuments in the world, the Taj Mahal is but one. Their nominal supremacy in India was from 1526 to 1857 but the zenith was the rule of the six Great Mughuls from the arrival of Babur in 1526 until the death of Aurangzeb in 1707. A slow disintegration followed until 1857 when the last Mughul, Bahadur Shah, an old man more interested in poetry than power, was exiled to Rangoon by the British after his defeat in their Indian Mutiny, known to Indians as The First War of Independence.

The *charbagh* arrived in India perhaps as early as 13th century with the first invasion and subsequent domination of the Indo-Gangetic plains by Islamic rulers. The garden plan was then re-introduced by the Mughuls. Babur defeated the ruling Lodi Dynasty at the Battle of Panipat near Delhi in 1526. Descended from Genghis Khan, he was sixth in line of descent from Timur, or Tamerlane. He was greatly influenced by Persian culture, and passionate about gardens which he established wherever he went.

A miniature painting shows him celebrating the birth of his first son, Humayun in 1508 in a Kabul garden, typical of any royal Mughul garden. Their walled spaces were microcosmic familiar worlds, reproduced in many cities in the Empire, later copied by Hindu rulers and even finally by the British. They were the location for diplomatic receptions and all kinds of celebrations. In the painting Babur sits on a *chabutra* or raised stone platform covered with a flowered carpets, art copying nature. Shade is provided by chinar or oriental plane tree, cypress and a *shamiana* or tent ceiling. Indian tents are splendid and in the National Gallery of Australia's collection there is a beautiful late Mughul *q'anat* or tent wall panel. Its form echoes an architectural arch or niche and the flowering plant or tree of life growing from a rocky bed is the Persian adaptation of a Chinese theme.

In Pakistan we bought a marvellous tent which was used for happy family events. It came in several parts—*shamiana, q'anats* and long diagonally striped 'socks' to hide the tent poles. In those days the design was big geometrical patterns in primary colours, machine-sewn, but the cheaper option now is to use printed cloth. At the Kumbh Mela I saw *q'anats* printed with a luxurious green plantation of banana palms which may have appealed to Babur, given his attraction to Indian bananas. He found its strange maroon heart-shaped flower fascinating and said 'The fruit has two pleasant qualities, one that it peels easily, the other that it has neither stone nor fibre.' A banana palm in our garden in Vientiane had ghastly seeds, black, round and hard as shot, highly dangerous for the teeth of the unwary.

At Babur's celebration visitors approaching the garden gate bring gifts. There is food and drink and entertainment from musicians and dancers. The classic garden design shows water channels flowing into a square tank with a central splashing fountain. All is geometric with the central water channel crossed at right angles by smaller channels, each section enclosing a flower bed. The geometry was retained in the Indian *charbagh* and the use of water was emphasised. Successive Mughul emperors designed increasingly ambitious gardens using wider channels, rows of fountains, waterfalls, cascades and chutes. A small pavilion might be added to the *chabutra* allowing shelter and privacy and this would become the garden's social centre. Larger pavilions sometimes had a system of basement pools and channels. In terraced gardens, the central water channel fell from level to level, gently or rushing in cascades, activating fountains on the way. Parterre gardens were divided by narrower channels laid at right-angles to the main channel and shady trees lined the paths.

Years ago while working at the National Gallery, an Air India calendar arrived in our office. At first glance each month's fascinating image seemed to come from India's past but it was very much a reincarnation, set mostly in England but extending exotically to Lugano and Manhattan. *Indian Summer at Dhigpal Nivas (1994/5)*, by Rabindra K.D. Kaur Singh, is an avatar of Babur's garden party. Rabindra and her identical twin sister Amrit are London-born Birkenhead-raised artists who paint images of contemporary life in the tradition of Indian miniatures. Equally talented, they work as one, challenging stereotypes of heritage and identity by combining aesthetic elements of west and east in a highly decorative, symbolic and witty style which they call Past-Modern.

The early response to their collaborative and collective work in a Eurocentric atmosphere advocating self-expression was hostile The sisters set out to expose narrow-minded, hypocritical critics while bravely asserting their identity as British Asians, artists and twins—now aged 50 they still make a statement of dressing alike. In their Indian summer garden they wear cream-coloured full-skirted *shalwar kamiz* as they flank their bearded doctor father, the quasi-Emperor in splendid floral trousers. Sikh relatives cook kebabs on a portable barbecue, eat samosa and vanilla ice-cream cones while sitting on the grass, having abandoned cricket match and tricycle. The Mersey provides the great central water channel of the *charbagh* but in a comfortable and enclosing arc, there are few straight lines in the garden. Small cypresses inhabit curving beds, shady trees border the fence, a fountain splashes and the tiled terrace merges with pretty annuals as an extended parterre. A fox family hides in a corner and a cat sleeps on the velvet lawn. Amrit and Rabindra say their role is political and social, documenting and commenting but all seems peaceful and happy at Dhigpal Niwas, their version of the paradise garden.

When travelling through his empire, Babur keenly observed local flowers, plants and trees which he noted in his diaries. He listed flowers, fruits and trees never encountered before—the hibiscus, lemons and limes, the banyan and the *pipal*. Thanks to the journals and chronicles left by the Great Mughuls, together with the gardens which survive in their original form, the history of the development of Mughul gardens is well documented. Elizabeth Moynihan, an architectural historian whose husband was US Ambassador to India between 1973 and 1975, spent 30 years on the subject. She painstakingly traced Babur's movements and located one of his earliest Indian gardens, said to date from 1527, at Dholpur, a former princely state in the south-eastern corner of Rajasthan. Today most of the garden is buried beneath the village of Jhor where villagers look on curiously as visitors view the scant remains.

The Raj Niwas Palace at Dholpur is now a hotel with luxurious modern pavilions each with an inviting little pool, and sensational rooms in the old building. A tiled inscription in the floor of what is now the office, says that the palace was constructed in honour of the visit of the Prince of Wales, Prince Albert Edward, in 1876. The functional red brick exterior of the palace belies the rooms within. The reception rooms downstairs are splendid enough but it is the extraordinary tiled bedrooms that are so oddly beautiful. Designs like Escher wood-cuts are mesmerising while other tile schemes of Dutch dairy cows, windmills and sailing boats are odd but fun. Some colours are somewhat repellent—mud for instance! But the best are a riot of fabulous colour—peacock and jade right up to the immensely high ceilings. The huge lotus blooms painted in the three storey stairwell are utterly gorgeous and outside the gardens are green and lush.

Babur created ten gardens with reasonable ease in and around Kabul but gardening in India was far more challenging. The flat terrain around Agra meant there was a lack of rising ground necessary for terrace-making and there were few natural streams for irrigation. Previous rulers had constructed canals and artificial lakes but water was generally raised from wells by the use of what is still called the Persian wheel in rural India. Babur was discouraged by existing Indian gardens which without walls, seemed to him charmless, chaotic and disordered. He found them 'so bad and unattractive we traversed them with a hundred disgusts and repulsions'.

His solution in Agra was to use the undeveloped banks of the River Yamuna for a series of large *charbaghs* enclosed by high walls and watered from wells. Nobles were required to follow his example and before long the neighbourhood of the old Lodi fort was dotted with similar gardens. A plant exchange began between India and Kabul. Plantains, sugar-cane and a particular red oleander were sent back to Kabul. Rose varieties arrived in India and a champion melon-grower was brought from Balkh, a city renowned for the melons which Babur missed greatly. He was very taken with the

Indian mango which *is* the best in the world. Even Pakistanis in unguarded moments concede this. Fruit trees were important in Mughul gardens as the Qur'an said that as well as green pastures and palm trees, there should be two kinds of every fruit. The sale of fruit from the royal orchards helped defray the cost of garden maintenance.

Invading Muslims prior to the arrival of the Mughuls demolished temples then used the stone to construct Islamic monuments, evidenced in the buildings surrounding Delhi's 12th century Qtub Minar. Babur, more enlightened and politically astute, required new material to be used and encouraged local masons to use familiar Indian motifs. The lotus pool at Dholpur is an example of this.

He ordered the construction of walled orchards and gardens throughout the empire—the Persian word *paradise* actually means walled garden. These secular gardens represented his imperial presence, defining imperial territory and imposing a sense of order in what he viewed as Indian disorder. Their presence made a political statement of the landscape without being overtly Islamic. A small mosque might be built within the garden but behind tall walls, it did not dominate. Later rulers were more interested in overt religious symbolism but these atavistic semi-nomads continued camping in their gardens, a small corner of paradise, when on tour for war or peace, work or pleasure. Beautiful tents reinforced the idea of formal garden and noble architecture, one paradise garden within another.

Although the occasion of his birth was such a cause for celebration, Humayun did not become an illustrious ruler, neither was he very interested in gardens. But he was the father of Akbar, the greatest of all the Mughul Emperors and his tomb in New Delhi is a superb example of Mughul architecture. Restored over the past few decades by the Agha Khan Foundation in collaboration with the Archaeological Survey of India, it is the earliest intact Mughul garden of the classical *charbagh* design and is the model for later garden tombs. Sometimes construction began during the lifetime of the eventual occupant so he could enjoy its earthly delights but Humayun was not so lucky. His reign was marked by bad judgement and ineptitude, punctuated by defeats. In exile for 15 years he regained Hindustan only in the year of his death. It is said he died heeding the call to prayer, falling down stairs in his beloved library, his arms full of books. Another story says the fatal fall may have happened as he observed the movement of the planet Venus from the vantage-point of his roof when he is said to have tripped on his robe at the sound of the *azan*. Less sympathetic reports say he was under the influence of either opium or alcohol or both.

Humayun was buried temporarily in Delhi's Purana Qila or Old Fort, moved once and then finally in about 1572 to his spectacular red sandstone and white marble tomb. It is one of the first important Mughul buildings, purely Persian architecture with additional Indian elements such as the slim lotus-topped octagonal minarets. It took eight years to build, the enormous cost entirely paid by his first queen, Haji Begum, with her stepson Akbar's approval. It was after all a political statement, proclaiming the power of the dynasty, but was also an act of homage to Hazrat Nizamuddin, the famous Sufi saint, whose tomb is close by.

The garden today, as well as the tomb itself, is in good condition after the massive restoration. The centuries had taken their toll with the grounds suffering particularly when used as the site for a refugee camp at the time of Independence and Partition in 1947. Begun in 2001, the garden's rehabilitation involved the removal of 3,000 truck-loads of earth. Three kilometres of pathway edging stones were reset to define divisions of the complex *charbagh*. It was impossible to change the course of the Yamuna River which had moved away from the eastern wall but internal channels were repaired and water quietly ripples again. Fountains play, perfumed flowering shrubs and fruit trees have been replanted and work continues on the gateways. The original four squares had been further bisected into 36 squares. The central water channel appears to flow beneath the tomb recalling a verse in the Qu'ran which says rivers flow beneath the Garden of Paradise. All is not concerned with the past, a micro-habitat zone has been created in the adjoining nursery and a socio-economic development project begun in the nearby crowded neighbourhood.

Akbar the Great was more of a builder rather than a landscape designer but he loved gardens all the same. In 1589 he became the first of the Mughuls to visit Kashmir. He found it utterly delightful and referred to it as his private garden. The Mughuls who found the heat of Hindustan's summer almost unbearable, considered Kashmir's climate perfect. Unlimited water and a terrain ideal for terraced gardens beautifully emulated paradise. Akbar's son Jahangir adored Kashmir and continued his great-grandfather's passion for plants and flowers and gardens.

Centuries later the British escaping the heat of the plains, would also fall in love with Kashmir. Prohibited from building houses and making gardens, they overcame the problem by camping in the mountains and staying in house-boats moored along the edge of Srinagar's lakes. By contrast Simla, in the south-western ranges of the Himalayas, developed into a thoroughly British creation and in 1864 became the summer capital of the Raj, to which the Government of India migrated en masse. The former Viceroy's residence, now houses the Indian Institute of Advanced Study. Its gardens were created by shearing off the top of Observatory Hill to provide a plateau. The immense stone Jacobethan pile of Viceregal Lodge was built here between 1886 and 1888 at a cost which astounded the India Office at home. The original Victorian garden needed armies of *malis* to tend it but today it is vastly simpler. It is obvious how well some plants will grow in the cool of the hills, a banksia rose had climbed to about three storey height against a tree on the edge of a lawn.

Akbar, although illiterate, was a great patron of the arts, illustrated books in particular. He had taken great interest in European printed books introduced by Jesuit missionaries in 1580. Akbar included the Jesuits in multi-faith gatherings at his capital, Fatehpur-Sikri. Old manuscripts were copied and Babur's memoirs, the *Baburnama*, were translated into Persian from the Chagatai Turkic language in which it was originally written. Superb miniature paintings illustrating the books are a great source for the details of plants and trees, garden design and even maintenance.

More than a century later Emperor Shah Jahan was very

concerned with both religious and political symbolism. In 1648 he moved his capital from Agra to his splendid new city, Shahjahanabad in Delhi. In Agra the Taj Mahal was well underway and his Red Fort was mightily impressive, but the second Red Fort at the heart of the new capital, was larger than any contemporary European palace and full of gardens. Architectural historian, Ebba Koch, sees one of these gardens, the Hayat Baksh or Life-giving Garden, as a representation of Mughul imperial power and an example of garden imperialism like Louis XIV's Versailles. Huge in size with ranks of fountains, rigid geometry and shrubs arranged with military precision, the gardens were meant to overwhelm the common man. Another historian, Eugenia Herbert, argues however that the common man was never going to view such glories and be thus overwhelmed. The garden was one of the most private spaces within the palace, meant solely for the royal family and their servants. Few others saw the Hayat Baksh where it was said the season of spring came off second best to the skill of the Emperor's artists who adorned the walls and ceilings of the garden pavilions with flowers in pietra dura, bas-relief, painting and gilding. Only the Emperor could use motifs of plants in art and architecture, lesser beings had to be content with nature itself. The inscription over the Diwan-i-khas, the Hall of Private Audience, said 'If there is a paradise on the face of the earth, it is this, it is this, it is this.' The British would later supervise the philistine destruction of much of the Delhi Fort's beauty. They also sought to subdue the Indian garden, imposing the undoubted beauties of their own in an Albion version of garden imperialism.

The *charbagh* was for the Mughuls the ideal garden, an earthly paradise and perhaps the first architectural expression of the new Indian empire. In the Qur'an Paradise is a garden filled with abundant trees, flowers and plants, a place where water played a very important part. As eight terraces existed in Paradise, each more beautiful than the last, garden designers would aim to lay out eight or even nine, attempting to surpass the sublime. Four rivers find their source at a central spring or mountain and in their ideal form are laid out as a square divided into four equal parts. The rivers are represented in the classic *charbagh* as water channels separating the gardens and flowing towards the cardinal points. They symbolise the promise of water, wine, milk and honey which the righteous will receive on their entry to Paradise. The garden's centre at the intersection of the four divisions is important in this symbolic map. In an ideal design, a pavilion, pool or tomb would be situated here. The garden mausoleums of Humayun and Safdarjung in Delhi and Akbar at Sikandra near Agra, follow this pattern with the tombs rising as sacred mountains above the fourfold confluence. Tomb and garden design were treated in unison, each enhancing the beauty of the other, embodying the perfection of the Islamic ideal, the ultimate paradise garden surrounding the dead Emperor for ever.

Long before the Muslims arrived in India with their geometrically precise form of garden design, India was certainly not a wilderness. Gardens in the Hindu epics are mentioned as places of great natural beauty where groves of trees were decked with flowers or laden with fruit. Temples were built near springs or rivers and stories of gods and goddesses often take place in verdant glades and dense forests and on flower-strewn banks bordering rivers whose limpid waters were dotted with lotus flowers. Rama and Sita first meet in a garden 'so rich in bud and fruit and flower that its abundance put to shame even the trees of paradise.'

Royal gardens were settings for dalliance and seduction, the pastoral beauty of a primeval landscape tamed but sensuously welcoming. The *Kamasutra* detailed densely shaded bowers, glorious scented flowers and a swing as essentials for a Hindu prince's garden. Other texts, both Hindu and Muslim, gave advice on planting a pleasure garden with highly scented plants to assist seduction. The Mughuls wholeheartedly adopted one particular of indigenous Indian gardens, the Moonlight Garden. Here after the intense heat of summer days, white blossom and flowering trees scented the cooler night air. They added pools, fountains and cascades and outlined raised paths, platforms and pavilions with small lamps in cusped niches.

Shah Jahan built such a garden across the Yamuna from the

Taj Mahal. Its main purpose was to view his magnificent creation, built as a memorial to Empress Mumtaz Mahal, his chief consort and greatest love. Her name meant most excellent of the region. She gave birth to 14 babies in the 19 years of her marriage. Seven died at birth or early infancy but one would become the last of the Great Mughuls, Emperor Aurangzeb. She died at Burhanpur, giving birth for the fourteenth time. She was buried there in a pleasure garden but her final resting place is surely the world's most beautiful mausoleum. The tomb is not located centrally in the garden but at the farthest point from the entry with the river behind it. Perhaps this was due to the presence of many secular gardens along the river in Agra, Babur's clever innovation to compensate for the flatness of the countryside. Another explanation could be that the river provides the central channel of the *charbagh* and the Moonlight Garden on the other bank is the continuation of the fourfold plan. This would add to the perception of Shah Jahan's power, displaying the ruler's dominion over all of nature, including the rivers. Mumtaz' garden, created after her death, replicated the beauty of paradise where it would have been assumed she existed already.

Lotus, iris and crown imperial lilies appear on bas-reliefs on the tomb's exterior and the form and decoration of the dome refers to the lotus, a Buddhist and Hindu symbol of fertility, purity and enlightenment. Within the mausoleum the surrounding screen and the tombs (Shah Jahan also rests here) are decorated with exquisite pietra dura. Inlaid jasper, jade, carnelian, turquoise, coral, lapis lazuli, onyx and amethyst become honeysuckle, jasmine, pomegranate blossom, lilies, iris, poppies and narcissus. The ephemeral spring flowers symbolically refer to life, death and regeneration, sadly meaningful in a memorial to the Empress who died while giving birth.

The gardens of the Taj were always described as magnificent but today are not as Shah Jahan knew them. The changes were largely made by Lord Curzon during his term as Viceroy of India from 1899 to 1905. In a Balliol rhyme, a form of doggerel originating in the Oxford College where Curzon studied as an undergraduate, he was described:

> My name is George Nathaniel Curzon,
> I am a most superior person.
> My cheeks are pink, my hair is sleek,
> I dine at Blenheim twice a week.

This stuck for the rest of his life and his connection to Balliol remains, his portrait hangs in the Hall today.

He was a 'most superior person', brilliant, eloquent, presumptuous and self-assured. People could never be half-way in their feelings for him, he both attracted and repulsed. His Viceregal term, it could almost be termed as his reign, was full of amazing events and glorious spectacle. Curzon unsurprisingly identified easily with the Mughul emperors, such was his power and such the pomp and splendour. Both the Mughuls and the British came from cultures obsessively interested in their gardens, seen as instruments of civilisation, ordering indigenous chaos. Reprising Babur, Curzon boasted he had turned dusty wastes into green parks and gardens. His great obsession was to preserve the architectural and archaeological heritage of India and one of his triumphs was the Ancient Monuments Bill of 1904. The focus of his passion was the Taj Mahal. It had always been protected but Curzon did not see himself as a mere caretaker. His imperial aspirations were to demonstrate the superiority of British civilisation, its respect for the greatness of the past and its ability to mould native peoples into loyal British subjects, beneficiaries of its enlightenment and refinement. He made changes.

Everyone knows just how beautiful British gardens can be and one of the most important features is the lawn. All over Australia at the end of summer our lawns can look from a distance like drifts of sand. If we live in drier regions and are obedient, we don't water them when it doesn't rain, and they don't like it! Many gardeners have given up trying to maintain a greensward, turning grass into lawn with the Victa, surrendering to tan-bark or native grasses which need neither much water nor any mowing. But for any proper English garden, the lawn was and is the essential element, almost like the wall for the Mughuls. It was the proud heart of the garden where croquet or cricket could be played, afternoon tea taken in cane chairs or the location for a large party. Old photographs from the British Raj show sweet families on small patches of turf with hoops set up for croquet, and uniformed servants steadying wobbly little children on ponies. Images of grander gatherings capture well-dressed groups watching events from comfortable seats or promenading at viceregal parties on great sweeps of lawn. It was the primed canvas on which could be painted tall trees, flowering shrubs and beds of annuals, varieties from home struggling for survival alongside stronger natives. It was an oasis and absolute necessity even if tough local sod replaced the soft English grass which withered in the heat.

When I first visited India I saw lawn-mowers being pulled by oxen in Delhi parks. Another variation had one man pulling a rope to the fore with another guiding the mower from behind. Noisier machines are seen and heard these days. Our miniscule patch of grass in Peshawar was kept neat by the otherwise extremely lazy helper, Waqar. His first dedication was to sleep and several times I had to scale our 10' high metal gate, no mean feat, to find him dead to the world under a cooling fan, oblivious to my ringing the bell at the gate. Apart from stealing a photograph of our daughter, he was always well behaved and provided some amusement. He had a deep appreciation of our dining chairs, always saying 'Beautiful chairs' in his deep voice as he passed them, and he seemed to enjoy trimming the lawn with my kitchen scissors, his idea not mine. It was a tiny garden with a slender, young mulberry tree against the front wall and along one side, a bed with three or four bush roses. The flowers were perfumed, small and cream with a faint pink tinge and for the eight months we lived in the house, they bloomed without ceasing. It was a generous delight.

Curzon's taste in gardens was 18th century in the style of Capability Brown where vast expanses of lawn, dotted with majestic trees lapped the walls of splendid mansions. He had little interest in flowers and garden beds at all. He had grown up in such a landscape, at Kedleston Hall in Derbyshire which oddly enough was the model for Government House in Calcutta, built in 1803 and occupied a century later by Curzon as Viceroy in a tenancy seemingly predestined. Both the enormous house and the garden of the original Kedleston were designed in the Palladian style by Robert Adam. The ethos was rather like a Mughul garden tomb, an integration of nature and the works of man. It is austere, rather like Capability Curzon himself, the grounds very unlike the Victorian gardens of his time with their crowded herbaceous borders, profusion of bedding plants and topiary.

Old paintings and engravings of the Taj Mahal painted by such artists as William Daniell at the end of the eighteenth century, show the building framed in a romantic style by large spreading trees which almost encroach upon the building. Some of the trees were said to be mahoganies. It was not Curzon's style, either personal or imperial. In deciding what the visitor might see, he exercised a similar control to Shah Jahan's design for the view *his* nobles might see from the garden across the river. Curzon swept away all the orchards and the shady bosky woods, those 'tiresome little flower beds' with their 'garish English flowers' and put down lawn.

These flowers, seen in any English cottage garden and so despised by Curzon, persist today in India—hollyhocks and phlox, Sweet Alice and Sweet William, larkspur, stock and carnation and wonderful red salvia. *Cur moriatur homo, cui salvia crescit in horto.* Why should a man die who has salvia—i.e. sage growing in his garden? I met a friendly gardener, hard at work planting salvia in the Lodi Gardens. He would certainly never have heard this Latin quotation from the 12th century didactic poem Regimen Sanitatis Salernitanum, the Salernitan Rule of Health. But he knew a thing or two about planting salvia, running a string along the bed, walking along it to impress the line into the soil, removing the string and then planting the frail little seedlings.

'Sage the saviour', 'salvia save us'—the word comes from the Latin salvere, to feel well and healthy, to be saved. Sage was considered to have important curative properties in ancient and medieval times. The bedding plants do not have any therapeutic value but it is comforting to think they have a guardian role in the garden. The earliest British botanists in India were often Scottish surgeons employed by the East India Company. The Scottish universities in Edinburgh, Glasgow and Aberdeen offered the best medical education of the time and botany was an important part of the syllabus since plants were the primary source of medicine. Herbal treatments are a very important part of India's ancient healing tradition, Ayurvedic medicine, so there was much to learn for British doctors with open minds.

I have a pot of a pretty tall waving variety of salvia on my veranda, more graceful than the stiff little firecrackers of municipal plantings. I had a pineapple sage once upon a time and like its namesake, the king of fruit, the plant originates in Brazil. In his memoirs, the Emperor Jahangir wrote that his father Akbar planted pineapples 'found in the Franks' ports. It is extremely good-smelling and tasting. Several thousand are produced every year in the Gulafshan Garden in Agra.' This was quick off the mark for Akbar who ruled from 1556 to 1605. Christopher Columbus, the first European to write of seeing them did so on 4th November 1493 and it took some time for the first fruits to arrive in Europe and take it by storm. John Rose, gardener to the Earl of Essex is credited to have raised the first pineapple in England which was given to King Charles II in 1661.

Another endearing virtue of salvia is that hummingbirds are drawn to it. We had occasional hummingbirds in our Port-of-Spain garden though bananaquits were much more frequent visitors. They were dear little neat birds about the size of a sparrow — white, grey and black with yellow breasts and rumps. Their slender curved beaks are designed for extracting nectar from flowers and puncturing fruit in order to feed on the juice. They become very fearless and we were adopted by a brave mother bird. She flew into our house while we were away for a weekend. Glass did not exist in all our window frames so it was easy access for small creatures. She was very busy during our absence in a nasty pendant light fixture in the middle of our sitting room and we felt her nest greatly improved the decor. She laid three eggs in the nest. They hatched and the babies were doing well until one morning Petitpuss, our pampered and naughty cat, decided in a fit of jealousy to commit murder. Poor mother bird. We kept the babies alive for a few days but they succumbed and we sadly removed the nest.

Curzon micromanaged the Taj Mahal garden project and seemed particularly preoccupied with the cypresses, where should they be planted, how densely and could they not be larger? On the cool winter afternoon of my first visit to the Taj Mahal in 1969 there were very few visitors. A kind official invited us, three young foreigners, into his office in the gate-house for a cup of chai. Displayed on the walls was an interesting collection of old photographs. They were all frontal views of the building taken at every stage of cypress growth from small and slender to tall and dense. Some of the photographs may have dated from Curzon's day and maybe even some of the existing trees which have a long lifespan. The Mughuls probably introduced the cypress to India. They are symbolic of eternity and alternating cypresses and fruit-trees symbolised life, death and rebirth. In the late 18th century the garden contained thousands of orange trees as well as guava, apples, pomegranates and lemons. Though Curzon removed all fruit trees, pomegranates and guavas have returned, growing in plantations on the sides of the formal garden.

Curzon flattened the elevated paths, once raised well above both the water channels and the colourful parterres which had been filled with tulips, lilies, tuberoses, balsam, anemones, violets, sunflowers, marigolds, poppies, carnations and iris. The aerial view would have been like looking down on a flowered carpet. I love the idea of aerial views of flowers. It is the reason that Hmong mothers in Laos embroider beautiful hats for their little ones, to fool malevolent spirits flying about on high, into thinking their babies are simply flowers. Some parterres have been restored within Agra's Red Fort, bordered by the gardener's favourite, celosia. Humayun recorded the use of cockscomb or celosia and ancient carbonised seeds have been found in excavations of Shah Jahan's gardens. Today they are planted widely in the gardens of Agra and Fatehpur-Sikri and as well as providing vivid splashes of colour, their seed is attractive to songbirds. A *mali* may sidle up to visitors with a surreptitious 'ssssssssst' seeking to sell a pinch of seeds folded in a piece of paper.

Scented flowers were considered important as gardens were intended to appeal to all the senses, particularly the sense of smell. Champa, either a native magnolia or exotic frangipani introduced by the Portuguese, roses and jasmine had been planted by Shah Jahan but all were swept away by Curzon. Like the fruit trees, flower-beds have returned and a small invasion of an almost domestic cluster of terracotta pots on an iron stand lies just inside the gateway to the Taj. Gerberas, petunias, geraniums and red salvia were interspersed by some kind of bromeliad on a five-tiered display. Curzon like his monarch would not be amused.

Today the Taj is visited by two to three million tourists each year. The delights of sound and smell from tinkling fountains and perfumed flowers are absent, but the overwhelming beauty of the building remains. Each time, that first glimpse of the building floating at the end of the vista makes my heart leap. The Taj Mahal and other magnificent Indian monuments are included on the UNESCO World Heritage List. Their grounds, and dozens of others under the protection of the Archaeological Survey of India are delightful, with sweeping lawns, shady trees and beds of flowering canna. Despite the beds, I think Curzon would generally approve, as vista has eventually trumped historical accuracy and the imperial English lawn, which Constance Villiers-Stuart described as 'the universal virtue of mown grass' has triumphed in the end.

About 50 miles north-west of Islamabad on the Grand Trunk Road, the gardens at Wah date from Akbar's reign, built in 1581 by one of his Generals, Man Singh who was posted at the strategic point of Attock a little further to the north. Man Singh's brother-in-law was Akbar's son, who became the Emperor Jahangir. In 1607 he stayed at Wah on his way to Kabul and wrote of seeing many fish in a pond. He carefully caught ten or twelve in a net which were returned to the water after pearls had been sewn on their noses. Shah Jahan stayed here in 1639 and had the garden extensively redeveloped with *baradaris*, channels, waterfalls and baths with hot and cold water. Walls were painted with floral designs and the garden was said to be heavenly, a true earthly paradise. The exclamation 'Wah!' means pleasure, appreciation and surprise—

perfect if you like—and is the word a dancer, singer or musician loves to hear. The gardens at Wah must have been so thoroughly beautiful, visitors could not help but exclaim.

Shah Jahan subsequently stayed there four more times, breaking journeys to Kabul. His successor Aurangzeb also visited but after his death the gardens deteriorated. When our children came for school holidays in Pakistan for the first time, we stopped at Wah for a picnic lunch on our way home to Peshawar. The day was hot but it was cool enough beneath the shady trees. We saw no bejewelled fish but were greatly amused by boys having huge fun in the pond. Wearing only their baggy *shalwar* they leapt into the water, the impact forcing their trousers to blow up like balloons keeping them afloat. It was very funny.

If we were driven from Rawalpindi or Islamabad to Peshawar, the driver's preference for a chai stop was Hasan Abdal, 10 or 12 kilometres on from Wah. It has been a holy place since at least the 7th century when visited by Buddhist pilgrims. It later became a sacred site for Sikhs because of a rock which bears the handprint of their founder Guru Nanak. Though almost all the Sikh population left Pakistan at the time of Partition, twice a year Sikh pilgrims from all over the world visit the Hasan Abdal Gurudwara. It was deserted whenever we visited but once we were allowed in by the caretaker and shown the handprint.

In the small town there are Mughul era tombs and in a pretty walled garden, the tomb of Lalla Rookh, the eponymous heroine of Thomas Moore's epically long poem. She was the daughter of Emperor Aurangzeb and her name meant 'tulip-cheeked'. The poem tells that she was betrothed to the young prince of Bokhara and set off on a long journey to Kashmir for their wedding. On the way she falls in love with a poet called Feramorz. The doomed situation is saved by the revelation that poet and prince are one and the same.

In Peshawar we sometimes walked in the Khalid Bin Walid Bagh, also known as Company Bagh, originally a Mughul garden, located in the *saddar* or British town. There were fine roses and old shady trees and in the late afternoon vendors sold gigantic *pappadams* for snacks. We went to the autumn flower show in another garden where there some of the largest dahlias I have ever seen, arranged in circles in one class and slopes in another. Their handsome Pathan propagators looked much the same as plantsmen in any country.

In 17th and 18th centuries some princely states remained independent of Mughul rule. The Kshatriya or warrior caste Rajputs who lived in what are now the modern states of Rajasthan and Madhya Pradesh were often preoccupied with war but were also great patrons of art and architecture. Schools of miniature painting developed and craftsmen adorned their splendid forts and palaces with intricate and beautiful designs, very often botanical in nature. There were certainly similarities to Mughul buildings but the Hindu Rajput palaces are more complex and less symmetrical.

Much of the great Fort Palace of Amer dates from 17th century. In the *Diwan-i-Am* or Hall of Public Audience, the decorations were so beautiful that the envious Emperor Jahangir contemplated having the building destroyed. Across the courtyard is the delicately painted *Ganesh Pol*, a vertical field of flowers. Beyond it are the private quarters of the Maharaja containing a glittering *Sheesh Mahal* or Mirror Palace, the *Sukh Niwas* or Hall of Pleasure and a sunken garden laid out in the style of an informal *charbagh*, small and pretty. Without concern for the Islamic imagery of paradise and the rivers of life, there are stone walkways instead of channels and at the centre, an octagonal platform instead of a pool, surrounded by ponds in the shape of a star.

If the ascent to the fort is made by elephant, the birds-eye views of the gardens below are almost unique in India. It is an island garden called Mohan Bari meaning charming and delightful, located in the Maota Lake. There are three terraces, the uppermost being a regular *charbagh* whose channels cascade to the lower levels. It might have been a moonlight garden, planted with scented white flowers to be enjoyed in the evening. But its name, Kesar Kiyari meaning saffron flowerbed suggests it was planted with colourful blooms which when viewed from the palace would have resembled another splendid carpet. Other gardens were built along the edge of the lake.

For the Hindu Rajputs at least, the *charbagh* lost its meaning as a vision of Islamic heaven. It was not exactly appropriate for temples but as happens so often in India, concepts are absorbed and evolve into something different and suitable. A lovely garden around the big temple of Govind Devji in Jaipur refers to the *charbagh*. Govind Devji is a version of Lord Krishna and the garden is seen by devotees to relate to the forests in which Krishna, the divine lover, dallied with the *gopis* or milkmaids at Vrindhavan.

The most elaborate of palace gardens in Rajasthan was built at Deeg in the south-east corner of the state in the region of Vraj, Krishna's youthful stamping-ground. It was created for the Jat ruler of Deeg, Suraj Mal, in about 1760, located near the bastions of earlier fort. The design of the central area is a large *charbagh* with deeply sunken gardens. It is almost surrounded by pavilions and substantial buildings sited between two large bodies of water. Two pretty pavilions with *bangaldar* rooves flank the Gopal Bhawan on the edge of one of the tanks, Gopal Sagar. Gopal is one of Krishna's 108 names. The pavilions are called Sawon and Bhadon for the months of the monsoon. The bank of buildings are mirrored perfectly in the tank and the pavilions look as they were intended, like house-boats floating on the water.

The monsoon for which they were named, is the season when life-giving rains fall on India's parched plains. There was and is much to celebrate in the monsoon. Forest and field are refreshed, peacocks dance and lovers watched the weather from the shelter of pretty pavilions. It is a time for dalliance and even the lowliest peasant might have some spare time for relaxed contemplation of the world. Poets and artists delight in it and it was the time for the ancient Indian game of snakes and ladders, a version of which was much enjoyed by Jains. In the desert state of Bikaner, within the old palace a beautiful room is painted with monsoon murals. On a deep cobalt blue background swirling circular clouds look fluffy and benign, like white-edged listening ears. Here and there are curling dragon's tongues of lightning, red with an internal stripe of yellow. Closer to the bottom of the wall, the cloud ears that have turned into open watery mouths from which dense spears of rain fall towards the red and green borders and the floor, the earth. The paintings showed this strange beauty to the little palace children for whom rain was a rare phenomenon and who might have been frightened by the power of the lightning and the noise of the thunder.

At Deeg there are 500 fountains, dry now except for what must be a fabulous spectacle held during the monsoon each August, when coloured water shoots again from the jets. They are fed from a 600,000 gallon capacity reservoir in a nearby building. To fill it, water is drawn up in large leather buckets by oxen laboriously trudging up and down a slope. The entire palace which became the Maharaja's summer residence after his move 25 miles away to Bharatpur, is a celebration of the monsoon which could be summoned up at another time of the year in microcosmic form.

This feat took place in the Keshav Bhawan, a grand summerhouse, named for Krishna, Keshav being yet another of his names. The building is a *baradari*, which literally means twelve doorways. On first inspection Keshav Bhawan has twenty but within the outer square colonnade there is an inner square with twelve cusped archways. It is located at the opposite end of the garden to the Gopal Bhawan facing the other great tank, the Rup Sagar. A channel almost a metre wide runs between the colonnades, with fountains in the centre and hundreds of tiny jets along the sides. When the maharaja was masquerading as the controller of nature, a magician able to summon up an unseasonal monsoon, the fountains would play and the jets would spurt. In the ceiling, piped running water agitated heavy stone balls creating a noise like thunder and a curtain of water would fall from the eaves like sheets of rain. If the day was sunny a rainbow might even result and then the maharaja could, if he so desired, order the reservoir refilled so it could happen all over again.

The deeply sunken gardens and water channels show how many reconstructed Mughul gardens would have looked at the time of their creation. The position of certain trees at Deeg suggests a Mughul design and there are traces of the adopted form of the moonlight garden. The whole complex is exceedingly beautiful and surpassed any contemporary late Mughul buildings. Some marble architectural details used in the buildings, a few adorned with pietra dura, had been looted from Mughul buildings within the Delhi Fort. A marble *hindola* or swing in front of Gopal Bhawan has a Persian inscription dated 1630 which is during Shah Jahan's reign. Some say it belonged to Nur Jahan, twentieth and favourite wife of Jahangir and the aunt of Mumtaz Mahal.

The Monsoon Pavilion at Deeg hints at another Rajasthani tradition, the *jal mahal* or water palace. This is a single structure or a series of pavilions located on an island taking up all its space and seeming to float on the surrounding water. The Jag Niwas, now the Lake Palace Hotel in Udaipur's Lake Pichola is a well-known example and a second, the Jag Mandir, lies in the same lake. On the road from Jaipur to Amber, another floats serenely in a lake called Man Sagar. It was built possibly as early as the 1730s when the capital moved from Amer to the planned city of Jaipur. Departing Amer meant leaving behind the pretty complex of gardens and the island could have been a substitute built by Maharaja Sawai Jai Singh II in about 1734.

Its history is unclear and it may have been a later construction by Maharaja Madho Singh I in c.1775. If this is its origin, the link with the Jag Mandir in Udaipur is personal as the Maharaja spent his childhood there. Madho Singh was 6'6' tall and 250 kg in weight. One of the more curious articles in the textile and costume collection at the Jaipur City Palace is a pair of his enormous pyjamas. Despite ascending the throne after a bitter and bloody struggle with his brother, he made great contributions to his state in art and architecture, literature and religion. He also created the Sisodia Rani Ka Bagh, a garden complex on the Agra Road.

The Jal Mahal looks more a palace than a garden but the building is in truth a very substantial folly. It has a solid earth and rock core which supports the weight of the garden and its pavilion on the top. In the 19th century it was turned into a hunting lodge and languished. The first time I saw it, the lake-bed was dry and we bumped in a car across bleached grass to visit the building. It was ruinous but up on the top men were playing cards and smoking, enjoying the breeze and the shade of the trees. The lake area became an environmental disaster and it was a huge job to repair. The depth was increased by more than a metre and two million tonnes of toxic silt was removed. A water treatment system was developed and local vegetation and fish were reintroduced. The surrounding wetlands were regenerated and nesting islands created to attract migratory birds. A modern secular sculpture by Frenchman, Christian Lapie, stands shrouded in vegetation and apparently facing the wrong way, at the Amer corner of the lake, installed there in 2006 at the same time as a much larger cluster of similar powerful stones on a gentle hillock in Jaipur's Central Park *In the Path of the Sun & Moon: Universal Being,* monumental and abstract but human and spiritual.

The lake has been full for years and after the monsoon when the water is highest, the lowest storey of the building is submerged and acts as a cooling system for the whole building. Brigid Keenan and I took a few hours off from the Jaipur Literature Festival to visit the Jal Mahal in the final stages of a magnificent restoration in 2011. We were rowed across the lake in a Rajput-style boat made in Krishna's town of Vrindhavan. The view of the Aravalli hills, crowned by forts and temples is splendid. A wealthy Jaipur businessman had undertaken the project directed by Delhi architects and Mitch Crites, American anthropologist and landscape architect. He lives in a beautiful old *haveli* within Jaipur's old walled city and has worked on dozens of fascinating projects.

He thought the remains of the garden indicated a *charbagh* and has recreated this with additional Rajput and modern elements. It is called Chameli Bagh or Jasmine Garden. The plant choices come from the old moonlight gardens, white jasmine, poppies, bougainvillea and wisteria. Inside artists have created breathtakingly beautiful decorations. Most are based on flowers— gorgeous tawny iris with sinuous stems, sprays of imaginative calendulas, celosia and marigolds bending into classic 'paisley' *guls,* fanciful gilded blossoms on a dark maroon background, regular lines of bright red tulip shaped buds with stems like sprays of neem leaves. Enchanting green pilasters with trompe l'oeil niches frame perfect trees, one a banana so fascinating centuries before to Babur. Above it the underside of cusped portico arches glowed with the same greens as ribbed banana leaves and a long-tailed green bird flies away from a banana palm painted around the corner of a wall.

Another beautiful Rajasthani oasis garden is a development of both *charbagh* and *jal mahal* in the central section of the Sahelion ki Bari, the Garden of the Maids of Honour in Udaipur. Built around 1720, the water channels of the *charbagh* have disappeared and the body of water instead of surrounding an island garden, is internalised as a pool within a courtyard. In the heart of the garden, the central pavilion resembles a miniature *jal mahal*. It sits in the pool like a tiny palace, topped with a little bird turned by the force of the fountains. Kiosks are adorned with carved lotus and recessed seats in the walls meant for lazing, have assumed a more prosaic role—potting sheds which when I last visited were full of healthy cineraria and salvia—salvia save us!

Umaid Bhawan Palace in Jodhpur was the last of the splendid palaces built for an Indian prince. Now a superb hotel, it was built between 1928 and 1943. It is very different architecturally from all the others in Rajasthan being Art Deco in style though so sumptuous it really needs the additional descriptive of Palatial Art Deco. It was one of the largest private residences in the world and one section is still occupied by the present Maharaja and his family. The construction was a form of famine relief for thousands of workers engaged on the project. Money was not spared on any detail and this extended to the gardens. Jodhpur, surrounded by desert, is regularly beset by drought so the variety of grass had to be selected carefully. A hardy variety was imported from East Africa, but not only that, so was the soil! The 26 acres of garden is formal and planted with dry heat survivors such as bougainvillaea and an enticing drought-resistant shrub with bright yellow crepey flowers and a subtle perfume called Tecoma stans. It is not a native but is encountered all over India. Perhaps we could grow it here—it would do well in Australia.

Nagaur lies about 90 km northeast of Jodhpur. It was a small princely state, strategically placed on trade and invasion routes and its history is full of struggles for control. Though officially Mughul territory, it was given to Maharaja Bakhat Singh by his brother the Maharaja of Jodhpur and here he ruled for 25 years until 1752. He built a magnificent garden palace within the fort which has recently been restored after the army vacated many of the beautiful buildings. Some wall paintings survived and others have been restored. Bakhat Singh also commissioned the most fabulous paintings on paper, now part of the Maharaja of Jodhpur's collection. A superb selection came to Sydney in the exhibition *Garden & Cosmos* shown at the Art Gallery of New South Wales in 2009/10.

It is easy today to identify existing buildings portrayed in some of the paintings though they seem somehow lifeless without the presence of the Maharaja and his beautiful female companions. In the paintings both the gardens and the floral designs on garments, architectural elements and furnishings are totally desirable and strangely timeless. Blockprint designs on bed-covers look exactly like contemporary Jaipur textiles. In one painting the larger than life Maharaja is playing Holi in a pool with crowds of courtesans, suggestively aiming a water pistol. His palace is transformed into a heavenly realm, another paradise garden, and he is Krishna surrounded by adoring *gopis*.

Umaid Bhawan was the new dwelling for the royal family who previously lived in the Meherangarh Fort Palace situated on top of an enormous rock on the edge of Jodhpur. The old palace is now an excellent museum where some of the Nagaur paintings are always on display. There are no gardens within the walls of the Fort, built as it is on a barren rock, but far below is the Chokelao Bagh, a pretty 200-year-old terraced *charbagh,* restored over the last decade. The planting is so dense in part that visions of Krishna and the *gopis* are conjured up again, this time in their nocturnal forest trysts. The restoration has focused on trees and plants that can withstand the long months of dry heat without too much watering. On a spur beyond the main part of the fort another garden surrounds the *chatri* or cenotaph of a 19th century Maharaja. This and the Chokelao Bagh are, like the Umaid Bhawan garden, great luxuries from the past.

In an effort to green the desert, the same Maharaja who built the great art deco palace, had large areas aerially sown with seeds of mesquite, a tenacious Mexican native. A British advisor had told him about this miracle plant which could thrive in harsh desert climates, prevent soil erosion, provide fodder for stock and give humans a source of food and fuel. The landscape certainly did become green but the effect on local ecology was disastrous. Rather than merely thrive, it invaded with such vigour it was given the name *baavlia*— the mad one. It looks similar to *babool,* an Indian acacia. Both are spiny with twice-feathered leaves but *babool* seems to have more redeeming qualities as a native although it is also invasive. There is not huge interest in growing natives in India where unlike Australia, they are not nearly as easy to find in local nurseries. But there are a growing number of ecological restoration projects in India with different aims ranging from beautification to creating awareness about native flora to species conservation.

One such project began in Jodhpur after the 2005 restoration of the city wall surrounding the fort. The land lying within the wall, freed from the possibility of human and animal encroachment, was to be improved and Pradip Krishen, the Project Director, was asked to turn it into a forest. He had different ideas. Rather than battling with the rocky, eroded landscape which would have needed millions of tons of soil, he suggested returning the area to what it would have been 600 years earlier. He is a film-maker, photographer, wood-worker and environmentalist. His interest in botany started as a hobby as he learned to identify trees in his quest to 'get to know the forest'. His writing is whimsical and *Trees of Delhi: A Field Guide* (2006) is a wonderful book which I consult far more frequently than I'd ever imagined.

Eradicating the deep-rooted mesquite was dreadfully laborious and initially unsuccessful. Ring-barking was ineffectual and machinery or dynamite shattered the rock, defeating the whole idea of regeneration. Eventually the team worked with a group of 15 *khandwaliyas,* traditional miners from Jodhpur's sandstone quarries—most of Jodhpur is built of local stone. The rock at the garden site is volcanic rhyolite, hard and brittle and the outcrop, the Malani Igneous Suite as it is called, which forms the entire five square kilometres within the Fort walls, is so geologically important that it has been declared a National Geological Monument. I wish I could tell this to my geology teachers. At my old-fashioned girls' school, our headmistress considered geology a far more suitable subject than biology which involved such bold topics as anatomy and worse, procreation!

The *khandwaliyas* could tell from the sound of hammer striking rock, how it was laid down and how they could get in with chisels and hammers to drag out the mesquite roots. It was very slow with 12,000 extractions in the 70 acres, but the work was done and two men are still on the job. Vinod Puri Goswami took me round on my first visit in 2010, soon after the end of the rains. It was hot and humid in the storm-water gully where the women dressed in brilliant colours, weeded and snipped. As we paddled around in the water Vinod's enthusiasm was infectious and he pointed out beautiful species. A great source of indigenous plants was found only 6 km away on a hill behind the stables for the Maharaja's Marwari horses. This is now also the site of another good hotel, where the bedrooms are luxuriously converted stables. Seeds were collected and grown in the garden nursery where more than 20,000 plants have been raised. The collecting continues, of species found in other parts of Rajasthan as well as Jodhpur. Nearly 300 species of tree, shrub, climber, herb, grass and lithophyte have been planted, some in convenient mesquite extraction holes, and six years after the project began, Rao Jodha Desert Rock Park, named for the founder of Jodhpur, opened to the public.

Rao Jodha in order to build his new fort strategically on top of the great rock in 1459, had to move a hermit, known as the Lord of the Birds, who lived there in a cave. One story states that the old man reacted angrily at the intrusion of his solitude. He cursed Rao Jodha, saying his citadel would ever suffer from a scarcity of water. He was later placated by the construction of a temple and a pond but the curse lingers and is the reason given for droughts which occur every three or four years. Average rainfall is about 18 inches per annum though it is very variable and in one famine year there was less than an inch. There is still no water within the Fort.

Last year a very charming young man, Denzil Britto, the resident naturalist, talked about the garden in the Visitor's Centre. One common desert plant, the succulent *thhor*, a kind of euphorbia, grows energetically on rock all over Rajasthan and other arid areas of India. The cool shade it casts and the protection offered by its spines provides a microhabitat for other plants. These attractive qualities have led to it becoming the park's emblematic plant. Another very common plant is the *aak* or giant milkweed. Little bunches of its pretty little purple flowers were sold outside temples in Laos so it seems to be able to live in places with a much higher rainfall. A white variety has been introduced in Rao Jodha's garden. It is an ingredient in ayurvedic medicine and fibre from its stem is used to make robe, fishing line and other strong stuff.

India's textile traditions are one of its greatest glories. Each region has something unique that has been magically created for centuries. In the Punjab, which is the last location in this paradise garden ramble, it is a special form of embroidery called *phulkari* which literally means flower-work. The embroidery adorns large shawls which were often started by a grandmother at the birth of a baby granddaughter to eventually become part of her dowry. The ground cloth is coarse *khadi*, hand-loom cotton cloth, strong enough to hold the weight of the silk floss thread. The embroidery is a darn stitch, scarcely visible on the wrong side, with all the glory of the silk seen on the top. They are extremely beautiful and now even more highly treasured because they have not really been made since 1947 when the Punjab was divided. Jasleen Dhamija, an expert on the technique, says the unfortunate decline started before this time. How could anyone resist something called flower-work? And when the stitching completely covers the ground, the work is called a *bagh* or garden.

Pictorial shawls from East Punjab show village life—women churning butter, wrestlers and *sadhus*, farmers and cowherds, men on horses, people playing games, peacocks, elephants, lions and dancing bears. They are lively and amusing but I love the abstract shawls from the west. The first ones I bought were in Islamabad. One is unfinished with only a few little golden blossoms completed between the long regular rows of larger magenta flowers on a white ground. I wonder what happened to the creator. Another is much finer fabric, worn and fragile, is a veil rather than a shawl, with isolated motifs looking almost Chinese. Small aberrant shapes or colour variations in an otherwise very regular pattern might mark an event in the family of the embroiderer; a birth, a death, a move, a wedding. The stitching of the phulkari doesn't attempt to portray conventional blooms, the geometric shapes are triangles and pyramids, squares and chequer-boards, hooked whirligigs, arrowheads and diagonal stripes in bright magenta, orange and luminous gold, startling white and sometimes touches of pale green, black and navy. They convey the creators' delight in the essence of life, from the spring of a young woman when all the buds are blooming to the autumn leaves of a mature woman.

Chandigarh's rock garden is very different from Rao Jodha's. It has sprung from the dreams and imagination of one man, Nek Chand Saini. With his family he arrived as a 23-year-old refugee in India at the time of Partition, from a village which had suddenly become part of a foreign country, Pakistan. His masterpiece is almost yet another country, perhaps the re-creation of not only his childhood home but his entire childhood and family history left behind in the catastrophe of Partition where 14.5 million people were displaced. Some see it as something grander, a hope for universal harmony through creativity? But Nek Chand does not intellectualise his work. He says he did it as 'a hobby' and that he made the garden because he wanted to.

The state of Punjab was riven in two at the time of Partition, the east went to India and the west became the easternmost province of the new Dominion of Pakistan, now the Islamic Republic of Pakistan. The old capital city of Lahore lay within Pakistan so a new capital was needed for the Indian state. A site about 230km north of Delhi was chosen, on gently sloping terrain with the foothills of the Himalayas to the north. The city was to be called Chandigarh, Chandi was the name of a goddess worshipped locally and *garh* means fort. Prime Minister Nehru saw the new town as symbolic of India's new freedom 'unfettered by the traditions of the past' and 'an expression of the nation's faith in the future'.

In 1950 an American company was commissioned to draw up the Master Plan but after the unfortunate death of one of the principal planners, the company withdrew. In 1951 the commission passed to a team led by Charles Edouard Jeanneret, Le Corbusier, pioneer of modern architecture and town planning. It was conceived as a garden city with self-contained neighbourhoods separated by green space. Le Corbusier was dedicated to providing better living conditions for residents of crowded cities. His ethos fitted perfectly with Nehru's optimism for the future and the giant Open Hand monument that looms over Chandigarh's administrative buildings is his symbol of peace and reconciliation, the hand open to simultaneously give as well as to receive.

India's states are based on linguistic regions and in 1966 a new state called Haryana with a majority of people who spoke Hindi rather than Punjabi, was carved out of the eastern part of the Punjab. Chandigarh lay on the border and became a Union Territory to serve as capital to both the Punjab and Haryana. The city is spacious, green and clean, but suffers criticism like most planned cities, of being dull, new and too regular. Residents of Canberra where I live, know all about these criticisms, ignorant people in other states bag our city all the time, unwilling or too smug to take the time to explore our riches.

Originally planned for about 300,000 people, Chandigarh is now home to a million. Today the Capitol Complex with three signature Le Corbusier buildings, the Secretariat, the Parliament and the High Court, is under tight security so it no longer fulfills its designer's vision as a citizens' focus for celebration and activity. On my first visit in 1969 we entered at least one of the buildings. It must have been one of the courts because I can see in my mind's eye a small cocoon-like chamber, not a large assembly hall with tiered seats. We wandered through corridors and I remember being struck by what seemed piecemeal furniture, old filing cabinets and bashed up desks. Now I read that Le Corbusier designed all the furniture so perhaps it had already started to disappear by then. Original furniture and design elements down to humble man-hole covers from the streets, have found their way to auction houses in Paris and London where they have been sold for high prices, a significant loss to Chandigarh.

Nek Chand's family settled in the town of Gurdaspur, close

to the new international border. In 1949 he joined the Highway Department through the Refugee Employment Program and by 1951 he was a Road Inspector with Chandigarh's Public Works Department, scrutinising work on the construction of roads in the new city. This put him in a perfect position to spy likely materials for his dream. A small PWD store stood at his official site, within forest on land which he knew was not zoned for construction. Here he transported his objéts trouvés by bicycle to work most nights for four hours by the light of burning bicycle tyres, creating sculpture which was located in a patch of cleared jungle. As it was government land he was violating the strict planning laws protecting Le Corbusier's 'City Beautiful'.

Using neither sketch nor plan, Nek Chand's garden just evolved until today the garden spreads over more than 12 acres in a series of interlinked courtyards populated by thousands of sculptures. For Nek Chand, the garden is Daavtaon ki Nagri, a kingdom of gods and goddesses. Passages and doorways are low, requiring visitors to stoop and thus make obeisance to the gods. Around every corner something brings a smile. The miscellaneous materials include smashed crockery and sanitaryware, oil drums, tiles, bricks and brick dust, metal rods, foundry slag, condensers, bottles, pots, bicycle frames, exhaust pipes, wire, electrical fittings and tube lights. At first it came from the rubble of twenty villages demolished to make way for Chandigarh. Later booty came from construction sites and unusual discoveries like buckets of broken glass bangles after festivals. Nek Chand observed construction in the new city and developed his own techniques. He used jute sacks to mould concrete walls and pillars, wire was formed into frames then clad with cement and pebbles. His studies in hydraulic engineering enabled him to design efficient water-pumping and recycling systems for the waterfalls. Near miniature palaces and temples are throngs of animals, phalanxes of men, congregations of women and gangs of children, flocks of peacocks and geese, monkey armies, herds of horses, dogs and oxen. Tree roots are made from cable, bears from bicycle frames, walls of clay pots and women of glass bangles. Nek Chand's artistic talent and technical competence is incredibly impressive and the garden is magical.

I have visited twice, the first time on a beautiful sunny day when tribes of school children on excursion were having a wonderful time propelling themselves as high as the sky on long swings, overlooked by a line of sculpted guardian horses. Visitation has reached 12,000,000 but the history of the garden's survival has not been easy. Government employees spraying for malaria on the city's outskirts first discovered the secret garden some eight years after it was begun. 1973 was an important year when at the conclusion of the construction of a large road, Nek Chand's PWD hut was due to be destroyed. This is when the administration became aware of the so-called 'Store Garden'. Chandigarh's Chief Commissioner and Chief Architect were first amazed and then delighted by the unique creation. Rather than demolition they decided on preservation and in 1976 it was inaugurated and opened to the general public. Nek Chand was given the first of many awards, a cash prize and more importantly was released from other 'mundane duties' to devote all his time to his garden as Sub-Divisional Engineer, Rock Garden with a work-force of 50 labourers.

Several serious threats have been averted since then. Avaricious politicians and others have brought in the bulldozers, to be faced once by a barrier of hundreds of protesting school children. Funds have been cut off, the labour force disbanded and vandalism sustained but a popular revolution has saved it. Now a London-based foundation deals effectively with problems and international volunteers come to the magical kingdom to work in programs involving local people, even squads of soldiers from nearby army bases. They are engaged on the world's largest mosaic project, in the Third Phase of the Rock Garden. Nek Chand, now in his 90s, regularly visits his creation. His kingdom of the gods is his paradise garden.

The Palace at Deeg, Rajasthan

An audience at Nek Chand's garden, Chandigarh, Punjab & Haryana

So You Can See In The Dark

Yesterday afternoon I was propelled into the kitchen by an unseen force which told me it was imperative that I make jam or chutney or pickle—in short a preserve of some kind. It is an automatic thing that has happened at moments of stress over more than forty years. Several meanings of the word 'preserve' perhaps fit exactly what I was doing, not only capturing the essence and flavour of fruit and vegetable, but safeguarding myself as well. I was already a little tense as a suitcase containing my very best clothes and even more distressing, my address book, had been missing for more than three days, lost by an airline. My jewellery had fortunately been in my handbag and I was quite resigned to living without the clothes, even my marvellous magenta suede stilts, but the address book was a great loss and already that particular day I had needed to go to it no fewer than six times. But then to make matters far worse, I heard that one small grandson had broken his arm and my daughter was with him in Casualty at our local hospital.

The fridge and the fruit-bowl were not immediately inspirational but I knew I had enough empty jars for a batch of something and I was determined to fill them. The only possibility was carrot jam—I had plenty of carrots and plenty of lemons. Alas not enough sugar but a walk up to the shops this morning fixed that and now I have seven jars full of glorious orange goo. I didn't start a moment too soon. The family situation greatly worsened in between jam procedures. My daughter became very ill herself so there was even more impetus to get on with the jam.

You might not think that carrot jam is very exciting but I can assure you it is extremely good. Now I'm writing this I have just realised that in my two-stage and somewhat distracted manufacture I have completely forgotten to add the brandy which is a final delicious addition, though not entirely necessary. So this batch is a teetotaller's version. My recipe is an old one from Warwickshire and came from a very small, three inches square, cookbook of just twenty-four pages, the sort of publication stocked in the giftshops of National Trust properties in England. The only drawback I can see to carrot jam is that it cooks in a heaving mass a bit like the boiling mud pools at Rotorua and has an amazing range for dreadful blistering splats. If you don't partially cover the saucepan, the kitchen will be adorned with orange splashes and the floor will be a sticky quagmire. However, if you can dodge the splats, the jam is quick and easy and a brilliant colour. One of the nicest things about the production of preserves is the sight the filled jars present at the end.

I made all kinds of jam and pickle when I lived in Pakistan but my cooking in India was very rudimentary. I had hardly any equipment, my kitchen was extremely basic and I had neither the time to cook nor the friends to entertain. My houseguests were few during the four months I spent in a flat, just my daughter and her two little boys and a great friend from Sydney. Nobody expected lavish meals and I didn't have much equipment. My friend Annie searching the kitchen for plates on her first morning failed to recognise the stainless steel *thalis*! I didn't run much further than providing breakfast for house-guests or a drink on the roof for others, and when I did eat my solitary meals at night they were usually omelettes and salad. A former tenant had left behind a small square sandwich-toaster-type contraption. I cooked my toast on it in the morning and it was good for browning the top of various concoctions cooked in the one small saucepan owned by me and the little frying pan which had also been left behind. The sandwich toaster was extremely temperamental and would only work when it felt so inclined. I used to leave the room or turn my back on it or stand on one leg. I never raised my voice and generally it would see its way clear to working.

I developed a taste for tinned sweet corn which was my first meal in the flat, that, followed by a banana. I did make a kind of baba ganoush now and then, cooking the eggplant against the naked gas flame which gave it a wonderful smoky flavour. I bought beautiful little cauliflowers which can be eaten in one helping, gorgeous mushrooms when they were available and excellent green peas from the vendor who sold vegetables from a barrow outside the nearby supermarket. It is a great thing in India to be able to buy delicious ready-shelled peas which saves a lot of time. At home when I've had more time and the peas aren't shelled, I've made a good curry from the pods—*mattar chilka kari*. The virtue at not wasting all those lovely green pods is only marginal compared to the great fag of removing the hard inner linings of the pods which break your thumb-nails.

Because I grew up in an all-electric kitchen I have an understandable fear of gas. The gas stove in Peshawar was terrifying. Lighting the oven involved crouching behind the oven door, putting a match to the end of a whole rolled up broadsheet issue of the Frontier Post, extending an arm around the door to thrust it into the stove and waiting for the subsequent explosion. The Jaipur flat had a hob attached to bottled gas. The thought of running out of gas was too frightful to contemplate as my flat was located up five flights of metal fire-escape stairs. The stairs were a great incentive not to forget anything when I set off for work each morning and they provided another good reason not to cook. When my daughter came to stay, she and her little sons preceded my son-in-law by a few days. She was very adventurous and took the boys all around the town—to the zoo and the planetarium and all the way to Jaigarh Fort in an auto. The boys were in the midst of a stage of fiendish naughtiness and one evening when I arrived back from work I found a very woebegone trio. Em was furious with them for some misdemeanour but the situation had all been made far worse as I had forgotten to tell her to turn on the gas bottle before attempting to light the burner and the children were halfway through eating cold baked beans for their evening meal. Oh dear, what a drama. But Em had a gin, I had a whisky, the boys had a glass of milk and we all felt better.

In the summer and autumn months if I arrived home at a reasonable hour I would go up to the roof to enjoy the marvellous view with a whisky and soda and some peanuts. I looked out to the hills in one direction and up and down the length of a leafy street in another. I had a very good address, in the pukka location of Civil Lines where the residences of both the Chief Minister and the State Governor were located just across the road. Each evening as the sun set, thousands of birds would flock to the telephone wires just to one side of my rooftop vantage point. Their deafening chattering lasted until as though at a given signal, all would stop. Not a peep from a solitary bird would be heard. They ceased with such perfect timing any conductor would have welcomed them to his choir.

When I moved into my flat it was a week or so before Diwali, the happy festival of lights which encompasses a number of celebrations and events from Hindu mythology. The most important day for most is the third, called Amavasya when Lakshmi, the Goddess of Wealth, is welcomed into every household, thoroughly cleaned in anticipation of her arrival. She is then at her most benevolent and devotees hope she will fulfil their wishes. The name Diwali means a row of lamps and the festival involves the lighting of small clay *diyas* or oil lamps, which line the parapets and verandas and roof-lines of even the humblest home. They signify the triumph of good over evil. The lamps are kept burning through the night and houses cleaned in order to make the goddess feel welcome. There is of course another dimension to the festival of lights. The most significant spiritual meaning is the personal awareness of an inner light and the idea of victory of good over evil also refers to the power of enlightenment over ignorance.

Fireworks are lit in order to drive away evil spirits. Everyone who can afford them wears new clothes and shares sweets with friends and family. The sweet shops in Jaipur are wonderful at any time but at Diwali they are truly amazing and crowded with purchasers. Overflow stalls appear up and down the footpaths to cope with the crowds of purchasers. In another section of the bazaar little shops selling ledgers and account books do a brisk trade. Traditionally Diwali marks the end of the financial year for businesses connected to the agrarian cycle as it marks the end of the harvest season for farmers. The books are bound in red cloth stitched by hand and make wonderful day books for any purpose. As the famers might give thanks for a good harvest and pray for another yet to come, businessmen invoke Lakshmi to bring wealth, prosperity and success to their endeavours.

These days the firecrackers are so powerful the noise is something like World War III and thanks to electricity the illuminations are very elaborate indeed. In Jaipur that year extraordinary sculptures also appeared — a green Statue of Liberty at Badi Chaupal, a leaning Tower of Pisa further down the bazaar and a small Taj Mahal. Flashing lights depicting Lakshmi in all her glory, lotus-borne and flanked by lustrating elephants, appeared on one business in the old city and across the road on another old building a huge luminous peacock spread his marvellous tail in a sequence of flashing lights. It all looked wonderful and the excitement was infectious. I certainly had to join in. I bought yards of plastic tubing which encased tiny little light globes and strung it around the top of my building and on the stairs to the roof. From here I could see the little Moti Dungri Fort on a hill in the middle distance illuminated for the festival. It looked like a fairy castle in the darkling sky and at the dead of night it was like a *vimana* or celestial chariot for a god, hovering over the hills. I would wake up just to look at it.

Every night was punctuated by the comings and goings of the many trains that passed through Jaipur. Civil Lines is located close to the railway line and not far from the station. I walked over a nearby level crossing each day on my way to and from work. At night when the town was sleeping, the warning bells of the crossing would ring out. It always seemed to sound like the start of Liszt's *La Campanella* which I would finish off in my half-asleep state. I loved it. In Peshawar we were woken by the call to prayer from a nearby mosque and in Vientiane it was the drum of the wat just over our back fence, rousing the monks at the start of another day.

In Jaipur I don't think I ever cooked carrots although I bought them to eat raw, but in Peshawar they were often on the menu. They are the beautiful rosy-coloured variety, not the orange which the Dutch developed in the 17th or 18th century. We discovered a very scenic place in Peshawar, perfect for an afternoon tea picnic.

It was on the river banks close to a rustic old rose-coloured stone bridge which dated from Mughul times. Under the bridge in the lengthening shadows, farmers who had driven their carts to the water's edge washed their harvested carrots, similar in colour to the bridge itself. It was a scene straight from a painting by a South Asian Constable. The farmers were very friendly and insisted we take some carrots as a gift.

In the winter the great treat from the bakery near our house in University Town was a dish of *gajar ka halwa,* the rich and addictive pudding made of grated carrot cooked very slowly in milk, butter and sugar with the addition of raisins, almonds and rosewater. Just the thought of it makes my mouth water. I have cooked it often in Australia and eat it whenever I'm in India in the winter. It is one of the ways carrots are most commonly eaten in India and they are also the main ingredient in a delicious *barfi* or sweetmeat, popular at Diwali. I recently bought some in Lucknow made from black carrots and it was very good. I would never have identified it myself or even found it at night in the dimly-lit winding lanes of the old part of the city called Chowk, but Cyrus Kherawala, a Parsi gourmet, knew just where to find the old man selling it on a dark corner. These black Lucknow carrots are also used is in a spicy drink called *kaanji*. A friend's mother makes it and he swears it is delicious, tasting something like pickle and prepared in a similar Indian way, by being left in the winter sun for a couple of days. It turns a lovely reddish colour, a little like red wine. Indian restaurants rarely serve carrots as a solo dish. They frequently brighten up a vegetable *biriani* and come in mixed vegetable curries but apart from *gajar-ka halwa,* their use must be mainly in dishes made at home.

MasterChef Australia was a prime-time ratings winner in India for some years and then came an Indian equivalent. The winner of Season Two of the show in 2013 was an extremely brave young woman called Shipra Khanna. She says she started cooking interesting 'outside' food when warned not to allow her delicate daughter to eat outside the home for fear of infection. She experimented and taught herself how to cook Chinese and

Italian foods and all kinds of bread and cake in her own kitchen. She credits her success to her daughter and the inspiration of MasterChef Australia. Caught up in a nasty domestic situation and an acrimonious divorce, cooking has transported her to a new and optimistic world and she has now opened her first restaurant in Ahmedabad. Her winning eclectic menu included a Garam Masala Carrot Cake! Garam Masala is a beautiful aromatic mixed spice — the *garam* means 'hot' but in fact the heat seems to evaporate if added early during the process of cooking rather than at the end. Recipes vary and the mixture can include peppercorns, cardamom, cinnamon, cumin, coriander, cloves, fennel, turmeric, chilli and nutmeg. In haste when making either my Christmas pudding or cake I usually throw in a spoonful or two rather than opening several jars of cinnamon, cardamom and allspice.

Prime Minister Moraji Desai came to Sydney for the CHOGRM meeting in February 1978. This was the first convening of a Commonwealth Heads of Government Regional Meeting, a regional off-shoot of the better known CHOGM. The meeting was sadly marred by a bomb explosion on 13 February, outside the Hilton Hotel, the site of the meeting and where most delegates were accommodated. Three people were killed and eleven injured. Arrests were made and over many years, trials, enquiries and a Royal Commission investigated the crime. Mr Desai claimed that members of the Ananda Marga sect had targeted him with intent to murder because of the imprisonment of the organisation's spiritual leader, Prabhat Ranjan Sarkar. Before this very regrettable tragedy took place (the poor men killed were two innocent garbage collectors and a policeman) members of Australian government departments had been exercised by several requirements for the Indian leader.

Mr Desai was a longtime advocate of urine therapy and practitioner of that unusual regime. He had publicly stated that it was the perfect medical solution for the millions of Indians unable to afford more mainstream medicines. As I have a great interest in pineapples, I was amused to find that if there is a need to adopt the habit of drinking one's own urine, the easiest method is to start with pineapple juice as it looks much the same. I haven't had the desire to test the theory.

I expect Mr Desai looked after that article of diet himself but not so easy was the fact that his consumption of milk had to be very, very, fresh, unpasteurised and from a cow facing in a particular direction, the east perhaps. This was eventually accomplished by diligent members of the Ceremonial and Hospitality Branch of the Department of Prime Minister & Cabinet who located a cow on a vast green sward at Sydney University, only about two miles from the Hilton. This happy ruminant was daily milked for not the 'King's Breakfast' à la A.A. Milne, but the PM's. The other requirement concerned carrots. They were an important part of his diet but they *had* to be red carrots which proved entirely impossible to find here in the land of the orange variety.

Strangely the cow part of that story had a connection in the leafy suburbs of Canberra. Prior to the Sydney bombing, on 15 September 1977 the Ananda Marga were alleged to have been involved in an attack and kidnapping of a diplomat from the Indian High Commission and his wife. It was a nightmare for the poor couple who were abducted from their home in the suburb of Red Hill. The gentleman was stabbed but somehow his brave wife managed to overpower the driver of the car in which they had been bundled and the pair were put out on a lonely country road in the dark of night.

The Canberra stabbing had unexpected repercussions. After his recovery, the gentleman was tailed by security for his own protection. What came to light was a spot of infidelity. When his long-suffering wife learned of this she sought help from friends and family at home in the Punjab. One good friend went to her guru and explained the situation far away in Australia. 'Oh well,' he said, 'this is just a passing phase. Time will cure the problem. All will be well. But in the meantime tell her it would be just as well to help things along the way. For six weeks she should place under his pillow every Tuesday night a small packet containing *roti, ghee* and *gur* (unrefined sugar). Then on Wednesday feed this to a passing cow.' This is all very well if you lived in India where passing cows were not an unusual occurrence. If you were an army officer living in a nice cantonment, you might even have your own dairy cow in the garden of your bungalow. But not so in suburban Canberra and even if you had a nodding acquaintance with a few cows in nearby paddocks, they would more than likely kick up their heels and run away when faced with hand-feeding of such unusual nourishment. Fortunately for the poor wife, she knew me quite well. She asked for my help and how could I refuse? So each Wednesday I would go into town and pick up the roti parcel to give to our milking cow who had been bailed up in the cattle yards for the purpose. All went well until the sixth and last week when I arrived home with the children, too late to trek up to the yards in the dark to thrust the offering into the cow's mouth. I placed it on the roof of the car and planned to do the needful in the morning. But daylight revealed one of our cats had enjoyed a fine midnight feast. We said a mantra over him and hoped for the best.

The indigenous or *desi* carrot of India is greenish-white in colour and probably originated in neighbouring Afghanistan where there was also a purple variety. These original wild species reached Greece and Rome before the Christian era and by the 10th century at the very latest, were found in north-western Europe. The Moors may have brought a purple variety from North Africa to Spain soon after this and it was the Dutch who developed the orange-coloured variety as late as the 17th century. The colour was particularly appropriate and symbolic in the Netherlands for the Royal House of Orange. Carrots were originally grown for their aromatic leaves and seeds rather than the roots and they are related to parsley, fennel, dill and cumin. It's easy to recognise the family resemblance in the botanical cousins and pretty Queen Ann's Lace is also related. Fronds of carrot leaves were once worn as ephemeral decoration in hats.

The indigenous Indian variety had little flavour in comparison to the orange European variety although the 16th century Portuguese physician, naturalist and pioneer of tropical medicine, Garcia da Orta, wrote of good ones in Surat and even better in the Deccan. The *desi* carrot wasn't the type the British had come to know and enjoy, the improved hybrid versions having increased sweetness and minimised the woody core, so along with other vegetables they brought their own varieties. The carrots failed dismally in the plains but were grown successfully in Darjeeling and other hill stations and acclimatised seed was introduced all around the country.

The carrot in the past had rather a contemptible place in Indian cookery as well as folklore and colloquial expression. *'Gajar-mooli'*, which translated means 'carrots and radish', a metaphor for an extremely insignificant and foolish person and is used to describe someone with bit of a personality by-pass. *Mooli* or radish was used as a term of derision for Shah Shuja, the powerless puppet ruler placed on the Afghan throne by the British in 1839. The Chinese have always given disparaging names to foods from foreign lands—the tomato is called a barbarian eggplant and the carrot a barbarian radish. Further bad press for the humble carrot.

Children the world over have been urged by their mothers to eat up their carrots so they can see in the dark. Can anyone really see in the dark? In a work by James Turrell in the Art House Project on Naoshima Island in Japan, the viewer's perceptions of light and dark are challenged. It is part of his *Aperture* series and is located in a tall dark wooden building designed by Tadao Ando. A large door is the portal to a huge darkness, so deep and dense it is impossible to see one's hand in front of one's face or certainly to find the way out. The sense of direction is lost as an attendant ushers shuffling viewers towards invisible benches. The ability to see is lost completely and there is a sense of dissolving into the deep, but after ten or fifteen minutes a discernible light hovers at the end of the vast expanse of black. Somehow it is easier to see it by looking at the side of its source in a sneaky sort of way. It is very curious and leads to questioning all the senses.

And carrots helping with seeing in the dark? A friend told me her grandmother would say after the injunction to eat up them up, 'Have you ever seen a rabbit wearing spectacles?' This was along with eating spinach to be as strong as Popeye and remembering all the time the starving children in India who had nothing to eat at all. The huge amounts of carotene contained in carrots converts into Vitamin A which is essential for good eyesight. Carrots also contain Vitamins B and C and are a good source of potassium, folic acid and can help lower cholesterol. Pureed carrots are an easy thing to cook when starting babies on solid food and an old wives cure for simple diarrhoea is to cook finely diced carrot in the starchy water saved after cooking boiled rice.

I have several Indian cook-books and the oldest, dog-eared, stained and falling apart is *Cooking the Indian Way* by Attia Hosain and Sita Pasricha, with a spelling mistake on the cover in one of the authors' names. My edition was published in 1969 the year I returned from my first visit to India. It is such a marvellous book and I have used and adapted many of its recipes. One such is *alu methi*, potatoes with fenugreek which is just as good when made as *gajar methi*, substituting carrots for the ubiquitous potato. In the simplest of roadside *dhabas* and restaurants, potato is the most likely vegetable to find in India. I once had a very ordinary set meal in a Bundi hotel where three of the four dishes served at dinner contained potato. It was actually my birthday, celebrated completely by myself and as I rarely eat potato in any form, it wasn't a brilliant feast.

Vijay Prashad is an eminent academic in the field of South Asian History and International Studies at Trinity College in Hartford, Connecticut. He is a self-described Marxist, and a co-founder of the Forum of Indian Leftists or FOIL, a journalist and commentator and the author of several books. He seems an unlikely link to my favourite Indian cookbook but in a review he recently wrote on a new American Indian cook-book I discovered he is the grandson of Sita Pasricha. He tells the story of his grandfather, posted as a doctor to the Indian High Commission in London. Grandfather neglected his own health and died not long after the family's arrival on posting. Prashad's resourceful grandmother decided to remain in England and took in paying guests to help with the finances. In 1962 she teamed up with her friend the writer Attia Hosain, who had also stayed on in London. The result is a simply marvellous book. They said it was written 'with the problems of housewives abroad in mind', those who wanted to cook Indian food without being able to buy all the ingredients. In our penurious winter of 1981 in Norfolk the shopping situation was not so different from London in the 1950s. Apart from the cook at the local Chinese takeaway there were no Asians in the town in which we lived and I wasn't able to buy many ingredients I needed. Even in Norwich, shops in those days were not very focused on exotic cuisines. Mushy peas were a feature of food stalls at the market. It was thrilling one day to find a Cypriot grocer in another part of the city who sold wonderful figs and olives. Meanwhile in Drearham, the name we gave to our temporary home, I adapted Sita and Attia's *bhaji* of spring greens to brussels sprouts and my children who had hitherto hated all possible variations of sprouts, devoured them happily.

Prashad says he used to have a photocopy of the book, the only available form since it went out of print in 1970, until his sister found a few copies on the internet. I've since looked it up and find I could buy one on Amazon for $100 new or slightly less for a second-hand book, so my copy is really quite valuable even if it looks quite dreadful. The price on the back for Australia and New Zealand is 95 cents—amazingly good value for a dollar spent all those years ago.

Another even more treasured little book is just a few years younger and in a similar state of decrepitude, the mark of a well-used cook-book. *Mirch Masala: One Hundred Indian Recipes* by Surayya Tyabji was given me in September 2004 by the author's niece, my dear friend Shama Chowdhury. It was a very touching and sad last meeting we had as Shama died just two months later. She was very ill that day, far too ill to sit at the lunch table at her home. One of the dishes was the utterly delicious *Baigan aur Dahi*— slices of spiced eggplant, fried in oil, drained and then floated in yoghurt seasoned with spices. It was perfect and I went back to Shama's bedroom after lunch raving about it. 'Zai' she said to her sister, 'get that little book and I'll give it to Claudia.' And so she did and wrote in her neat hand, 'Passed on to Claudia with much love as always, Shama.'

Her death was such a blow—Zai rang me at my desk at the

National Gallery in Australia. We had all first met in Port Moresby where Zai and I were living at the time, twenty-five years before. Shama and I met just twice then but we became good friends and I saw her every time I visited India—once in Bombay, once in Ahmedabad and many times in Delhi. The visit to Bombay was with my mother and the children then aged 9 and 10. Poor Shama was in a fit of nerves about cooking for us—she was living in her family's flat where she hardly cooked at all. But together we managed to conjure up some good meals and Mum and I were amused that Shama had learned how to cook Indian food from one of Charmaine Solomon's excellent books, published in Australia.

Shama was a very fine writer. In an article about her in 2006, two years after her death, when Penguin India published four new editions of her work, Nilanjana Roy, a marvellous journalist and literary critic, said 'She had made a name for herself as a reviewer of rare sensibility and unshakeable honesty, and as a gifted teacher, but she came into her own as a writer relatively late.' Of the four books, two are her novels, *Tara Lane* and *Reaching Bombay Central*, there is a volume of collected essays and reviews titled *The Right Words* and the fourth is *Frontiers* a collection of stories. Other works by Shama including children's stories, a play and beautiful translations of poetry by Meerabai *In the dark of the heart: Songs of Meera* are still in print.

At the time of the new publications I was working in Jaipur for the Jaipur Virasat Foundation. I received an email from Penguin India, inviting me to attend the launch of these four books of Shama's work. The email had done a couple of circuits around the world, sent first to the National Gallery in Canberra and then back to me in Jaipur. The launch was to be held in Delhi two days hence on a Saturday. In the lead-up to the Jaipur Festival in January I was really frantically busy and I thought to myself, oh dear what a shame but I just can't go—we worked six days a week including Saturday. I continued on with whatever it was that I was doing and soon enough it was time for lunch. Another reason why I didn't have to cook much in my flat was that my lunch was generously provided at work. It came from the Anokhi Farm kitchen and was always absolutely delicious—simple vegetarian dishes, different every day. We used to eat in an area behind the office, roofed but opening onto a patch of lawn.

That day a group of five musicians were seated on the grass playing and singing most beautifully. As I sat and listened, lovely Mamta, the office administrator, explained to me that significantly, although the musicians were Muslim they were singing hymns by Meerabai. Meera, a 16th century mystic of aristocratic birth, was a devotee of Lord Krishna to whom she wrote 1000 *bhajans* or hymns in passionate praise. Of course I thought immediately of Shama, whose translations were for her a way of bridging the two worlds in which she lived as a writer in English in India. She had made a conscious effort to improve her Hindi in order to more deeply understand Meera's poetry and like the musicians, Shama came from a Muslim family.

The music was captivating and I found it quite extraordinary that they were singing words that might have been translated by dear Shama. It simply brought tears to my eyes. Mamta looked stricken and asked whatever was wrong and I explained. 'Well, you must go to Delhi tomorrow,' she said. 'No, no there's too much to do and tomorrow is Saturday.' 'Don't worry about that,' she said, 'this is far more important.' So I bought a ticket for the bus the next day, almost missed it through no fault of my own, finally reached Delhi just in time for Victoria to pick me up at the Bikaner House terminus, whisk me home so I could change my clothes and get to the Habitat Centre in time for the evening. It was indeed far too important to have missed.

Shama was gentle and gracious but an incisive observer of people and place and the subtleties of everyday situations. She quietly addressed problems of corruption, insecurity, inequality and intolerance in her writing while dealing with smaller, seemingly insignificant details of life. She became Professor of Western Drama at the National School of Drama in Delhi. Always encouraging to young writers for whom she somehow made time, she ran a welcoming hospitable household for her husband Javid Chowdhury, two dear children, Rishad and Shaheen and Javid's sister whose name is also

Shama, a loved extra member of the family. *The Right Words*, the title of her book of selected essays, is a description of Shama. She always found the right words. I miss her still.

Somehow I met, although not through Shama, her cousin Laila Tyabji, a most fascinating and talented woman and the little cookbook given me by Shama was written by her mother. Laila is tiny and as elegant as any Indian woman can be. Her saris are always superb, worn with matching interesting jewellery and wonderful hair which always look as though it has just been professionally styled. Tiny impressive women are sometimes bossy and noisy but not Laila who breathes quiet, calmness and dignity. Trained in art and design in India and Japan, she is Chairperson and one of the founders of Dastkar, a Society for Crafts and Craftspeople. She has worked with artisans over the last thirty years, speaking on their behalf in policy planning for the craft and development sector by Government and non-government organisations. One of her great passions is textiles, she is an embroiderer herself and is often seen with a beautiful bag she has made slung over her shoulder.

Like Shama, Laila is also a fine writer. She sent me two published essays she had written about her fascinating extended family and the wonderful food they consumed. *Mirch Masala*, her mother's little book, has been reissued in a smarter, more up-to-date format which I should buy for my daughter and daughter-in-law. I could never part with my own original with its funny illustrations by the Goan artist, Mario Miranda (1926–2011), of a gentleman eating his way through the book, section by section, growing steadily more rotund watched by a waiter in an old-fashioned uniform with buttons and epaulettes—alas no cockaded turban and cummerbund like some branches of the India Coffee House restaurant chain. Mario Miranda's cartoons in mural form look as though they will live on for ever on the walls of the famous Café Mondegar in Bombay where I bought a couple of plates to further remind me of *Mirch Masala*. Carrots do not feature greatly in that little book but thinking about them has led me in this essay to recollections of some very special Indian women, definitely in no way *gajar-mooli*!

Here are three very good and varied carrot recipes, for balance perhaps not all to be eaten in the same meal!

Gajar Methi—spicy fried carrots

500 gm carrots

2 teaspoons dried methi (fenugreek) of 2 handfuls fresh

60 gm ghee or butter or 2 tablespoons oil

½ teaspoon turmeric

1 teaspoon chilli powder (or to taste)

Salt to taste

Scrub carrots, cut into 1 cm rounds. Place in saucepan of cold water and bring quickly to the boil. Remove from the heat, drain and allow to cool. If using dried methi soak in a little water and strain though this is not absolutely necessary as the steam in the cooking will reconstitute the leaves. Wash and chop fresh methi if used. In a frying pan heat the ghee, butter or oil, add the carrots and turmeric and sauté, stirring for two minutes. Add the methi, chilli powder and salt and fry for another three minutes, stirring the while. Lower heat and cover the pan until carrots are cooked and there is a wondrous aromatic smell. Serve with other vegetable curries, rice and pickle.

Gaja-ka Halwa—carrot pudding

1 kg carrots

1 litre milk

250 gm sugar

250 gm butter

60 gm ground almonds

60 gm sultanas or raisins

½ teaspoon saffron threads

1 dessertspoon rose-water

Scrub carrots then grate on a coarse grater. Wet a heavy saucepan and place in it the carrots and milk. Bring to the boil then lower the heat and simmer for two hours. Stir with a wooden spoon occasionally to ensure the mixture does not stick (wetting the saucepan helps with this). After two hours the mixture should be a thick pulp. Add the butter and sugar. Turn the heat up and cook for 15 minutes, stirring the while. Add ground almonds and sultanas. Stand the saffron threads in a tablespoon of boiling water for a minute then add to the carrot mixture. Mix well then remove from heat and pour into a bowl to cool. Sprinkle with rosewater and serve at room temperature.

Carrot Jam with Brandy

Carrots

Sugar

Lemons

Brandy

Scrub and chop carrots and place in a saucepan with water to cover. Bring to the boil and simmer until soft. Drain and process to a purée. If a little liquid is required to assist, use a spoonful of lemon-juice, deducting the quantity from the juice required in the jam. Weigh the puree. To every 500 gm of carrot pulp allow 500 gm of sugar, the grated rind of one lemon and the juice of two. Place all ingredients in saucepan, bring to the boil, lower heat slightly and cook until set, stirring occasionally to avoid sticking. Add brandy if desired—2 tablespoons to the above quantities. Stir well. Pour into warm jars and seal.

PS I recently visited somewhere I lived for a while and remembered a carrot encounter. New to the city and somewhat friendless I joined an auxiliary of one of the state institutions. I was prepared to do anything in a voluntary capacity and was directed to the Craft Group which is the sort of thing I usually avoid. I can sew so I thought, why not. I was in my early 50s but everyone else present was in the 70–90 bracket and two ladies, brought along by their friends for a therapeutic outing, did not seem exactly sure where they were at all. We were given orange and green felt, cut to shape and told to make—yes—carrots! We had to sew them neatly in buttonhole stitch and stuff them with dried rosemary to be sold in the organisation's little shop. I guess I could add this skill to my CV but somehow I haven't and I didn't return for second helpings.

Carrots and cauliflowers at Kota, Rajasthan

Waiter at Indian Coffee House, Gwalior, Madhya Pradesh

A Big Tamasha

Free speech and sectarian tensions at the Jaipur Festival 2012

This year's Jaipur Literature Festival (20–24 January) more than lived up to the Indian Ministry of Tourism's slogan—'Incredible India'.

The festival was established in 2006 as a component of the Jaipur Virasat (Heritage) Festival, an arts event founded in 2003 to showcase the varied and colourful Rajasthani culture. Performances of classical music and dance were held in the forecourts of old temples and folk concerts attracted crowds of thousands in city squares. Craft bazaars, art exhibitions, workshops and many forms of theatre took place in dozens of locations around the city—in former royal palaces, forts and gardens, a modern amphitheatre and galleries in an arts complex designed by architect Charles Correa, even an ancient reservoir, everywhere laden with atmosphere. It was brilliant, exotic and in the smaller venues, surprisingly intimate.

The advent of a rival cultural festival inaugurated by the Rajasthan State Government brought serious funding and sponsorship difficulties as previous supporters defected to the Government festival. But the literature section with its broader national and international base, soon overtook all but the evening musical events. From a modest program of eighteen writers at a single venue in 2006, Jaipur has become Asia's largest literary gathering. This year more than 250 writers spoke at four concurrent sessions over five days—truly a big *tamasha*.

When Maharaja Sawai Jai Singh II shifted his capital from Amber to Jaipur in 1727, Rajput noblemen were required to build official residences nearby, and Diggi Palace, the festival location, has its origins from this time. Home still to the Thakurs (rulers) of Diggi, a *thikana* or sub-state located about 50 km from Jaipur, the attractive collection of 1860s pavilions, courtyards and walled gardens became a hotel in 1991. It is reached by a lane, in years past choked with people, cars and auto-rickshaws. This year it was virtually vehicle-free and where previously anyone could enter freely, this year rigorous security prevailed. There were some 500 police on duty throughout the festival. Dozens manned barriers at the main road, dozens more young volunteers issued free passes after sighting photo id of attendees encouraged to have registered on-line. Policemen and women checked bags, there were metal detectors and finally bar codes on the festival passes were scanned. Inside the gateway the police presence was again obvious but unobtrusive.

The 2011 festival attracted publicity after alleged racism and a stoush between those who saw themselves as true founders of the festival, but this was just a whisper compared to what happened when it was revealed that Salman Rushdie was to attend in 2012. Long after the withdrawal of the notorious Iranian fatwa in 1998, Rushdie continues to be pilloried in India and elsewhere because of his book *The Satanic Verses* (1998).

Rushdie had in fact attended the 2007 festival on which I worked for six months. Concern for his own personal security was of course uppermost in the organisers' minds but there was no incident whatsoever. The author was genial, affable and accommodating, the audiences enthusiastic. This year protests soon arose, first from Maulana Abul Qasim Nomani, head of the conservative Darul Uloom seminary in Deoband in the state of Uttar Pradesh. He demanded Rushdie not be granted an entry visa to India despite the fact that, as a PIO (Person of Indian Origin) he did not need one.

Initially Rushdie was asked to delay his arrival while festival directors endeavoured to defuse the situation and organise added security. The Rajasthan Congress Party State Government, citing security problems, suggested Rushdie stay away and the Chief Minister met with Union Home Minister in Delhi to inform him of 'prevailing sentiments'. The Central Congress Party Government sounded an alert about plans by the outlawed Students Islamic

Movement of India (SIMI) to target Rushdie, but sought to distance itself. Then so-called reliable intelligence sources in Maharashtra and Rajasthan reported that three assassins from the Mumbai underworld were travelling from Mumbai to in Rushdie's later words 'eliminate me'. The origin of these reports is unclear but the Rajasthan State Government conveyed the advice to festival organisers. Maharashtra's Director-General of Police subsequently denied any part in communiqués which were also forwarded to New Delhi. Rushdie had his own sources in Mumbai investigate this rumour about the putative hit men. Two appeared to be fictitious and the third was a member of the banned group SIMI. Rushdie accused the Rajasthan Police and the State Government of concocting the whole threat to keep him away from the festival. He lamented that politicians 'are in bed with religious extremists groups' for 'narrow electoral reasons' and that these extremists, whom he regards as the real enemies of Islam, are thus able to prevent free expression.

After airing these serious reservations 'about the accuracy of this intelligence' he decided 'it would be irresponsible of me to come to the festival in such circumstances'. The simmering situation lost a little heat but death-threats were made against Festival Directors, writers Namita Gokhale and William Dalrymple and Producer Sanjoy Roy. Despite the doubtful reports, the directors—sensible, tactful and discreet—altered the program and the festival opened on time with a decided flourish.

Most observers believe that the machinations were very much connected to the State elections in neighbouring Uttar Pradesh where the Congress Party is in opposition. Congress General Secretary, Rahul Gandhi was actively campaigning as was his mother, Sonia Gandhi, President of the Indian National Congress Party and widow of the assassinated Prime Minister, Rajiv Gandhi. Unusual consequences followed when the BJP and other conservative Hindu organisations were vocal in their defence of Rushdie's freedom of speech, somewhat embarrassing to the liberals. By contrast some secularists, unwilling to offend Muslim sentiment, found themselves defending the ban. Conservative Muslims have exploited the Rushdie affair to create a common voice but the question on many lips is just how many offended Muslims have actually read *The Satanic Verses* in order to be so angered by its content. The greatest loser over the whole affair is surely Rajasthan Chief Minister Ashok Gehlot, seen as cowardly in a state famed throughout history for chivalry and fortitude.

Editorials and articles poured scorn and derision on State and Central Governments and questions of democracy and freedom of speech pervaded many excellent sessions. *The Argumentative Indian in Ancient India* discussed the doubt, dissent and argument which were at the very origin of Indian thought and in *Creativity, Censorship and Dissent* Kashmiri, Tamil and Bangladeshi writers examining the delicate balance between responsibility and freedom in issues of state, academic and social media censorship. Where is that ephemeral line?

Richard Dawkins blasted the 'lamentable disgrace' of Rushdie's enforced absence which he attributed to 'the virus of faith', drawing parallels with 16th century Catholics considering the murder of Elizabeth I as a commendable act. Several Pakistani writers—Fatima Bhutto, Ayesha Jalal and Mohammed Hanif at different sessions expressed their hopes and fears for their own troubled country. Mohammed Hanif called the Rushdie affair disgraceful and referring to the Deobandis, said 'their cousins in Pakistan recently issued a fatwa and banned hair transplants. Nobody took them seriously.' The Arab Spring was often invoked with Simon Sebag Montefiore, Karima Khalil and Max Rodenbeck from Egypt, Palestinians Raja Shehadeh, Sari Nusseibeh and Karl Sabbagh, Iranian Kamin Mohammadi and Lebanese Hanan al Shaykh. As well, Indian Muslim writers and thinkers were high profile in the very balanced program.

Tension reignited at the end of the first day, when—quite separately and unbeknown to each other—two pairs of writers, Hari Kunzru and Amitava Kumar at one session, Jeet Thayil and Ruchir Joshi at another, read from *The Satanic Verses* in protest at recent events. Because of the ban that has been in place since 1988, all four, it seemed, had broken the law. Several First Information Reports (FIRs) were lodged by citizens with police against the writers as well as the three festival directors, who were thus at risk of police arrest. The four writers hurriedly left town after signing a statement that the festival was not responsible for their actions.

Writers, academics and critics promptly petitioned the Government demanding that it reconsider the ban on *The Satanic Verses* and support 'the right of all artists and writers to freedom of expression'. It said 'Within India, in the 23 years since the ban, we have witnessed an erosion of respect for freedom of expression, as artists like MF Hussain, and Balbir Krishan have been intimidated and works of writers like Rohinton Mistry and AK Ramanujan have been withdrawn because of threats by groups claiming to be offended. India is one of the very few countries in the world where the ban stands, placing us alongside Egypt, Pakistan, Iran, Malaysia, Liberia and Papua New Guinea among others. We submit with respect that there is a democratic need to review and re-examine the circumstances that led to the original ban of the Verses in 1988, which have changed greatly over time.'

The technical term for banning a book in India is 'forfeiture'. Under Section 95 of the Criminal Procedure Code every copy of a banned book may be seized wherever it is found in the country. India has the dubious reputation of being the first country in the world to ban *The Satanic Verses*, nine days after its publication in Britain, but the ban was actually on the book's importation from the London-based Viking/Penguin Group. Penguin India's then consulting editor was the now venerable Kushwant Singh, whose 97th birthday card I signed in a Delhi bookshop. He cautioned it would offend the religious sensitivities of India's large Muslim population and Penguin India declined to bring out a local edition. Copies already in the country were not subject to the ban and sold like hot cakes. Today's technology provides the possibility for anyone to download a pirate copy of the book. The four protesting authors had done precisely this and read from sheets of A4 paper. So in effect, they had no case to answer.

After a quick program change, Rushdie, via a video link, was to appear on the last afternoon, 24 January, in the largest venue, a shaded area where 4500 can be squeezed. The session, *Midnight's*

Child, was to cover the author's childhood, his writing, the many problems faced over the years and the film adaptation of *Midnight's Children*. However, the very prospect of the sight of the author on screen was apparently intolerable to some. Onto the stage came the Directors and senior organisers. Ram Pratap Singh Diggi, the owner of Diggi Palace and a vital part of the Festival, announced that the video-link would not proceed following advice from the police that protestors had already infiltrated the property and large groups were massing in nearby parks to march on Diggi. It was a charged and emotional moment. There were certainly suspicious-looking young men in the crowd, not present for the love of literature. One of them, seated next to me, distracted and restless, started a conversation in poor English. I explained that the advertised session *Reconstructing Rumi* had been changed, he didn't seem disappointed, indeed he had never heard of Rumi.

During the final session, an Intelligence Squared Debate, the exchange was understandably tense. Several firebrand writers and journalists opposed representatives of the Muslim community and demanded to know whether freedom of expression really existed in India. Phrases like 'It's a huge defeat' and 'It's a triumph of bigotry' peppered the dialogue. Debaters denounced the government and the banning of an author, not his book. They also pointed to the low education rate and the deprivation of women's rights among the Muslim community. The overwhelming popular verdict supported Salman Rushdie.

As I departed Diggi Palace at the end of this intense afternoon, a young man gave me a copy of the Holy Quran and told me I reminded him of his grandmother! And in another defusing of tension, the Festival Ball, held later in the evening in the splendid sixteenth century Amber Fort outside the city, saw authors and others kick up their heels and enjoy a very good party.

While all these dramatic twists and turns developed, the festival continued seamlessly, much to the credit to the embattled organisers. But what of the other writers and what they had to say? Sometimes a choice of session was impossible with the crush of humanity so many chose to sit tight in one venue for three in a row. One such brilliant morning started with James Shapiro on *Contested Will: Who Wrote Shakespeare?* which referred to his book *1599: A year in the life of William Shakespeare*. William Dalrymple followed with a riveting preview of his forthcoming study of the disastrous retreat of the British from Afghanistan in 1841 *Return of the King*, and then came Lionel Shriver in conversation about *We need to talk about Kevin*.

David Remnick, editor of *The New Yorker*, Joseph Lelyveld, journalist and author of the controversial book on Mahatma Gandhi *Great Soul*, banned in Gujarat last year, Philip Gourevitch, Jason Bourke, Samanth Subramian and Pulitzer Prize winner Katherine Boo made an illuminating panel on *Journalism as Literature*. Michael Ondaatje on *The Cat's Table* was great. I did not make Oprah Winfrey's session through a princely mix-up but the Maharaja of Jodhpur and 4500 others attended and loved her. The lone Australian writer was Richard Flanagan who was excellent in two panels *Thugs, Emperors and Convicts: the art of Historical Fiction* with Michael Ondaatje and others and *A Small Island: Writing and Insularity* where his Tasmania met Antigua, Sri Lanka and Mauritius.

Amy Chua talked about Dragon Mothers; Rushdie's ghostly presence at many sessions was certainly evident at *The Chutneyfication of English*, a term he invented; A C Grayling and Steven Pinker discussed enlightenment, reality and the meaning of life; David Hare and Tom Stoppard talked about theatre.

In the centenary birth year of Sadat Hasan Manto, the Indian writer who became a Pakistani after Partition, there was a reasoned and fascinating examination of his short story *Toba Tek Singh*, a work which has achieved cult status. The program stated that the story which deals with madness and dislocation is 'a refracting metaphor for our troubled times'. Three of the panellists were Indian but the fourth, Israeli Achia Anzi, is currently visiting professor of Hebrew at Jawaharlal Nehru University in Delhi and translating Manto into Hebrew. Jaipur saw the discussion become even more pertinent.

Namita Gokhale described the festival as the Kumbh Mela of literary festivals. The Kumbh Mela is one of the world's largest gatherings where Hindu pilgrims bathe in the holy water of the Ganges. Those crowds are quite extraordinary, tens of millions. The comparison is somewhat dangerous for the Kumbh has a history of stampede and scuffle and potential for an accidental ugly outcome. Seventy-five thousand literary pilgrims made the journey to Jaipur and Diggi Palace performed its annual enlargement miracle. Now it is in the lap of the gods as what will happen in 2013.*

---

* This article appeared in the March 2012 issue of *Australian Book Review* as 'Letter from Jaipur'. Peter Rose had commissioned a short article on the Festival before I left home in January but as events unfolded in the Australian media, he emailed to say, don't worry about the length!

Festival Directors announce there will be no videolink with Salman Rushdie

Police security at the Jaipur Literary Festival, 2012

The Kumbh Mela

The first time I heard of the Kumbh Mela was when I read *Portrait of India* by Ved Mehta in 1975. Published originally in 1967 it later came out in Penguin paperback. I read it when we were engaged in an arduous savings campaign to finance a family trip to India the next year. We lived very frugally, cutting corners everywhere and had many little schemes to raise the money—my husband chopped fire-wood and sold ute-loads to people in town and I made batch after batch of Anzac biscuits—nearly 6,000 of them—which were consumed at a gallery coffee-shop where I had a job a couple of days a week.

In his essay *The Sacred River of the Hindus* Mehta writes of his experiences at the 1966 Kumbh at Allahabad and recounts what happened at the previous festival in 1954 when unofficial estimates put the number of those killed in a terrible stampede in the thousands. The official figure was 500 with those injured at about 1000. Whatever the numbers, the story is shocking.

Our eighteen months of money-making schemes were successful. We arrived in India from Burma in December and travelled from Calcutta to Puri for Christmas where Santa Claus managed to find his way to deliver some funny little presents to Jamie and Emily, aged 5 and 4. They wore their home-made batman capes and masks all day long and a splendid silver kite was launched on the long stretch of beach in front of our guest-house. The New Year was welcomed in great style in Assam and then we set off on our first very long train journey from Calcutta to Delhi. As we rattled along on in the night my husband suggested we hop off the train in Allahabad and go to the Kumbh Mela. I wouldn't have a bar of it—risk my two precious little children in a colossal crowd like that? No thanks, we weren't ready for that. Besides Em had been terrified of Santa Claus, men in busbies and bagpipes for the first three years of her life, whatever would she make of all those naked *sadhus*? And what would I for that matter?

Since then I had never been in India at the right time but to be absolutely honest, I had never really yearned to attend a Kumbh. If I had been really dying to go to one, then I would have looked up the dates and made plans—and I simply hadn't. In the article I wrote on the 2012 Jaipur Literature Festival for the Australian Book Review I quoted in the final paragraph the words of Namita Gokhale, an eminent Indian writer and one of the Festival Directors. She described it as the 'Kumbh Mela of literary festivals'. I felt that this was something of a dangerous analogy even though the Kumbh Mela has become a metaphor for a huge crowd even in India, the home of huge crowds. Colossal gatherings are regular occurrences in India that is true—there were 100,000 at this year's Jaipur Literary Festival. But given that Jaipur often seems to attract controversy and that the Kumbh has had instances of stampede and scuffle, the potential for a metaphorical link to an accidental ugly outcome is not something to contemplate lightly.

My friendship with Robyn Beeche is what changed my attitude. Robyn, an Australian who became an internationally acclaimed photographer in London in the 1980s, lived part of the year in an ashram in Vrindhavan, the Krishna pilgrimage town situated on the Yamuna River near Agra, south of Delhi. Vrindhavan is located in Vraj, a region dotted with small towns and temples associated with the stories and worship of Lord Krishna, an avatar of the God Vishnu, one of the Hindu Trinity. Robyn and I had talked about the *parikrama* or spiritual progress to holy places in Vraj which she has done and I hope I will do one day. And what of the Kumbh Mela—that huge gathering that takes place every twelve years when those who bathe are cleansed of their sins and given blessings which extend for generations? It came up in conversation and for the first time had sounded like something I wanted to attend. Somehow impending family visits, the approach of Christmas and all manner of things piled up towards the end of 2012, but lurking at the back of my mind was Robyn's invitation to stay in the ashram's camp at Allahabad for the 2013 Mahakumbh Mela.

The real spur to finally committing to be part of it was sitting next to a friend at a luncheon who said that Christiane, his wife and my friend, really wanted to go, so why didn't we go together. I mumbled a feeble reply but later thought well for goodness sake, why not? After so many trips to India there are still plenty of gaps for future investigation, but this was a big one. I would be far too old to go next time — not too old to go to India itself, but at the age of 77 would it be sensible to attend my first Kumbh? Not really and twelve years is quite a long, imponderable time in anyone's life. The invitation was just too good to miss. It wasn't just a matter of having somewhere safe to stay. Above all it was the fact that Robyn would be there — such an insightful, clever, generous and caring person. Knowledgeable without being a know-all, incredibly aware of everything that happened around her, organised, sympathetic, capable and amusing, *and* she had been present at the last Kumbh Mela. So she, if anyone did, knew exactly what to do.

The word *mela* can be translated as a festival or a gathering and the Kumbh Mela is the biggest gathering of humanity in the world. This year probably 100,000,000 people gathered on the river banks at Allahabad over the 55 days of the festival. On the main bathing day, the Mauni Amavasya Snan, the crowd was estimated at 30,000,000. One BBC report claimed 35,000,000 but 30,000,000 is good enough for me. This year's festival was a Maha Kumbh Mela which takes place only every 144 years, twelve times twelve years, which would explain the record numbers. In an editorial in the Times of India, Gautam Siddharth said that the Mahakumbh is the closest that Hinduism comes to being 'organised'. It also serves he says 'as a reminder of how order and organisation flow out of apparent chaos'. It is a magnificent celebration of the eclecticism of Hinduism.

The *kumbh* part of the title is the name for a vessel, an urn, pot or pitcher. Shrivatsa Goswami, spoke at the ashram camp one evening in an interesting, inclusive way which the several non-Hindus present could easily understand and enjoy. He is a member of a traditional priestly family which serves at the Sri Radharaman Temple at Vrindhavan and is the Director of the Sri Chaitanya Prema Samsthana Ashram (known as the Gambhira) in whose camp we were staying. He became well known in the 1970s when he was visiting fellow at the Harvard Divinity School's Centre of Study of the World's Religions and remains a highly respected academic and author. In his illuminating talk he said that the *kumbh* philosophically contains all the waters of the earth and individually we are all like such a vessel, containing soul and spirit, a fraction of the absolute existence.

Reinforcing the eclectic nature of Hinduism, there are many, many stories about the discovery of *amrit*, the nectar of immortality, contained in the original *kumbh*. One concerns the sage Durvasa, an impatient man, always ready with a curse. One day, feeling particularly and unusually happy, he went to the god Indra with flowers and a garland. Arrogant Indra took them and gave them to his elephant, the white many-headed Airavata, who first trampled and then ate the offerings. Durvasa, highly insulted at this lack of grace, cursed the god and brought a great famine down on his kingdom. A shaken Indra went to the god Narayan—this is Vishnu—and Shrivatsa said it was actually his eighth incarnation, Krishna. Narayan had witnessed both the insult and the subsequent reaction and suggested that the cosmic ocean should be churned to counteract the situation. While this mammoth effort was taking place, Lakshmi arrived, rain fell and the famine was relieved. However, when it appeared, the demons ran away with the pot of nectar taking it to the underworld where it was guarded by a serpent. Krishna sent Garuda to retrieve it and the great bird on such a long journey needed to rest four times on his return, in Haridwar, Prayag—the ancient name for Allahabad, Ujjain and Nasik, now the holy sites where the Kumbh Melas take place.

A second story focuses on the sage Kashyapa and his two wives Kadru and Vinata. Kadru, the mother of all snakes, was envious of Vinata, the mother of birds, who was modest and good. Kadru's son, Vasuki who was the king of snakes, and Vinata's son, the great eagle Garuda, were natural opponents and fierce rivalry existed between them. Kadru, always scheming, invited Vinata to compete with her in guessing the colours of the horses of the chariot of the sun. Whoever was mistaken would be the loser and be punished.

Kadru guessed black and Vinata said white. Kadru then had the *nagas*, the great snakes, create dark lines around the sun giving the impression of black horses so Vinata lost out to Kadru on that round and became a virtual slave to her co-wife whose plotting was far from finished. When approached by Garuda who asked her to pardon and release his mother, Kadru agreed on condition that Garuda retrieve the pot of *amrit* from the heavens. He would have to defeat an army of celestials before approaching the *amrit* which was guarded by two ferocious serpents containing within them the venom of the entire universe.

Against all odds Garuda managed to defeat all the company of heaven and seized the *kumbh*. Indra however managed to snatch the pot four times on the bird's journey home and a little of the nectar spilled each time at four sites, yes you guessed it, at Haridwar, Prayag, Ujjain and Nasik. One of many morals in this story is that of the sacrifices mothers will make for their children. Vinata, the model mother, is rewarded by the devotion of her magnificent son Garuda and he in return is rewarded by Vishnu who grants him the privilege of becoming his vehicle.

A third story also has its origins in the well-known episode of the churning of the cosmic ocean in order to find *amrit*. The story called Samudra Manthan is found in the Puranas and in both the Mahabharata and Ramayana. At this time the gods or *devas* and the demons or *asuras* were constantly fighting, a metaphor for our own lives with our regular conflicts between good and evil. Evil seemed to have taken over when the demons defeated the gods. A truce was called and the gods were advised to keep a low profile. Mount Mandara became the churning pole and Vasuki, the serpent king turns up again, this time in the role of churning string. The mountain started to sink so Krishna placed it on the solid back of the great tortoise, Kurma, the second incarnation of Vishnu. As the churning by both gods and demons began, instead of the anticipated *amrit*, horrifyingly a frightful poison arose which threatened to engulf the universe. To save the world, Shiva swallowed the poison. His shocked consort, Parvati, leapt to his rescue and half-strangled him, a dramatic act which kept the poison from going any further than his throat. The potent poison caused his throat to turn blue but never mind, more churning produced the *kumbh* of *amrit* carried in the arms of Dhanvantari, the physician of the gods. Shiva survived with the immortal nectar-like water of the Ganga flowing from his head, unfortunately not like that which flows in the river today. The shaky truce fell apart, fierce fighting between the *devas* and the *asuras* started again, this time over the nectar which had been snatched from Dhanvantari.

To protect it Garuda came to the rescue and taking the pot, flew far away from the battle. Four drops of the divine nectar fell during his flight—on Prayag, Haridwar, Ujjain and Nasik. The four sites are unsurprisingly believed to have acquired mystical power and spirituality and in rotation are the locations where the Kumbh Mela takes place every twelve years. An *ardh* or half-*kumbh* is held every six years at two set locations and a *purna* or full *kumbh* is held at one of the four holy cities. But the holiest of holy is Prayag or Allahabad, located at the *sangam* or confluence of the holy rivers Ganga & Yamuna with the invisible Saraswati. Pilgrims believe that bathing here at this time will cleanse all sins and grant salvation from the endless cycle of reincarnation, not just for the bathers but for their children and grandchildren, generations on.

The Allahabad Kumbh Mela takes place in the month of Magha, a month in the Hindu Lunar calendar corresponding to parts of January and February. A holy dip taken at the *sangam* any time in Magha in any year is one thousand times as beneficial as a dip taken anywhere in the Ganga in the months corresponding to September/October and October/November and ten million times more beneficial than one taken in any other sacred river any time in parts of March/April or April/May. It is even more valuable than the donation of millions of cows. Indeed the benefits of bathing in Magha during a Kumbh Mela are so immense that not even Brahma could possibly count them. Taking just a single step in the direction of holy Prayag can be seen as expiation of one's sins and it is said that at intervals of twelve years the waters at the *sangam* acquire the properties of *amrit*.

Shrivatsa interrupted his discourse on the origins of the Kumbh

Mela to despair at the parallel unhappy state of the sacred River Ganges and the nation. At the time of the 250th anniversary of Jaipur in 1977, the then Prime Minister Moraji Desai was given a copper vessel by Maharani Gayatri Devi, the widow of Maharaja Sawai Man Singh II. Within it she said was a treasure. Maharaja Sawai Jai Singh II who ruled from 1688 until 1743 had kept 108 pots such as this in the cellars of the City Palace, 108 is a highly auspicious number to Hindus. The treasure within was Ganga water and an examination at the University of Rajasthan declared that it was of drinking quality even after more than a century. Another Jaipur ruler Maharaja Sawai Madho Singh II who ruled from 1880 to 1922 was the owner of the two enormous sterling silver vessels prized by the Jaipur City Palace Museum. They sit, reflecting the world as it passes by, in a pretty little terracotta, pink and white pavilion, marble-floored and hung with chandeliers, the Diwan-i-khas or Hall of Private Audience, in the centre of a courtyard. They are 1.6 metres tall with a capacity each of 4000 litres. Called *Gangajalis*, they were made from 14,000 melted silver coins without solder and are said to be the largest sterling silver vessels in the world. They were created so the Maharaja need not drink anything but Ganges water on his journey to England in 1901 for the coronation of King Edward VII.

The Maharaja knew a thing or two about Ganga water and Lord Shiva knew it too—that the Ganga was *amrita*, so what could a pot of poison do to it? In Shrivatsa's opinion, India far from being the shining jewel it was at the time of the amazing feats performed by the gods, it is today going through a huge crisis. He hoped that by coming to the Kumbh all of us in combination, might release the Ganga from the death threat of the dam upstream from Prayag. The nectar he said is obviously already dead otherwise Ganga water could have been sent all over the country to save countless lives.

Shiva was a great devotee of both Krishna and Rama. He asked Krishna why all the *lilas* or divine play was devoted solely to him and expressed the desire to see him in a special appearance in the company of beautiful women. It would seem that Shiva was intoxicated from what Shrivatsa described as poisons such as *ganja* to which Shiva was partial and this allowed him to make outrageous and uninhibited suggestions. Krishna agreed to this while the massive churning of the Cosmic Ocean continued—it took a millennium so patience was an admirable virtue. The *amrita* was slow to appear so Krishna impulsively took the churn into his own hands and the nectar appeared in a *kumbh* which the demons immediately captured. Two promises had been extracted—nectar for the gods and the Shiva's request for beautiful women.

Once they had the *amrita*, the demons started their habitual quarrelling which continued for twelve days and twelve nights, during which time four drops were spilled on those holy places. In the midst of the turmoil a beautiful woman called Mohini walked by. Her charm was so distracting that they invited her to take the pot. She organised a competition—something we now know that gods enjoy—this time of nectar-drinking. Her diverting beauty enabled her to quietly remove a cup of *amrit* which she took to the Gods. One of the demons then defected to the god's side but Shiva threw his discus and cut the quisling demon's throat. In revenge a total eclipse of the sun took place, probably relating to the snakes in the earlier story forming black rings around the sun. Mohini, who in fact is Krishna i.e. another form of Vishnu, now found herself in trouble. Shiva awaits her. Mohini/Krishna ran for her/his life but Shiva followed and grabbed her—let's say it was she Mohini! They entered a grove and Shrivasta says a hugely important thing happened. That meeting he said was the genesis of all the different children of India. It also was the nativity in a circuitous way of Hanuman, the monkey god and ardent devotee of Lord Rama. Important in the worship of Hanuman is his image in recumbent form which lies in the sands of the Ganga at Allahabad. Each year he is submerged by the waters of the monsoon-swollen river who, it is said, comes to touch his feet in worship. He is resting here in the Fort at Allahabad and some say that a holy dip at the Sangam will be fruitful only after seeking his *darshan*. Shrivatsa urged us to visit the Fort for this purpose, to see the Akshaya Vat or immortal Banyan Tree and most importantly the Saraswati—the remaining tiny visible trickle of the third river which is believed to join the confluence of the Ganga and Yamuna.

All these stories cataloguing slightly different deeds at different times in different places, become intertwined and confused but conclude with much the same answer. They can really be called a confluence of stories of both Shiva and Krishna, a meeting of Shaivite and Vaishnavite traditions like the confluence of India's most sacred rivers, the Ganga and the Yamuna. It is rather a confusing merge with endless variations. Dhanvantari turns himself into a rook or a crow, snatched the pot and took twelve days to carry the *amrit* to heaven; Garuda in another version is the bearer. Whichever magnificent bird it was, the journey took twelve days and one day for a god equals a year for a human which accounts for the twelve year cycle and the sequence of stars.

The relevance of twelve is strong throughout the stories—the great bird's twelve day flight and the fight between gods and demons over the *amrit* which lasts twelve days and nights are stated periods of time. Also relevant is the twelve years of study which must be undertaken by serious students of Sanskrit grammar before attaining the title of *pandit* or *shastri*. There is also the mystical significance of Hindu philosophic belief of the twelve instincts in man—five senses, five motor organs plus the two mental instincts of perception and reason. All must be mastered in order to achieve perfect inner happiness. Twelve is the number of order and appears often in Christian texts. There are the twelve disciples and in the Revelation to St John he saw the holy city of Jerusalem with its great high wall with twelve gates and on the gates twelve angels, twelve foundations and on them written the twelve names of the twelve apostles. On either side of the river of life grew the tree of life with its twelve kinds of fruit, producing its fruit month by month.

The astrological calculation for the timing of the Kumbh Mela takes place in four ways. When Jupiter in Aquarius coincides with the Sun in Aries the Kumbh is held at Haridwar. When Jupiter in Aries coincides with the Sun and Moon in Capricorn, it is held at Prayag. The entrance of Jupiter in Leo sees the Kumbh held at Nasik on the banks of the Godavari River and at the entry of Jupiter in Leo and the Sun in Aries the pilgrims must journey to Ujjain on the banks of the River Shipra. Few know all these complicated facts.

In Mark Tully's essay on the 1989 Kumbh Mela in his book *No Full Stops in India* he says that the *pandits* had stated that year's festival was the most important for 144 years because of the auspicious positions of planets and stars. How then could our Kumbh also have this important status? Goodness knows but we read it in the papers! One of our lovely companions at the ashram camp, a very devout Indian woman rigorous in her religious observances, didn't know it was a Mahakumbh which was somewhat comforting.

As I write this I have had a few drastic computer days—new computer with attendant new problems, dead modem, dead mouse, disengaging connections—I'm completely fed up with it but getting back to writing this, somehow it all seems to fade into the realm of never mind. *Koi bata nahim*. When the internet failed and I couldn't check a few things I resorted to old textbooks. One volume, *Translations of Hindu Scriptures* with the price sticker saying $2.35 from the University Co-op Bookshop, has only made my confusion worse so I'm discarding it and others—in fact should I give them to the next book-stall at the church? Perhaps they will do some doubting Christian a lot of good. But what do I know anyhow? Some poor old superannuated India-lover with an imperfect understanding of anything much. The minute I give the books away doubtless I will need to consult the Rig Veda or one of the Upanishads so perhaps I had better keep it. My emails are not going out and that includes one I've written my son and daughter-in-law in Singapore and I've just been weeping with frustration at my total ineptitude at understanding anything at all—the philosophy and history of ancient India and the intricacies of 21st century high technology—oh heavens what a combination. I'm really a total failure in the brain department. But in the meantime I found the email my son sent me in January in his role as Security Manager Asia Pacific for a big international company. It is about Prayag, oh I should get back to modern times, Allahabad in January. He sent this to staff members who might be affected.

'Significant disruption should be expected in the northern city of Allahabad (Uttar Pradesh state) from 14 January to 10 March, during the Hindu festival of Maha Kumbh Mela. Tens of millions of pilgrims, including 60,000 foreign nationals, are expected to attend the event, which happens once every 12 years. Hotels in the city are fully booked for the period and finding transport is likely to be difficult. Travellers should reconfirm all bookings, ensure their itineraries are flexible and be prepared for major and protracted disruption.

The festival will take place at the point where the Ganges and Yamuna rivers meet, but most pilgrims will pass through Allahabad. Particularly large crowds are expected to arrive in the city on important dates during the festival, including 14 January, 27 January (Paush Purnima), 6 February (Ekadashi), 14 February (Basant Panchami), 17 February (Rath Saptami), 18 February (Bhisma Ashtami) and 25 February (Maghi Purnima). Around 30m people are expected to arrive in the city on 10 February for the Mauni Amawasya bathing ritual, the most important day of the pilgrimage.

The authorities are expected to deploy thousands of additional security personnel to maintain order. While such measures will also serve to mitigate any potential incidents of terrorist violence, the vast number of attendees and the religious significance of the event mean that it represents an attractive target for Islamist militant groups. Furthermore, the convergence of such large crowds may also trigger stampedes, which could pose risks to personnel. Travellers should avoid getting caught up in large crowds wherever possible as a security precaution.

For those wishing to attend the festival, the authorities have set up a Foreign Resident Registration Office (FRRO) that will allow foreign nationals to register at least 24 hours before their arrival for the pilgrimage. A special helpline (+9132-2548833) and email address (dmall@nic.in) have also been set up to assist tourists.'

My son, daughter-in-law and two grandchildren live in Singapore and my journey to India for the Kumbh Mela started with a happy few days in Singapore which included Amanda's 40th birthday. When I returned for another few days on the way home to Canberra, Singapore was an extraordinary contrast to the huge tented pop-up Sangam City. One afternoon I went with Amanda to collect the children at school. Coco, aged 10, was heard to say to a little gang of her friends, 'that's my Grandma, she wasn't killed in the stampede.' So perhaps despite my failings in understanding the complexities of Indian philosophy and spirituality, at least in my grand-daughter's eyes it seems I'm a survivor and almost famous! But I'm getting a long way ahead of myself.

After an interesting few days travelling in UP to Lucknow, Faizabad, Ayodhya and Kanpur, we at last arrived in Allahabad. We had driven from Kanpur that morning and had even stopped along the way for Christiane to buy some stainless steel bowls and *katoris*. Once in Allahabad we had lunch, visited Anand Bhavan, the home of the Nehru family and found the house in which Kipling was a paying guest during his last year in India.

Four kilometres from the city our first sight of the huge expanse of tented camp made us gasp. Our car arrived at the top of a long embankment where a wide road led gently down to an extraordinary temporary metropolis. It was known as Kumbhnagar at earlier *melas* but this year's popular title in newspapers was Sangam City. Even from our low viewpoint the 20 square kilometres sprawled out beneath our feet in a huge multi-coloured pool as far as the eye could see. We could scarcely glimpse the Ganges but the tall spans of road and railway bridges marked its location. We leapt out of the car. It was really hard to believe that we had arrived. Policemen politely urged us back into the car and we rolled down the hill into the throng of tented camps, tall pavilions like palaces where holy men would speak to devotees and where songs of praise would be sung all night. Everywhere there were flags and banners and huge photographs of famous *gurus* to whom pilgrims would flock.

What did we take in on that first sight? Row upon row of tents, large and small, vendors with their wares spread out on cloths on the ground lining the wide roads, all with names on sign-boards and arranged in an orderly grid system. Everywhere there were throngs of people. We crossed the Ganga on one of the fifteen pontoon bridges—huge grey-black torpedo-like iron balloons holding up the pathway of the bridge, strong enough to support cars and trucks going in one direction only, foot traffic went either way. It all had an unearthly feeling. We bumped over the pontoons to roads where we slowly turned corners to reach our destination more than seven kilometres from the Sangam. The broad roads had been laid with metal sheets to provide a better surface on the fine, grey, silty sand, sparkling with spicules of mica, which had been watered to lay the dust.

The Gambhira Ashram camp was on the far perimeter of the Sangam site. Robyn had sent me a text with directions as if we would enter from the Varanasi side which we were not. The driver was somewhat doubtful as we had earlier said our destination was simply a Vrindavan ashram's camp. Our new directions were perfect. 'Near the cross streets of Gangeshwar Marg and Tulasi Marg in Sector 7, near the Administrative Office and Uttari Jhunsi Police Thana, Kumbha Mela, Prayag.' Our camp was surrounded by a high wall of corrugated iron. Within were 17 white canvas tents able to house either four people. Six of dormitory size could sleep eight, though on several nights one accommodated twelve. There was also a large performance and worship hall and a dining pavilion. No. 13 was our tent. A deluxe tent of the Swiss Cottage variety, it had three commodious rooms *and* had its own en suite bathroom.

The large main room was in the centre, lined with a mustard yellow cloth, block-printed with black and red paisley guls, curling with flowers. Thank the Lord it *was* lined which meant it was marginally warmer than the small entry and the third room. The contractors who constructed the camp can supply absolutely anything in a range of degrees of luxury—for example presidential or ordinary blankets were available. Our huge wooden beds were located in the third room, the mattresses covered in army camouflage material, but we moved them into the large central room where there was also a far better light and a Godrej lockable steel *almirah*. There was still tons of room for four.

The fourth in our tent was Andrea Baqai, a GP from the Lakes District in England. Robyn and I felt that we should really only ever camp with two doctors in attendance. Christiane who is an eye specialist had every medical possibility covered in her bag of tricks. And the en suite? Before I left home the most common question asked, accompanied by horrified looks, was 'what will you do about toilets?' The toilet situation seemed to preoccupy the thoughts of many and when told of the possibility of flush loos some said they would have to see photographs as proof before leaving home. The houseboats on lakes in Kashmir used to have great signs boasting 'Flush toilets' or sometimes 'Flashing toilets'. The HB Arizona on which I stayed forty years ago was thus equipped and yes it did flush but it seemed that the contents of the lake entered not the loo but through the wooden floor flooding the entire bathroom. As occupants of a deluxe tent at the Kumbh we had our very own ablution block. Across from the tent flap at the rear of our abode, was a partitioned construction made of corrugated iron. On one side of its central wall was a tap with a bucket and dipper and a couple of bricks on which to stand—this was the bath. And on the other side was a brand new flush loo of reddish maroon colour with a tap and bucket. The flushing mechanism was manual, provided by womanpower and bucket, absolutely fine and perfectly functional.

When we arrived Robyn was out shooting photographs so we went on a walk around our block. As the sun sank, the lights came on and the world was almost as bright as day. An incredible forest of 22,000 halogen street lights stayed on all night and were given to town councils around India at the conclusion of the Kumbh. Electricity was cut off during the day as a safety measure. In our neighbourhood there were tented camps, mostly more humble than ours, and temporary structures called *pandals* which are created with great style all over India for religious observances and weddings. Made of cloth on a wood and bamboo framework, they look far more substantial as though made from bricks and mortar and meant to last for all time. Almost all the Kumbh Mela site is constructed out of bamboo, cloth and tin. Plywood is used in only a few more permanent VVIP areas and the hospital. The bamboo and cloth creations are like unattainable dreams—pretending to be palatial, desirable and grand but as ephemeral as the leaves on an autumn tree. The predominant saffron colour could also be described as autumnal but in India we were nearing the end of winter and the start of spring where the colour is yellow, *basanti*—the colour of the flowers of mustard and also the word for spring.

Saffron or *bhagwa* is the most essential colour in Hinduism and is one of three symbolic colours of the Indian flag—saffron, white and green. All over the site of the Kumbh were glorious splashes of every shade of saffron—pure ripe persimmon, bright tangerine, tawny sunset, darkest variants almost red, palest apricot and peach. Hindu saints and teachers wear robes of the colour to mark their renunciation of material life and for the nation's leaders it should remind them to be diligent in their dedication and indifferent to material gain. It is the colour of *agni* or fire which reflects the Supreme Being and lightens the darkness, symbolic of knowledge burning away ignorance thus representing enlightenment. Evil is removed by casting objects into a fire and saffron as the colour of the flame, takes on this symbol of absolution and resulting purity. A *pandal* close to our camp had a triple-storey façade, of burnt orange with buttercup niches flanking the entrance and apricot lancet windows in the upper tiers. It was strung with garlands of lights and flags fluttered in the slight breeze. One side displayed a huge photograph of a guru, almost two storeys tall.

People were walking fast in all directions, some stopping to buy fresh vegetables from vendors on the side of the road. Music and discourse came from loudspeakers fixed to every *pandal* and the noise was intense. Somehow I hadn't thought much about the noise but with so many millions of people of course the atmosphere had to be noisy. Some of the music was incredibly loud and so were sermons being broadcast close to our camp which continued all night but it didn't worry me at all. The first night I felt very gritty and could feel grit on my face and in my teeth, but I didn't notice it again. Perhaps more water had been poured on the roads. Within our camp one day some young men were pouring a slurry of probably cow-dung and sand onto the pathways between tents to make a firmer surface.

If I had a small complaint about anything at the Kumbh, it is entirely my own fault because I should have thought more sensibly about the weather. Fortunately the very unusual thunderstorms and record-breaking rains that we had experienced in Lucknow and

Kanpur had not fallen in Allahabad though it had been dreadfully cold and everyone in the camp caught nasty chest infections. By the time we arrived the weather each day was beautifully warm by late morning and into the afternoon but it was truly perishing at night and I could hardly sleep for the cold. I should have brought a down sleeping bag and I should have had some warmer thermal clothing. The beds were large and there were thick blankets and quilts but even so, I lay curled up in the narrow sliver of tepid warmth in my bed, head covered and breathing into the interior of my cocoon, hardly able to change position and getting stiffer by the minute because of that. My three companions who had more sensible thermal night-wear were sleeping side by side—my bed was perpendicular to theirs, at their feet. Christiane wore an eye-shade, Robyn had ear-plugs and whilst Andrea was not gagged, it was amusing to think of them as the three wise monkeys, seeing, hearing and speaking no evil. Each early morning I was absolutely dying to go to the loo but the thought of leaving even my luke-warm few inches was unbearable so I waited until after daybreak for an effort of record-breaking duration. We were meant to receive a bucket of very hot water for bathing each morning but that didn't always quite happen so my daily bath on those days was somewhat sketchy. But somehow the water in the pipes wasn't nearly as freezing as might be after the overnight cold—nothing like Canberra in June for instance. I suppose the earth in which the 550 kilometres of pipes were laid is never as cold as the frosty subterranean depths of my home town in winter.

Statistics of infrastructure for such a colossal gathering can't help but be fascinating. The home interest in lavatories seems to be shared world-wide for the numbers of these comforts were easy to find. The organisers must be proud of the fact that they built 35,000 single-seat toilets, 340 blocks of 10-seat toilets and 4,000 urinals in the mela grounds. Suresh Dwivedi, the officer in charge of health and sanitation, was quoted as saying that all faecal matter went into underground pits where it would start to decompose in a few days with the addition of bleach, lime and other hastening agents. I'm sure this was true enough but despite the huge number of loos, any open space became a dumping ground and you would walk there only at your peril. Everywhere along the major internal roads were small corrugated iron structures with a picture of an attractive happy-looking rather androgynous person denoting gender. The facial structure seemed to be much the same with just the addition of ear-rings and long hair in the case of female and a moustache for the male. One day Robyn thought she would make use of one of the elevated 10-seaters and climbed up the stairs, hastily retreating unsuccessfully, saying it was the most revolting she had ever witnessed in India! I held off drinking before long marches—it took some time to cover the distance from our camp.

During the Kumbh Mela Swami Chidanand Saraswati, spiritual head of the Parmarth Niketan Ashram in Rishikesh, one of India's largest spiritual institutions, ran a campaign to provide clean toilets in religious places. He has dedicated his order to saving the Ganga and this is part of his tactics. He recently entered into a memorandum of understanding with the Defence Research and Designs Organisation to use their technological research into bio-toilets in places where proper sanitation facilities are unavailable. The MoU will be of great help in the State of Uttar Pradesh and the mayors of both Allahabad and Varanasi had been asked to provide a list of sites where these loos are needed. The 2011 census revealed that 89% of homes in the state do not have a functional toilet. The Swami in a supremely realist statement said 'A clean body is the first thing to be able to focus on anything. Imagine yourself suffering from constipation and what restlessness it causes. It is more important to build toilets than temples.' He is particularly interested in the welfare of women, their safety, dignity and health in connection with the absence or scarcity of decent loos. His concerns were supported by an officer of the Ministry of Drinking Water and Sanitation who related the high incidence of anaemia and urinary tract infections among rural women to the fact that these women drink less water before going out to work in open fields in order to avoid the inconvenience of having to relieve themselves.

The *mela* grounds were very clean and everywhere sweepers wielding their long brooms corralled what was estimated at 40 to 50 tonnes of rubbish on an ordinary day (could there be an *ordinary* day at this extraordinary event?), rising to between 100 and 150 tonnes on the big bathing days. 10,500 sweepers were recruited for the job. Their piles of rubbish were often chiefly composed of shoes and leaf plates used for the free meals given out to pilgrims and holy men. There were mercifully no plastic bags due to a prohibition by the Government and the Honorable High Court for the *mela's* duration. On the big bathing day the piles full of enormous quantities of sandals and shoes were whisked away fast with an almost vengeful energy. So many of the pilgrims were people with little money so their lost shoes seemed pitiful. They must have been flipped off in the rush to either bathe or get away fast or else the owners were so jammed in a mass of humanity they couldn't bend down to retrieve them.

Pop-up is a word that popped up in the last year or so—pop-up shops, pop-up radio stations, pop-up art galleries, pop-up coffee bars. The Sangam metropolis was the mother of all pop-ups, a purpose-built settlement created in a few months to accommodate millions and millions of people for the 55 day period of the festival. The fascinating congregation, the world's largest religious festival, is not focused on a tomb or a cathedral, a cave or a temple, nor even a town. The sandy tracts on which the city springs up are either vacant or partly cultivated during the dry season and covered with water at other times. How does it all happen? How can the people be accommodated? Who would look after them? The whole throng is somehow unearthly, peopled as it is by thousands of individuals, so exotic and extraordinary, as to have the power to make others just stand and stare. One tour operator's blurb said 'Experience the Kumbh Mela. Meet Holy Saints. Bathe in the Ganges. Book now!' It is no wonder that the Kumbh Mela also attracts not only voyeurs and tourists but serious researchers as well as true pilgrims and holy saints.

Harvard University fielded a multidisciplinary team of more than 50 faculty, staff and student researchers in a year-long project to document and analyse the great gathering. The project was coordinated by the South Asia Institute at Harvard University and the Harvard Global Health Institute as part of their focus on Urbanization. Complementary disciplines focused on religious and cultural studies, environmental science and public health, technology and communications, even business. Their findings make interesting reading, discovering the mechanics of making the temporary city work. Some reports essentially strip the mystery or at least the mystique, from the essence of the Kumbh and reveal hard facts useful to some but irrelevant to millions more. While studying the urbanism of the tented city a team of graduate student researchers set out to map the Kumbh Mela using plans and sections, diagrams, perspectives, aerial photography and film. They studied two complementary conditions—first the physical structure of the settlements including the hierarchy of the residential sectors, the organization of spaces for public amenities and infrastructures and how close these spaces were to the actual *sangam*. Secondly they looked at how the festival was defined in more ephemeral ways such as the routes that pilgrims take between different areas of the site at the most important bathing times or to evening celebrations. The researchers sought to find how the two areas of study functioned together and to see if the results could be applied to sustainable urban design elsewhere in the world. It used to be hard to imagine where this could happen but refugee camps, some of which unhappily endure for decades, are a tragic fact of life today.

The Kumbh Mela is a unique, seemingly unmanageable event and most people would run a hundred miles at having to organise it. Indians do such things so incredibly well in their own idiosyncratic way. In small endeavours there is generally much frantic last minute activity which a cynic might describe as chaos. This tends to lead to palpitations for involved foreigners, particularly for the first time, but everything is usually all right on the night. Think of the 2010 Commonwealth Games in New Delhi, or *Monsoon Wedding*! Even if the Kumbh happens only every twelve years, there are other half-Kumbhs every six and the experts who know how to run them don't have time to forget details in between. Industrial fairs and expos, huge political rallies and annual national events do not need 40,000 loos or 550 kilometres of water pipe, but everything in India is on a massive scale.

Lalooji & Sons (LJS) are the historic contractors for the Kumbh Mela. There are several sub-branches of the original company started by cousins and brothers who compete against each other for contracts. They have set up *melas* all over India and they say that the very existence of the Kumbh Mela is because of them. Much of the success and speed of the organization is because members of the same families have been doing these jobs for generations, such an Indian characteristic—like medieval guilds. Imagine the horror at having to contemplate such a task for the first time but in India there is complete confidence in being able to achieve the gargantuan feat. People know exactly what to do.

Namita Dharia, who was part of the Harvard Graduate School of Design team studying the Kumbh Mela, wrote an interesting *Preliminary Report from the Field* several months before the start of the festival. In it she said 'Implicit understandings and a series of historic patterns are encoded into the locals and they operate on the same.' In March and April in the year preceding a Kumbh Mela, repair work is done on stores kept in Delhi, Haridwar, Nasik, Rishikesh and other *mela* sites. On 20 September 2012 contractors started the move of material and equipment to the site and ten days later work began. The contractors know exactly how long each individual job will take. For instance it is estimated that it takes 5 minutes to erect a bamboo and tin segment of a wall consisting of two bamboo poles and two or three sections of tin 10' x 2'. Nothing is guessed. It's the sort of effort we would associate with the Army in situations of strife. Rates for camps are fixed by the Mela Adhikari or administration but discounts are often given to holy men and some *akharas* are given significant discounts based on their relationship with the contractors.

A contrast to the sophisticated analyses of some of the Harvard research is the way local officials estimate crowd numbers. Alok Sharma, Inspector General of Police, Allahabad Zone was in charge of the 2001 Kumbh Mela at Allahabad and the 1998 and 2010 *melas* at Haridwar. His estimates are based on experience, helped by rough estimates from policemen under his charge who follow two methods. The first is to count people using the seven major roads leading into Allahabad, assuming everyone's destination is the *Sangam*. A 10 metre length is marked on each of the seven roads and the number of people passing these lengths each minute is counted. It is too difficult to count others entering by lanes and by-roads which probably accounts for about 30% of the traffic. The second method involves counting people after they have poured into the *mela* grounds from the three main roads from Allahabad. Combining the two methods and the number of people alighting trains at the Allahabad railway station is the estimated total number. But pilgrims using the pontoon bridges over the Ganges were not counted at least on the opening day and Inspector General Sharma said 'A real count is very, very difficult. And there is a tendency to increase the estimate.' Satellite imagery was used at Haridwar in 2010 but Sharma was not impressed with it. When asked the difference between the satellite-fed number and the manual calculations Mr Sharma said 'Just half or eight million'. Quite a margin of error.

An assistant superintendent of police, Hari Narayan Singh, spoke of the method of arriving at daily tallies of pilgrims. He was located in the control room that oversees the running of the festival, in touch with tall observation towers located near the bathing area. The count there is the result of a visual estimate of numbers of bathers going in and out of the water every minute. A calculation is made each hour, totalled at the end of the day. Mr Singh admitted 'No, there's no real science to it.' Pilgrims were urged to use the bathing areas nearest to where they were staying and as we walked in the darkness from our camp to the *Sangam* on the main bathing day there were huge crowds, colossal throngs of people, obediently bathing at all the designated places. Thousands immersing themselves in a place less likely to be as crowded as the confluence. So these people were not included in a count from the towers close the holiest place. So what's to worry about the science of missing a million or more in a visual count if all those others weren't included? I've often woken up in the middle of the night and found myself counting things, usually when I've been in the middle of a big catering job and nervous about falling short on something. That used to involve counting things in hundreds at the maximum. How pathetic! Those poor policemen must have numbers constantly in their heads and ant-like people walking across their line of sight even as they sleep.

30,000 policemen and security officials were deployed at 30 police stations, 40 police posts and 71 traffic police booths to provide security during the festival. They were drawn from the Central Reserve Police Force, the Provincial Armed Constabulary from both Uttar Pradesh and the neighbouring state of Uttarakhand and the Central Paramilitary Force. They were mostly men but plenty of policewomen were present and obvious. There were men from the National Disaster Response Force and divers who helped prevent drownings, flood relief battalions, mounted police on big, beautiful horses whose unpredictable hindquarters we gave a wide berth especially on the main bathing day. Commandos with guns slung almost casually over their shoulders were dressed in greenish battle fatigues with black bandanas on their heads, others had protective body armour over blue fatigues. In the midst of the crowds some of the troops sounded pretty fierce when dealing with Indian pilgrims. They were not so forceful with obedient foreigners and a smile worked wonders. I guess we were intent on not getting in the way. Police controlled all vehicular movement and car parks which had the capacity for almost 231,000 vehicles—buses, cars, tractor trailers and two-wheelers. It is said there is very little crime during the festival and much of the police-work was basically crowd control but in this day and age and in volatile India, there was the distinct threat of terrorism and everyone was on guard. Both the Dalai Lama and Congress President Sonia Gandhi cancelled their visits because of security concerns.

On our first morning we walked up the hill to the ancient site of Jhunsi or Jhusi. The prehistory of Jhunsi stretches back to the Neolithic era and archaeological remains have been dated to 7000 BC. Historically the town was called Prathisthanpuram. It was burned down by foreign invading forces in 13th or 14th century and came to be known as Jhulsi which is the Hindi word for burned. We climbed the steps to an elevation of 76 metres to see the view. The tented city spread out below us with a hazy hive of activity at the

Sangam in the far distance where the blue Yamuna and the brown Ganga meet. A higher band of green trees made a backdrop to the bathing site and this was the precinct of Akbar's fort built in 1575.

It was Akbar, the third of the great Mughul Emperors, who gave the city of Prayag a new name. He visited the town four times between 1561 and 1574, attempting keep the eastern provinces of his empire under control. During the 1574 visit he made the decision to turn Prayag into a military stronghold and laid the foundation of the great stone fort. Dates vary for this but 1574 seems most likely and it is probable at this time the town received its new name of Ilahabas or Ilahabad which means City of God or God's creation. Considering that in Hinduism there is a limitless number of gods but only one ultimate reality, the formless Brahman, eternal and the source of all existence, the informed unity of Akbar's name for Prayag, is appropriate in essence. An ecumenist might even think the first line of a Christian hymn written by an American called Samuel Johnson as a good description of the gathering at the Sangam—'City of God, how broad and far outspread they walls sublime.' It was one of the hymns we sang each year at Foundation Day at school.

At his magnificent capital of Fatehpur-Sikri, close to Agra, Akbar famously enjoyed ecumenical discourses with members of many faiths—Hindu, Buddhist, Zoroastrian, Jain, even Portuguese Jesuits from Goa. Disillusioned with orthodox Islam, he developed a syncretist faith known as Din-I-Ilahi or Divine Faith. His biographer, Abul Fazl, recorded the Emperor's desire to locate his new city beside the *Sangam*, the site so important to India's holy men. Just like the proliferation of stories explaining the origins of the Kumbh Mela, there are many to explain Akbar's presence. Myths say that he was the reincarnation of a Prayag hermit who jumped to his death to atone for having swallowed a cow's hair in a draught of milk which he considered tantamount to eating beef. It is said that when Akbar arrived in Prayag, many of the local rajas visited him to pay homage. The Raja of Jhunsi felt he had nothing valuable enough to present to the Emperor. His minister however arranged on a silver tray, a silver sledge-hammer and some sand from the banks of the Ganga with *tulsi* leaves and flowers. Akbar was perplexed at the unusual gift which he recognised as the *puja* items for a foundation-laying ceremony. It was a suggestion that Akbar should use Jhunsi land on which to build a fort.

On my first visit to Allahabad years ago, our bus drove down a road beside the walls of the great fort. We walked across the sand to the point of the *Sangam*, not at all crowded on a November day of little auspiciousness. Because the Fort is occupied by the Indian Army most of the area is closed to visitors. It is a convenient boundary to the bathing area and is probably a similar elevation to where we stood at Jhunsi, our view framed in the foreground by *pipal* trees.

High on the eminence was a very smart tented camp, the zenith of luxury for a stay at the Kumbh Mela. It was expensive but had every comfort (I wonder how their flush loos function) and possibilities for ayurvedic analysis and treatment. There is even a little encampment of *babas* at the bottom of the hill where an *aarti* or worship with lights was held every evening. Robyn had a close friendship with one of the *babas*, Ramanandagiri or the Hunchback Baba. He does have a hunched back but the name is not meant unkindly. When we met he was suffering from a cold but we had a happy conversation about this and that and he unwound his pale apricot-coloured turban and flicked back the mass of his long dreadlocks with a great flourish. A marvellous orange top-coat hung decoratively against the buttercup tent wall to protect him against evening cold, not new to him as his home is in the mountains where he looks after many of the holy men who have also made that place their home. Robyn often helped him with funds to buy food and other supplies.

Their little encampment was very colourful with bright yellow tent walls, orange and yellow patterned *dhurries* on the ground, orange mattresses and the *babas* were dressed in all shades of saffron. Some men wore turbans, others as they sat in the delicious morning sunshine had coiled their dreadlocks in a fat coif around their heads. In the centre of the shrine room was a hearth and a trident hung with a garland of marigolds. A large picture of the Hindu trinity was similarly garlanded. On a low divan near the hearth sat a naked baba deep in contemplation. Well, he wasn't quite naked, I have never seen anyone wearing more beads than he. His head was encased in a tall, rounded helmet-shaped coil of *rudraksha* beads and adorned with the crescent moon. His hair hung in dreadlocks down his back, a white beard straggled down his chest and around his neck he wore rope upon rope, perhaps thirty or forty strings of beads that hung down between his legs as he sat. *Rudraksha* beads are sacred to Lord Shiva. The *baba* somehow looked disarming, appearing more pensive than lost in meditation. He wore a smart gold watch on his left arm and an armlet on the upper right arm which ended in a stump. He had lost his hand and part of his forearm in a mining accident as a boy. He was a curious sight but we were becoming used to such things. Just before arriving at Jhunsi we had passed a *sadhu* lying on a tangle of ghastly thorns with a blanket of the same nasty, thorny stuff resting on his chest and modestly covering his body down to his knees. He rattled a little rolling drum, the sort that men with performing bears and monkeys used to carry, the same carried by Lord Shiva to provide the beat for the cosmic dance in which he destroys the world in order to create it again. Passers-by stopped and stared and some placed coins at his feet or notes in the thorny tangle. He had painted very unrealistic wounds on his thin, ash-smeared legs—a bit like the daubs of mercurochrome which miraculously cured our childish scratches. This bit of deception served to make him quite without menace, almost benign.

The senior *baba* at the Jhunsi camp had sustained a very deep burn on the back of his lower leg which Robyn had seen a day earlier. She wanted Andrea to examine it. It was dreadfully deep, third degree, but he said it wasn't painful. It had been caused by a hot water bottle while he was in a deep, almost anaesthetised sleep. Perhaps he had been smoking something potent. A thin-faced man sitting nearby had an incredible circle of dreadlocks wound neatly around his head. He, poor thing also had burns, on his hands from rescuing his dog and her pups from flames when his house in the mountains had caught fire. He spoke with a pukka accent and was clearly well educated but here he was in saffron robes, at the holy place waiting for the huge gathering, unworried about worldly things but still sad about the death of one of the pups in the fire.

Andrea rang her practice in England to speak to one of the sisters about the burn and returned later to treat the leg. Public health facilities at the Maha Kumbh were, like all the other statistics, startling in number and organisation. A temporary 100-bed hospital and twelve smaller health centres had been set up with 243 doctors, 257 paramedics and 600 other medical staff rostered around the clock, prepared for the worst in the form of stampede or bomb blast. The hospital which had opened in December had been receiving up to 1500 patients a day, both pilgrims and people from neighbouring areas who were taking advantage of the free medical treatment from paediatricians, gynaecologists, ophthalmologists, dentists and other specialists. X-ray, ultrasound and laboratory facilities were available. There was an intensive care unit, seventy-five ambulances and four river ambulances. Some of the Harvard team came from the School of Public Health and the Harvard Medical School. They saw the Kumbh as a model of how to support mass migrations of people into small areas in the event of war or a natural disaster.

Everywhere there were streams of people walking purposefully towards the confluence. Indians are expert at staring but somehow not here, either at us as foreigners or for that matter anyone, particularly at the bathing place. Pilgrims had come from all over India, arriving in family or village groups, carrying bundles on their heads, the women sometimes holding a corner of another's sari in order not to be separated. Streams of men in all those gorgeous shades of the holy colour, marigold garlanded and foreheads daubed with white, vermillion or saffron, passed us in an extraordinary procession. We peeped inside gates to see hundreds sitting cross-legged in rows, eating lunch which had been provided to them free of charge.

We crossed a pontoon bridge and on the other side it all seemed like a happy day at some unusual beach. A brass band, the members in red jackets and peaked hats, played the same sort of music as at weddings. Villagers sat while a priest organized their *puja* offerings of coconuts wreathed in marigold garlands. Nearby a *sadhu* was constructing a wonderful sand castle version of a Shiva *lingam* and women in red and yellow saris had just launched tiny paper offerings on the river, looking like baby boats, their masts of burning *agarbathis* and their cargo marigold flowers. Small children sought to have us buy some for ourselves. Directions to pilgrims advise them how to care for the river by not washing clothes on the banks or using soap while bathing. Another stricture said that 'throwing of materials used for worship or rituals in the river should be avoided.' There were surprisingly few—just these occasional small offerings and here and there—marigold garlands which had washed up from somewhere else. So many people were trying to save the Ganga. She is worshipped as a goddess and nobody wants to see a goddess suffer. But she is not in good shape.

Before leaving home, along with concern about loos, many had said with a meaningful look, 'well you won't bathe will you?' To which I answered 'oh yes I probably will' which generally caused an anticipated shudder. I had already bathed in the sacred Narmada River at Maheshwar at dawn one morning, as well as having a swim in it later in the day. The water seemed very clean, the strong current was the worry there. There were many more shudders when I returned home, having bathed, able to tell the tale and not dead yet from some water-borne disease. Despite the fact that the river is used for ritual bathing, the disposal of bones and ashes of the dead and even diseased corpses, and contaminated by sewage, the water is said to be quite pure. It is said that bacteria dies fast in Ganga water. Tube-wells were sunk to provide drinking water for the Kumbh and this is what came through our taps in the famous en suite. We did not drink it though. The camp had an endless supply of safe drinking water. We washed our metal cups and *thalis* in tap water and they dried in the air. I suppose boiling water would have done a better job or even the drinking water but nobody seemed worried to that extreme.

There were no cremation *ghats* anywhere near the bathing site and the water really did seem clean. It was the colour of weak black tea close to the sand-bagged shores but clear enough and it certainly didn't smell. I lived for many years on the banks of the Murrumbidgee River from which we drew our water supply. There were times when we were unable to drink that water without boiling it when the river was very low in the summer. We were more concerned about being able to find a swimming hole deep enough for immersion. On one famous occasion, a nasty tang did permeate our tap water. We turned on all the taps at full strength in the house and garden to drain the holding tank at the top of the hill. What should pop out flapping about on the grass in the garden but small silvery fish. That was certainly amusing but less so was a larger cousin who was too fat to fight his way out of the tap over the bath. Poor thing, stuck fast, he had to disintegrate a bit before we could clear the pipe which really was unpleasant. In country Australia when people clean out their tanks they invariably find a few possum skeletons which hadn't worried anybody's guts unduly. Of course a bit of organic matter like that isn't as bad as all the other things that can be found in the Ganges. Weeks prior to the festival, companies with factories on the banks upstream of both the Ganges and the Yamuna were warned against discharging pollutants. As well, reservoirs upstream had been ordered to helpfully discharge fresh water into the rivers ahead of the big bathing days.

Swami Chidanand's dedication to saving the Ganga, the river whose 'purity never ends' knows that the water is dirty. With his followers he is one of the leaders of the 'Green Kumbh' movement, new at the 2013 Maha Kumbh and part of a wider push for a greater consciousness in making pilgrimages more environmentally positive. The Union Minister for Water Resources, Harish Rawat, visited Swami Chidanand's Ganga Action Parivar Camp and officially launched the National Ganga Rights Movement. It is proposed to establish, secure and defend the inalienable and inherent rights of the Ganga, its tributaries and watershed and by extension, the rights of the people of India to a healthy thriving river basin. The Act would also establish the rights of the people of India and their governments to defend and enforce the rights of the Ganga. Along her course 660 million gallons of sewage is produced daily by cities on her banks and only a third is treated. At the *Sangam*, the level of organic pollution in the Ganges was double the maximum acceptable level after the first day of the *Mela* when

10 million bathed in the river. For Swami Chidanand it was deeds, not just words, and he and his followers staged 'symbolic action' by raking and burying piles of marigold garlands and picking up all kinds of rubbish.

One large section of the Harvard project studied religion and the humanities. Led by Professor Diana Eck, an eminent religious scholar who is Professor of Comparative Religion and Indian Studies. Her book on Varanasi, *Banaras, City of Light*, is considered brilliant by Indians in India who are highly critical of westerners writing about their faith and their country. Research topics undertaken by Eck and her students focused on religion and the environment which involved many aspects of the Ganges—the ritual use of flowers and its despoiling impact on the river and the effects of dams. The group looked at how hydroelectric schemes, canals and irrigation systems related to the sanctity of the sacred rivers.

River blight is not confined to the Ganges. The sacred Yamuna which is also worshipped as a goddess, is in a frightful state in Delhi. In his eccentric but probing look at the huge city *Delhi: Adventures in a Megacity* Sam Miller writes 'The Yamuna river is Delhi's shameful, rancid secret. This city would not exist but for the river ... But it has now become one of the world's largest open sewers, with more than two billion litres of untreated household and industrial waste flowing into it every day.' At Vrindavan, less than 100 kilometres downstream from Delhi, the river does not seem quite so ill although the whole stretch of river between Delhi and Agra has been declared unfit for drinking and bathing. It is far from the lotus-dotted blue stream seen in *pichhwais*, the glorious painted cloths sacred to Lord Krishna. It is sluggish and brown but I have seen turtles swimming in the river and out on a boat on its surface there is no unpleasant smell. This is partly thanks to the huge efforts of an organisation called Friends of Vrindavan, of which Robyn Beeche was a very active foundation member. They have initiated income generating projects for widows and members of sweeper families and organised a rubbish collection regime in some of the *mohallas* where such a service had never existed. Attempts are made to convince pilgrims not to throw garlands and other religious paraphenalia into the river, similar to the efforts at Prayag. One big success story at Vrindavan has been the manufacture of compost. From the organic matter collected from municipal rubbish the outcome is splendid compost, so highly prized by even tea gardens in the hills, that supply cannot keep up with demand.

There was a strong sense of purpose in the ribbons of people heading towards the *Sangam* or, having bathed, returning to their lodgings or even to the railway station—some people make an enormous journey just for one day at the holy place. With such huge crowds it is inevitable that a great number of people became separated from their companions. Volunteers kept an eye out for anyone appearing to be lost and escorted them to the Bhule Bhatke or Camp for Lost People. Umesh Tiwari who ran it this year, is the son of Raja Ram Tiwari who set up the first camp for the lost in 1946. Since that time a million adults and 20,000 children have been reunited, another astounding statistic. Close to the *sangam*, a loud-speaker blared announcements reporting people lost and found. Reunions are made easier by new technology. In 2001 police had land-lines and one digital camera. This year they were using WhatsApp to share information and had created an online photo gallery. The website showed photographs of those waiting in the tent, the found, looking disorientated and terribly unhappy. Those registered as missing were usually shown as silhouettes, the families not having a photograph to scan. Running across the bottom of the website were directions to pilgrims about not washing clothes or using soap in the river, also additional recommendation not to use plastic bags nor to encourage beggary. All useful information to be sure, but any poor family at wits end trying to find a lost relative would hardly need such advice. Most people were happily reunited but some elderly people were lost for days. Perhaps it might be a great way to part company with a troublesome old relative, lost at the Kumbh but in the most auspicious of circumstances when the celestial alignment of stars and planets would provide an accelerated journey to nirvana.

It was wonderful to be with Robyn and unashamedly copy her as she instinctively found fantastic photographic opportunities.

She was the person to follow. There was strict prohibition about photographing women bathers. Just days before a foolish foreign photographer had ignored this. His camera was seized, he was taken to a police station where he was questioned and bashed. Following this policemen were more vigilant in watching foreigners with cameras. As women, we aroused less interest and we had no interest in taking revealing shots. Very little is revealed by Indian ladies when bathing anyhow. By contrast most of the sadhus and nagas reveal all, and in common with most pilgrims, did not mind being photographed. Neither did we.

Itinerant vendors sold whirligigs, spinning frantically on long straw-covered poles, and strings of bright green plastic parrots which flapped idly in the light breeze. We came face to face with the effigy of A.C. Bhaktivedanta Swami Prabhupada, the founder of the Hare Krishna Movement, seated on a covered cart drawn by two handsome, pale bullocks and preceded by a bearded, long-haired man blowing a conch. Piles of plastic containers were offered for sale, allowing pilgrims to take Ganga water home and many vendors had large supplies of cord for new sacred threads. This surely was a very auspicious time to buy.

We stopped to try a very strange type of food. Several boys sat on the ground with two or three tall cylindrical shapes lined up on a ground-sheet. They looked like some kind of gorgeous drum — smooth dark terracotta on the outside and the cut top a bright white. We were told it was 'sweet wood' and were given a sample. That's exactly how it tasted, like sweet wood and I don't think it will set the world on fire as the new trend in snacks. Oh my goodness, where to spit it?

At last we could see the *Sangam*. A flotilla of small boats floated in the centre of the river where some pilgrims were bathing at the spot where the waters really meet. The shores of the Ganga were sand-bagged along its entire course through the *mela* grounds as a safety measure to stop the sand from melting away in the water under so many millions of feet. The bags gave a firm footing as pilgrims stepped into the water. We walked down the gentle slope where masses of clean straw had been laid to stop the area from becoming muddy and messy. Little hillocks of reserve straw provided a good soft spot for a nap for tired pilgrims and a place to drape damp saris. Other wet clothes hung on the wooden fences marking a race passage constructed to help with crowd control. Many saris had been laid straight on the sand but policewomen urged their owners to pick them up and make space. The air drying of saris formed wonderful moving patches of translucent colour. Two friends held an end of the five or six yards of vivid cloth, waving it in the air to speed the drying. The colours often seemed to match the dry saris of the wavers as though the whole endeavor was coordinated for harmony and beauty. Reds, oranges and pinks predominated. Someone at home had asked if bathing costumes were worn. *Absolutely not!* The nagas wear nothing except beads and some garlands but decorous Indian ladies take holy dip fully clad and then manage to change into dry clothes with no loss of modesty. Men for whom all such things are always easier, stride into the water stripped down to their inevitably dreadful baggy, daggy underpants.

Several metres from shore poles had been placed at regular intervals and loosely roped together to mark the extent of the bathing area from the shore. Here the water was very shallow and at the deepest it was only knee high for an adult of normal height, making it quite hard to immerse entirely and three times at that. The water level is controlled from upstream to minimize the chances of drowning. As a further precaution, boats moved around outside the flimsy barrier with men ready to rescue anyone presumed to be in difficulties. On main bathing days, police stood in the water and moved pilgrims on as soon as they have taken their holy dip. We stood and watched, nobody taking the slightest notice of us as they got on with the great immersion. What an exciting thing for the bathers, to think they had actually managed to be in the right place at this incredibly auspicious time. This holy dip was probably going to be one of the most significant things in their lives. An older man, a father but perhaps a grandfather, had two little girls aged about 6 and 4 with him. The little one bucked a bit and cried but he settled her. He led them into the water, swept the little one into his arms, the elder child holding onto him for security. He actually held the nose of each child and held them under the water three times while also ducking himself. Out they came—the whole thing took less than a minute. A woman near my feet had changed into dry clothes—a black and white choli and a bright magenta petticoat. She had a little paper boat laden with marigolds and dark pink rose petals. She lit some incense and sprinkled coloured powder in a private moment of worship.

The mood was one of quiet satisfaction and happiness. Further up the banks groups sat and waited, some eating, some dozing with their bags tied to their bodies, some just watched the world go by. By now it was well into the afternoon and the shadows were lengthening. The crowd was thinning and people moved away from the river when their clothes were dry and all their belongings packed up. Four little children dressed as gods ran up to us seeking rupees and eager to give us a bit of a blessing in return. Two small Shivas with strings of matted false hair made from jute and tiger stripe cloth wrapped around their skinny little hips adopted a one-legged pose and two slightly taller Parvatis, who could have been boys as well, accompanied them. Another tiny two year-old god, probably Krishna, unconcerned about heavenly things, sat licking the earthly delight of an icy pole. Past the small god impersonators we found ourselves following a thin ash-smeared *naga*, holding a brass *lota* in one hand and a piece of cloth in the other—it didn't seem at all odd to be walking behind a naked man. I've scarcely ever seen nude men outside my own family, or streakers captured on film at football matches. The scores observed every day at the Kumbh has greatly extended the incidence, perhaps enough for a lifetime!

Some experts think that Michelangelo's David is rather poorly endowed. One reason has been given that he was meant to have been placed on the top of the Cathedral and therefore endure fairly cold weather. Another theory is that a certain shriveling takes place in connection with fear and as he was just about to face the giant, Goliath, this could have been the reason. I don't think many of the *sadhus* were in a state of holy fear but the early morning temperatures at Allahabad could account for the generally unexceptional size.

Back at our camp, excellent musicians dressed each day in fine starched kurtas had been engaged from Vrindavan to join with Sri Venu Gopal Goswami, Shrivatsa's brother, in a seven-day reading of the Bhagwat Purana. This took place each morning for three hours in the large central communal tent in our camp. His voice was beautiful and much of the text was sung. His handsome face was shown on a banner adorning the outside of the camp walls. We listened one morning, seated on the ground with many of the other camp residents, among them a number of beautifully dressed women, disciples of Venu Gopal. At one end of the tent was a small temple made of thatch. Above the doorway was a painting of the images of Krishna and Radha which reside in the Radharaman Temple at Vrindavan, close to the Gambhira Ashram. The doorway itself was closed with the same gorgeous gold-printed saffron cloth that lined the tent wall behind the shine, it is printed by a devotee. Within it was a small image of Sri Krishna revealed at the appropriate times of worship throughout the day and beside it were articles used in the *puja*. Nearby on a tent wall hung a large *pichhwai*, a painting on cloth, of Shri Radha with the *gopis* or milkmaids. Seated under a tree at Bhramaghat beside the blue Yamuna, Radha seems to be offering spiritual advice to her friends but a closer look shows a dark bumble bee flying close to her feet. This is the playful Lord Krishna, beloved of all the *gopis*. Perhaps he is being welcomed but perhaps too he is teasing and Radha is sending him away. Elsewhere in the tent were banners displaying photographs of the image of Sri Radharaman in the Vrindavan Temple and of a painting of Shri Chaitanya Mahaprabhu, the Bhakti saint born in West Bengal in 1485 who is regarded by some as a full incarnation of Krishna. Chaitanya visited Vrindavan in 1515 with the idea of visiting the holy places connected to Lord Krishna. Vrindavan at the time had lost something of its vigour but the divine spiritual power of the saint enabled him to rediscover the energy and to reinvigorate the region of Vraj.

In our own tent we were often joined by Priya, Shrivatsa's pretty little grand-daughter. She attended an English medium school in

Vrindhavan and plied us each evening with questions from a quiz book, her current favourite. We had capital cities of the world and trick questions about animals and famous people—it was quite exercising. Our meals were wonderful. The cooks had come from Calcutta and according to Robyn, were streets ahead of those who did the catering at the last Kumbh. One morning we saw the *chowkidar* and his helper shelling the peas in the sunshine, they had become additional kitchen maiteys. The food was simple pure vegetarian, produced on the simplest of equipment in the cookhouse located next to the dining tent and was served to us from steaming stainless steel buckets by attentive boys. The foreigners constituted a bit of a problem as we chatted and lingered over our food. There were too many people to fit in the dining hall at once so we were rather gumming up the works. One night a rather bossy but highly efficient lady whom I have seen each time I have visited the Radharaman Temple in Vrindavan came to Robyn saying 'Robyn, may I speak to you in Hindi?' and raised the issue. After that we were much faster and more cooperative in our eating habits. It was so cold in the dining tent that we wore coats, scarves and hats so it was better to eat and run straight to the marginal extra warmth of our own tents.

Another day a long walk took us to a camp of one of the *akharas*. These are sects or monastic orders of Hindu holy men, probably founded originally by the great philosopher and reformer Shankaracharya, in the eighth or ninth century. The word *sadhu* means 'pious man' in Sanskrit and *sadhus* are described in devotional works as the male counterparts of the river Ganga seen as divine mother. Many *sadhus* connected to the thirteen main *akharas* are trained in martial arts, their militancy developed in the fifteenth and sixteenth centuries to resist interference by the Moguls into their practices, in particular bathing rituals. Their militancy however had sometimes been aimed at rival *akharas* and an order of precedence for procession to the *Sangam* had been established during the British era, to avoid the serious eruptions of violence that had occurred in the past.

Last year the Juna Akhara, one of the leading *akharas* and said to be the most fierce, issued a statement forbidding foreigners from entry to their 2013 Kumbh Mela camp. The reason given was that *sadhus* had noticed in recent years that foreign visitors were 'trying to pollute the atmosphere of our *mutts*.' A *mutt* or *math* is a monastic type of religious establishment, rather more formal and hierarchical than an *ashram*. The claim was that the foreigners brought drugs and liquor to seduce the *sadhus*. It had been admitted however, that certain *sadhus* had taken advantage of foreign women and seduced them in an entirely different way. Such aberrations had been expelled from the *akhara* including a polygamous *sadhu* who had notoriously managed to marry many times with a preference for Italian women. The directive was given in August 2012 but later it was reported that contrary to the earlier statement, those to be banned were only 'nefarious elements, who leave no stone unturned to lure and trap the gullible *sadhus*'. A kind of in-house constabulary of *kotwals*, was raised to keep an eye on suspicious or unreligious visitors, local and foreign, and to 'continuously alert and caution the saints and seers to refrain from falling into the traps laid by a few vested interests.'

The *akhara* camps were usually reached by passing underneath a great high arch, a triumphal construction made, like the rest of the pop-up city, of cloth and bamboo. We passed under one, with five chandeliers suspended from the archway like a *toran*, the sacred or honorific gateway in ancient Indian Buddhist architecture. Tinkling in the breeze, the chandeliers swayed alarmingly when a tall 4-wheel drive vehicle raced through at a ridiculous pace, bearing a company of *sadhus* armed with silver sticks or maces.

India is the home of the most wonderful tents in the world, pitched for weddings, political rallies and religious ceremonies, the ceilings and walls are separate and can be decorated in any number of ways. Some smart hotels in country or desert locations accommodate guests in glorious tents, fit for an emperor. In Pakistan we bought a super *shamiana*—the ceiling, and *q'anats*—the walls sewn in beautiful geometric shapes in primary colours and long striped socks to fit the tent poles. At extravagant weddings hundreds of metres of cloth might be artfully tied, pulled, draped and swagged to add wondrous dimension.

Inside the gateway a long marquee full of ambient saffron light ran down the side of the internal road. Within this were about a dozen small tents arranged like a housing estate with neat slanted brick edging to the front 'gardens' which were laid with carpets and cloth. Some had potted plants, palms and small conifers adding to the garden effect. The overwhelming radiance of every variety of saffron created a pervasive glow. There was no fire in any of the hearths that morning but big logs would provide warmth in the chill of the night where temperatures might descend to zero. The *trishula* or trident stood, hung about with strings of marigolds near the hearths. Now the morning sunshine filtered into the still somnolent atmosphere. One tall *sadhu* of fine physique stood grandly in his orange bath-robe, another, stout and white with ash sat with one leg upraised revealing a modest breech-clout. Some wore nothing at all, others were dressed elaborately. Several with long matted hair sitting in cross-legged contemplation looked exactly like old paintings of *rishis* by 18th century travellers. Some received visitors and gave blessings, some lay on *charpoys*, fast asleep. One with a wild rather bad-tempered look, his hair piled up in a large, untidy knot on the top of his head, shared a chillum with a comrade who looked distinctly unwell. A group of four men sat outside one of the tents, swathed in shawls. Weeks later when I arrived home and sorted out my photographs, I looked and looked at one of them. Surely we are a little alike! Perhaps it was our untidy grey hair, I'm sure there is a resemblance. Christiane and I had just been to Kanpur and visited the sites of what the British call the Indian Mutiny. In 1857 one of the events that most horrified the British took place at the Kanpur (Cawnpore) garrison. There was a dreadful massacre and almost the entire British population was lost. Legend persists that one of the daughters of the commander of the garrison, General Sir Hugh Wheeler, Margaret known as Ulrica, was rescued by an Indian cavalryman. Some stories say that she lived for another 50 years in or near Kanpur. My maiden name was Wheeler.

Robyn had seen vendors selling interesting beads from Ladakh so we went in pursuit of a bit of retail therapy. They looked rather like some I'd bought in Indonesia years ago which were made from melted down toothbrush handles. Elsewhere in the *Mela* grounds Colgate-Palmolive hoped to sell thousands of toothbrushes at discount prices as part of an advertising campaign. Toothbrush handle and Ladakhi or not, they were beautiful—long strings of large colourful beads. Rosaries of many kinds were sold by these vendors as well as less sacred adornments and after we had bought one or two, more and more appeared from bags and bundles. Other vendors sold a wide range of men's underpants, woollen clothing and shawls, religious books, idols and posters laid out neatly on sheets on the ground.

Perambulating sellers had peacock feather fans, bamboo flutes and tambourines. A boot-maker sat in the dust repairing *jutis* for a *sadhu*. The Prayag Dairy had numerous stalls dotted across the grounds and we stopped for delicious little cups of yoghurt. Other small shops sold bottled water, Nescafé or Horlicks with the added incentive of free biscuits. Coca Cola had 16 stalls across the *Mela* ground selling Coke at very cheap rates. Sales were reported to be high though several stalls we saw were deserted. This was great grist for the mill of the Harvard Business School researchers, a rather different persuasion to their colleagues studying public health, urbanism and religious topics. One HBS team studied the structure and governance of the Kumbh in order to understand how large-scale urban infrastructure can be deployed in a short time. The mission of one senior lecturer in finance was to turn the Kumbh's 'organized chaos into a Business School case study' and to see how it could fit into his belief that cities 'will become more powerful entities like the city-states of ancient Greece.'

A second team looked at the development of networks and issues of supply and demand. Young researchers found that simple assumptions about such elements as competition, could not be taken for granted. They found it very odd for example that people selling exactly the same things did not spread out to try and increase the odds of good sales by putting distance between themselves and other rival stalls. They were really stumped by the fact that along one particular stretch of a dusty internal road, one stall after another sold exactly the same delicious *aloo chaat*, a dish of spicy fried potatoes. It was identical with our bead sellers who were all selling the same merchandise. It was similar to the guild set-up in most Indian bazaars where everyone dealing in the same commodity occupies the same locality. It serves the customer well—instant opportunities of price comparison but as the customer knows, the prices in all the shops are always the same! So what to do?

More vital to everyday existence than beads and underpants were the multitude of small shops selling food and firewood. Beautiful vegetables appeared every day in the shops and on handcarts pushed around internal roads. Many pilgrims brought their own food and means to cook it but prior to the start of the Kumbh Mela, four warehouses were stocked with subsidized supplies to be sold at fair prices. It was estimated that ten million rupees would exchange hands at these shops during the mela. 16,500 tonnes of wheat flour, 9,600 tonnes of rice, 6,000 tonnes of sugar and 30,000 tonnes of food grains were stored ready to be sold. Retail prices were kept at the low rates of ration shops to be affordable to even the poorest pilgrims. As well, a mountain of 2,447 tonnes of wood was amassed. Some visitors had brought cooking equipment and a fire could be created on the sand shielded by a rock or a brick but small horseshoe-shaped clay fireplaces were available for sale in many locations to make cooking easier, providing a shield for the flame as well as a trivet to elevate the pan. Clay vessels of many sizes were available for sale and a great quantity of *chillums*.

In a campaign called Roti Reminder, Unilever paid 100 promoters in 100 food stalls at the gathering and elsewhere in Allahabad to brand their chapattis with a message of hygiene. An estimated 2.5 million *rotis* bought at these outlets would be consumed during the Kumbh Mela carrying a message stamped by an electric iron asking in Hindi 'Did you wash your hands with Lifebuoy?' Cakes of Lifebuoy soap were on hand at restaurants with washbasins. Since 2008 and the establishment of Global Handwashing Day, focused on the connection between hand-washing and child health, Unilever in its corporate social responsibility agenda has sought to use its brands to enact social change. Since their campaign began they claim the number of deaths of children from diarrhoeal diseases has fallen by half. The seed of the idea started in Burkino Faso in the 1990s and spread across the world until now on Global Handwashing Day, 15 October, 200,000,000 people in 100 countries are involved. Originally targeting children in schools, the campaign now reaches out to the whole community. The coalition of international stakeholders called PPPHW or Public Private Partnership for Handwashing, comprises governments, donor organisations, the private sector, non-government and community-based organisations.

With 8% of India's population present at the *mela*, advertising possibilities should have been brilliant. Experts agreed that there was big money to be made at the Maha Kumbh. The Associated Chambers of Commerce and Industry of India expected Uttar Pradesh's income to be boosted by Rs. 12,000 *crores* (a *crore* is 10,000,000). Many other sectors would benefit, especially airlines, airports and tour companies. Unilever may have managed to combine social responsibility with a clever channeling of propaganda, but other organisations found their expensive banners quickly disappeared, usually appropriated as building material. The most obvious advertising was the spiritual in the form of the huge photographs of saints and seers adorning poles and fences. Some looked beatific, some amused, one—gazing down with a very toothy smile at a baby in his arms looked as though he was going to eat it! Robyn found this phenomenon one of the big changes since the last Kumbh Mela, linked with the advent of digital photography and a consequent decrease in cost of creating the banners Saints in SUV's and the absence of elephants were other changes.

Without discussing it, Christiane and I had both decided not to bathe after our first visit to the *Sangam*. We felt we were voyeurs and tagging along on someone else's traditions. It was not due to lack of faith however, and when Robyn announced that she had decided that the right place for us to take holy dip was at a far less crowded part of the river very close to our camp at the extreme northern end of the mela grounds, we were at least interested to investigate. We visited it and on the spot jointly and severally changed our minds. It was perfect and as the auspicious day began at 4.23 pm on the afternoon before the huge throng at dawn the next morning, that is when we returned to our *ghat*.

The sun was still warm and there was plenty of activity. Marigolds and coconuts were for sale and tethered at the top of the bank were several small calves which a pilgrim could symbolically buy and then return in a rather feeble imitation of a highly meritorious act. A large group of people were engaged in a ceremony. They circled in a joyous dance, singing and holding aloft saffron flags and offerings. Round and around they went and then eventually most immersed themselves in the river. Others sat and watched, by the look of things having bathed earlier. There were really very few children present at the mela but some small ones sat here quietly with grandparents. Safety would surely have been a consideration in not bringing them into such enormous crowds. Older men came out of the water dripping and proceeded with the utmost decorum to dry themselves and dress again in many layers of clothes. *Banians* or singlets, shirts and vests, jackets and mufflers, dry *dhotis* replacing wet, some put on shoes and socks. Again the waving butterfly saris became gorgeous shimmering patches of colour. Why was it that today blues seemed to predominate? From even a short distance the river too looked blue, reflecting the pale azure wash of the sky. Some women disappeared into a roofless, canvas enclosure which we eyed off with a proprietorial view as to how we were going to manage our post-bathing clothing change.

Whenever I travel anywhere at all I always work out how I can jettison some of my gear. It might be just the toothpaste tube on a weekend to Sydney but in India my discards become more orchestrated and comprehensive. Apart from anything else, there is always someone either able to wear or at least profit from the abandonment of a favourite but ancient and faded shirt which if thrown out in Australia would just end up in landfill. Greatly loved but elderly Anokhi shirts and really the most favourite jeans in my whole life were the discard items for this trip.

Halfway through last year I had run an event at the National Gallery of Australia which had filled me with fear. I facilitate the NGA Book Club which is usually limited to about 16 people, the comfortable maximum to fit around the table in the Book Shop. It's a nice place to meet and over its five year history we have had some great discussions. We meet once a quarter to discuss a book that has a connection to art. We have read novels about Sidney Nolan, Clarice Beckett and Frida Kahlo, a collection of letters between Georgia O'Keeffe and Alfred Stieglitz, a biography of Modigliani, a book about art theft, one about the colour black and a very amusing book about life in Vanuatu. I try to choose books that either link with our wonderful collection or to a temporary exhibition on at the time and usually at the end of the discussion we look at works in the galleries that relate to the book. The huge volume of Georgia and Alfred's letters was something of a trial—it weighed more than 2 kilograms so was a difficult bed-time story. It was more than saved at our discussion which concluded with a visit to the Collection Study Room where Anne O'Hehir, curator of Photography, showed us Stieglitz photographs and copies of his lovely magazine *Camera Work*.

Not long before the Kumbh Mela our book of choice was *The Longing*, a novel focused on the life and paintings of a fictional character based on Eugene von Guérard, the Austrian artist whose paintings of the colonial Australian landscape may be found in all major galleries in our country. The book was a new release and we could time the discussion to coincide with the Canberra season of the excellent NGV travelling exhibition of works by von Guérard. The author, Candice Bruce, who had at one time worked at the National Gallery, agreed to speak about the book at the Gallery. Instead of a cosy cluster around the book-shop table, she and I sat 'in conversation' on a raised dais in front of the audience of about 50 in the Gandel Hall. It could have been totally terrifying but Candice was charming and a great speaker, the morning tea based on the tea-room fare described in the book was good and book sales were satisfactory for the shop. A good time was had by all. I invited Candice and some of our mutual friends to my flat in the evening and Candice gave me a tin of chocolate sardines. They looked so wonderful—chocolate fish shapes covered in shiny foil, packed into the little tin and far too good to eat. They remained untouched but for some reason I decided to take them to Robyn at the Kumbh and we then felt that consuming them after taking holy dip would be just perfect.

Our dip had to be recorded photographically for all time so we entered the river in relay. We chose the extreme end of the bathing area and our photographs give no hint that we were part of the largest gathering of humanity in the world's history. The scene looks almost deserted which suited us very well. My daughter had sent me a text saying that reports on Australian television showed what seemed to be a great deal of nose-blowing amongst the bathers and suggested we not swallow any water. Christiane had observed the bathing at the *Sangam* and felt that as the bathers were in the water for such a short time, there was scarcely time for them to pee. We weren't too worried about anything really. Someone the night before had demonstrated how to simultaneously pinch nostrils and plug ears. OK if one had huge hands perhaps but otherwise impossible and our resident doctors said we needn't worry about our ears, just to close mouth, pinch nose and not to open eyes under the water.

Christiane and I entered first, holding hands as we edged off the sand-bagged shore and waded in. We were to look at the sun, say our prayers and immerse three times. I knew I had all kinds of prayers I wanted to say but at the plunging moment they all sped out of my head into the holy ether. The water came up to mid-thigh, deeper than we had seen earlier at the *Sangam*. Even that depth made submersion slightly odd and very unlike diving with free arms into the sea at home at the beach. On my first submerging water poured into my right ear and I half-thought 'oh no!' but despite looking slightly murky, it was perfectly pleasant in feel and smell. In fact it was wonderful. We came out dripping and took over the cameras for Andrea and Robyn. In our photographs we all look incredibly happy. What was it that we had done? I don't for a second think I have been absolved from all my sins but I do think to have taken that dip was to affirm something important in life. Faith in action is such a fascinating thing and when there is no possible harm to another living creature, what can possibly be wrong with it?

In relay again we entered the tented changing area which was full of chattering, smiling ladies. They warned Christiane and me away from a vacant corner for some reason. There was nothing to be seen but obviously something was wrong with it. I was too intent on peeling off my wet jeans and undies to notice but Christiane said our companions were terribly interested in our bodies. Poor things, what sights! Robyn had given me strict instructions not to discard my clothes at the river as she had people in the ashram who could use them. So I rolled everything up neatly and stuffed them into my bag. I know I left nothing behind but when I went to rinse everything out later at the camp, I was minus my ancient knickers which must have been swiped from under my very feet. How funny. Reunited outside, we found it somehow extremely appropriate to each eat a symbolic chocolate sardine with enjoyment thanks to Candice.

Before the sun had set that evening we set off on another long walk across the pontoon bridge closest to our camp. With warm layers over our clean, dry clothes we joined streams of pilgrims and we were accompanied by Miss Priya. Her little sister was clearly not going to last the distance so she went home with her mother. Lights came on as we crossed the river and the pearly grey glow on the water was enchanting. Colour vanished after a few short moments— the scene was like a Whistler with every shade of grey, punctuated by red flags fluttering at intervals along the bridge. We walked a short circuit and on the other side we encountered processions of devotees, carrying images of gods towards the river for the evening *aarti* or worship with lights. Brahmins held candelabra, others carried vivid umbrellas, and an image of the god borne on poles by ten men, was smothered with garlands. Darkness fell quickly and the street lights cast long paths of illumination on the surface of river, twinkling as it rippled. When we arrived back at the camp Priya's mother was very agitated. We hadn't been away for long and she knew that her little daughter should have been safe with us but worry had got the better of her. It was sad to see but easy to understand as it was not long since the dreadful rape and murder of the poor student in Delhi and other terrible crimes of abduction and assault had been reported in the papers. All this had become somewhat remote to us in the safety of each other and the camp.

On the morning of the Mauni Amavasya Snan, we arose at 4.00. It was very cold and foggy as we left the camp for the long hike to the *Sangam* for the day of days in this year's Mahakumbh Mela. People swathed in shawls sat around small fires, warming their hands. Everywhere people were stirring. An elderly man dressed beautifully in a light sunshiny colour, hobbled painfully towards the river bank, holding a tiffin carrier. A young woman in reds and pinks helped an old lady bent almost double and leaning heavily on a stick. A trolley with a neat stack of pale cream sticks of sugar cane and a red wheeled juice extractor stood unguarded—it wasn't the moment for a cool drink. The sounds of a massive crowd were somehow subdued. There was no shrieking or shouting. It was more like the sound of a million bee hives. As we walked across a bridge we could see below us thousands of people already in the water, dutifully obeying directions to bathe close to their camps. It was a stunning sight. The line between shore and water was indiscernible. As far as the eye could see there were swathed figures, a blur of indistinct shapes and colours, illuminated in patches of light from the tall street lights. It couldn't have been more different from our sparsely populated patch of river the day before.

I'm writing this, turning the pages of my photograph album as I metaphorically advance towards the confluence. In parts, the series of stills gains momentum and I can see movement but the sound is missing. On the bridge people passed us shouting 'Har Har Mahadev', the immortal truth in praise of Shiva which can mean either 'Everyone's God' or 'God relieve us of our problems'. Here was a group of twenty or thirty men, waving flags and shouting. There several hundreds of people sat quietly waiting by the roadside. Under the railway bridge, the metal spans looming high in the dark sky, were brilliantly lit paintings of gods and epic events. Highest was an exciting version of the churning of the ocean of milk. The five great heads of a colossal snake rise up like the high stern of a surf-boat. White tipped waves crash over the part of his body not wound around Mount Mandara resting on the tortoise and three turbaned *devas* cling on like surf-riders. On the mountain itself a beautiful cow gazes serenely out as though nothing unusual is happening.

As we neared the *Sangam* the crowd became more and more dense as processions of saints and seers and their acolytes made their way slowly towards the river. In the past many would ride elephants but this stopped after the dreadful accident of 1954. The usual mode of transport now is some kind of motorized trailer drawn by a tractor. Wealthier groups make more effort at decorating and camouflaging the *raths* with umbrellas, cloth, garlands, bunting and flowers. The revered *gurus* sat enthroned at the top, some bare-headed, some wearing crowns and others in a variety of hats including one like an enormous Mexican sombrero. Followers carried saffron banners, standards and ceremonial fans and surged past dancing and singing. Some groups had brass bands, others had recorded music. There is a very definite protocol about which *akharas* lead the processions of naked *sadhus*. One group was led by several equestrian *nagas*. Naked men riding horses is rather an unusual sight. Covered in white ash one man had long dark hair trailing down his back and from the rear he presented a very curious image seated on a grey horse with a black tail, a strange variety of centaur. Another with a very wild look, played a loud staccato beat on kettle-drums lying either side of his bay mount's neck. Some people threw marigolds into the crowd. I tried to catch one and missed. A man on the carriage saw this and threw another directly at me. I bent down and scrabbled around on the ground to pick it up and immediately thought that was a foolish thing to do—stay upright at all times is good advice. But I picked it up and took it as a very good omen.

We found ourselves against a barricade that had been constructed to define long straight stretches of clear space available for crowd control in the event of a stampede. A young paramilitary officer in a bullet-proof vest paced within the space holding a plastic shield and a *lathi*. Near us another well-armed soldier had cannisters of tear gas in a labelled bag slung over his shoulder. Mounted police scattered the crowd on their big powerful somewhat frightening horses. Three photographers from our camp arrived, one of them Shrivasta's son Raju and another the experimental film-maker Ashish Avikunthak, said to become the successor to the great Satyajit Ray. It was a field-day for the camera and Robyn got some brilliant shots. We decided to move a little closer and by then had been joined by some others from the camp including a very tall young man—he must have been about 6'7'. Somehow I had got slightly wedged against the fence and took a moment to extricate myself and then my shawl caught on a nail. It was really only seconds lost but by then a policeman was stopping anyone else from moving forward. Oh dear, my friends are there I said pointing ahead and he let me through and I ran to catch them. Others ran too which was quite unnerving—it is better not to run—but I rejoined my friends and told the tall boy that I was going to hold onto his shawl.

Dawn was breaking and the street lights were extinguished. Wet people walked away from the river having bathed and didn't seem to notice the cold. Perhaps it is better to be clad only in ash rather than sodden clothes. The *sadhus* looked happy and triumphant, some holding swords, spears and tridents aloft, others waving their arms and shouting with glee. Some had marigolds slung casually around their hips or a *rudraksha* bead turban, some wore multiple strings of beads around their necks but most wore nothing other than a simple single string. By contrast most pilgrims wore, like us, many layers of warm clothes (I had six which I peeled off as the day advanced) and probably waited some time to approach to the water. Crowds surged in all directions, people in groups clutched each other tightly to avoid separation and simple country folk looked bewildered. Some ladies from western India dressed in gorgeously embroidered skirts and plain black *odhnis* posed happily for photographs displaying their beautiful silver cuffs. By contrast a rather angry-looking *sadhu* showed off a mean looking metal circlet tightly wound around and digging into his chubby abdomen. We saw a *naga* who had kept his arm raised above his head for so long that it had withered, his fingernails curled around like talons. Another with a useless polio-afflicted leg made a laborious journey away from the river, supporting himself with a long a staff and with a bottle of Ganga water slung over his shoulder. The sweepers wielded their long brooms creating hillocks of abandoned shoes and garments. Above us to our right was an elevated platform where the world's press was located. The amazing photographs of thousands of *sadhus* leaping into the water would have to be taken from a boat midstream. Does that mean a return journey for me I wonder?

Our route along the southern bank of the Ganga eventually led us to a flat sandy area where barbers were busily shaving the heads of many pilgrims, the shaven locks strewn on the ground. Nearby a throng of some 200 men stood in a circle. Their heads were newly shaven and they were all clad in pale cream-coloured *dhotis*. They were quite dark of complexion and had the look of healthy farmers. We found that they had journeyed from Nepal and this was their ceremony to honour the Ganga and the day. Two white-clad priests with pink turbans on their heads officiated and with five or six of the men, sat within the circle. Robyn and I were beckoned in and we took our place next to them. In the centre of the circle were dozens of offerings, stainless steel food carriers encircled with marigolds and other vessels wrapped in straw netting and similarly garlanded. The priests and the supplicants sang prayers back and forth and the men stood, raised their arms to the sky then knelt, bowing their heads to the ground. A hollow in the sand contained the sacred fire and vermillion powder had been sprinkled around it. Pungent incense was burned and the smoke rose, almost obscuring the circle of men and making our eyes smart. We felt so privileged at not only witnessing this beautiful ceremony but also to have been so generously invited into the inner circle. It was obviously so special but withal so manifestly honest and natural. It was our loss not to be able to understand exactly what was happening but the fervour and pride displayed by the men was unmistakable and a very interesting contrast to the sophisticated *akharas* to which visitors flock in order perhaps to see something freakish.

We felt almost overcome with the intensity. Nearby another smaller group of men seemed to be about to begin a similar ceremony. They were watched by thirty or so women dressed in beautiful saris, heads covered. It was almost sensory overload and we sat on the sand in the sun just to ponder what we had witnessed in the six hours since we set off in the dark. To bring us back to earth just yards away from us two women set about cooking lunch for their families. Potatoes and peas went into pans perched on the small clay hearths we had seen in shops. Spices were sprinkled from small cellophane packets and stirred in with long-handled spoons, water added and a lid popped on the top. So we went home for our lunch too.

Caste and status are to some degree levelled at the Mahakumbh as people from all walks of life, rich and poor, high caste and low, all come to bathe. The liberation for which believers hope has extended far into the stratifications of society. A group of 100 women from Rajasthan from a very low stratum of society, had made a long journey by bus to the *Sangam*. Once treated as outcastes and shunned by society, they were to perform a *puja* with seers in a significant break from tradition. A spokesman for the group, Bindeshwar Pathak, is a pioneer for social change in India, the founder of a great sanitation movement, Sulabh International. He believes that the toilet is an instrument for social change and by converting 1.3 million bucket toilets into flush models, he has helped free hundreds of thousands of people from the sub-human occupation of dealing with night soil. Sulabh has installed 8,000 community toilet blocks—I've gratefully used them in several parts of India—and 54 million Government toilets have been installed based on the Sulabh design. What a champion. He has been honoured worldwide for his projects and has recently been active in recognizing the plight of the large numbers of destitute widows living at Vrindavan, characteristically doing something practical about it. Welfare schemes have been established to improve their miserable existence. At the Mahakumbh 150 priests and religious leaders took part in a ceremony called 'Liberation of the Untouchables' after which the Rajasthani women were declared to be cleansed of their past. Many conservative Hindus will call this a stunt. Taboos entrenched for a thousand years are not broken overnight. The road ahead for these women will not be without problems but they have been encouraged to make a new start.

Paramahansa Yogananda, the Indian yogi and teacher who introduced many in the west to the teachings of meditation and yoga through his book *Autobiography of a Yogi*, died in 1952 a couple of days before Andrea was born. We had passed a tent where his books were on sale and strangely Andrea does look rather like him. On the day after the Mauni Amavasya Snan, one of his texts appeared in a column called 'Sacred Space' in *The Times of India* saying 'The sincere devotee loves God deeply whether he is non-active and silently meditating on God, or in the midst of a whirl of outer activities.' In all the whirl of humanity at the *Sangam*, in those eddying swirls of good-natured, devout people, this seems to encompass us all. We were there not only to witness faith in action but to examine ourselves as well.

Quoting from Gautam Siddharth's editorial again, 'this deeper organization of the teeming multitudes serves as a reminder of the permanence of ideas and the impermanence of place.' Organisation was such a key-word in any conversation about the Mahakumbh and it was all so magnificently achieved that the terrible thing which happened later on the main bathing day became even more tragic.

At 6.45 pm at the Allahabad Railway Station a stampede took place that claimed the lives of 36 people. At first it was claimed that an overhead footbridge had snapped sending people plunging to their deaths on the tracks but this was found not to be the case. A journalist reporting the next day found the footbridge perfectly intact. Huge crowds converged on the station at the end of that most auspicious day. Hundreds of additional trains had been scheduled but the numbers were still inadequate. They were also running so late that everything seemed to be at a standstill. The railways had planned for 350,000 passengers over four days and on the day of the accident, more than 160,000 passengers had already boarded trains. 300,000 people had jammed the station capable of handling only 40,000 commuters at a time. About 6,000 people were trapped on the overhead bridge. When crowds started jostling towards it and another platform, either those on the bridge panicked, stumbled and fell down the stairs, or else the panic was caused by police who had resorted to a *lathi* charge in an attempt to control the crowd. Authorities blamed each other for the frightful situation. The railway officials said they had not been consulted on crowd management plans, the Kumbh administration blamed it on the *lathi* charge. UP Minister for Urban Development, Azam Khan, stepped down as Chairman of the Kumbh Mela Committee, owning moral responsibility for the tragedy. In the aftermath of the disaster there is much resolve to understand how to prevent such a thing ever happening again. The Harvard School of Public Health research team found five simple ways—earlier crowd control, insistence that travellers hold tickets for reserved seats on the trains, better sharing of information between authorities, basic line enforcement with unidirectional traffic flow to avoid crowd surges and improved communication by means of phones and walkie talkies. Of course this is all too late for those who lost relatives and friends.

A tremendously sad photograph appeared on the cover of one of the newspapers two days later. Two dear old bespectacled men in their 80s, dressed beautifully, almost identically in white dhotis, starched shirts and turbans and brown sleeveless vests and both holding walking sticks, sat in the back of a van with the white wrapped body of their third companion. The three had been friends since boyhood and had gone together to Prayag for the Maha Kumbh Mela. Their poor old friend had died in the stampede and they were taking him home to Haryana, nearly 800 kilometres away.

Our car had stayed parked at the camp for the duration of our stay at Prayag because we needed to depart before dawn the morning after the main bathing day. The police had cordoned off seven kilometres around the *mela* grounds and traffic was not allowed in for 24 hours before and afterwards. Getting out was apparently not such a bother, or so they said. Our excellent driver, Anil, had enjoyed himself at the Kumbh and was up bright and bushy-tailed for us to leave at 4.30 am. Fortunately at our extremity of the grounds we were closest to the Varanasi Road. In the dark we set off with very little life stirring about us. We first took a wrong track and ended up at a dead end, our headlights illuminating a man taking a bath under a tap, his body steaming in the freezing morning darkness. Back on the right track we found the correct road but here we found a long line of completely stationary vehicles, mostly buses with drivers sound asleep waiting for dawn. Smart Anil, always thinking, found out about a secondary road and we hurtled off through a forest in the dark. Never mind a few wrong turns, he got us out in fine style and we arrived at the Varanasi Airport hours ahead of schedule.

Months later, it is quite impossible to comprehend the dimensions of that huge crowd. So many images from those few days at Allahabad will remain in my mind and everything that we experienced was so good. Apart from the terrible accident at the Railway Station the coverage by the world's press over the 55-day festival was overwhelmingly positive. The officials were gratified by stories hailing the Kumbh Mela as a great 'success story' and having gone off 'like clockwork'. The Chief Minister of UP, Akilash Yadav, was invited to Harvard to speak at the Business School which he boycotted after his colleague Azam Khan, who stepped down as chairman of the organizing Committee, was detained and frisked at Boston's Logan International Airport.

But now after the tumult and the shouting has died, the captains and the kings departed, what does it all look like? The description is more like an ecological disaster than the result of Allahabad's first 'green' kumbh. The cleanup has been hindered by the fact that the wonderful army of workers which kept the grounds so clean during the festival, was disbanded soon after it finished. The garbage situation is terrible as is the haze of the fires burning it. The Ganges which was reasonably deep and passably clean during the mela is no longer that. The artificially increased flow has ceased and the ban on factory pollution has lapsed so the water level has dropped and the quality has dramatically deteriorated. Daily fogging during the Kumbh kept mosquitoes and flies out of the area but now stagnant pools created by receding water have become perfect breeding grounds for insects. And all those toilets, the statistics which officials quoted so proudly, were really just holes in the ground with little treatment. Unfortunately for Allahabad the waste has been left to seep into the groundwater which is the main source of water for the city.

It is a shame to conclude on a negative note when the four days at Prayag were one of the great experiences of my life but how else to end? As we sat waiting for the plane to take us from Varanasi to Delhi thinking how amazing it had all been, Christiane received a text message from Thomas. 'What's this do you think?' she asked. The message was somewhat cryptic stating that the Pope had 'decided' and could the Kumbh possibly have something to do with it. Decided? Could he mean deceased Christiane wondered? She said 'Oh Thomas has such big fingers and maybe the predictive text had taken over.' (I always think of the word prescriptive rather than predictive—much the same really, it's such an irritating, autocratic thing.) She texted back seeking enlightenment and we found that Pope Benedict XVI had become the first Pope to quit in 600 years. Thomas' wry allusion to the *kumbh* was of course in jest. India's Christian population is 2.3% according to the 2001 census. Of the 24,000,000, more than 19,900,000 are Catholics, many in the south. The history of Christianity in India like everything else in the country, is very interesting but that's another story. The news of Pope Benedict made the front pages of all the papers the next day and so life went on.

PS Robyn Beeche's life was suddenly cut short when she died at Shoal Bay on the Central Coast of New South Wales on 13 August 2015, aged 70. A fine funeral service celebrating her life was held in the historic Anglican Church of St James in King Street, Sydney. Flowers, incense, bells and song united her two worlds, India and Australia. Her career as a photographer is recognized world-wide and her work is represented in many public collections. I treasure two of her photographs but more precious than that is the cache of marvelous images I have in my head, of time spent with her in India and Australia. As though seeing life through a finer lens than most of us, she absorbed detail of everything, storing them away in both document and memory. I miss her very much.

A baba near Jhunsi at the Mahakumbh Mela, 2013

Bathing with Christiane at the Mahakumbh Mela, 2013

Cautionary Tales & Ripping Yarns

The first Indian story I remember reading was *Louisa* by Mrs Hobart-Hampden, a story serialised in the 1923 bound annual of the children's paper *Chatterbox*. My book was given to my mother for her tenth birthday in 1924 and I read it more than thirty years later when I too was about ten. There is an inscription in the flyleaf 'To Twinkle from Joyce & Ruth, wishing you many happy returns of the day 8/1/24', the same birthday as Elvis Presley about which we teased Mum in her old age. I wish I could ask her now if she had read much of the book. *Louisa* with thirty-five episodes was one of two major serials for the year 1923. The other, also with thirty-five entries, was *Island Adventure* by G. Belton Cobb, a successful writer of adult crime fiction. Like *Louisa* it is an adventure with overtones of mystery. The setting at a lake in Westmoreland would have been familiar to many of the British readers and the three major characters, siblings Sydney, Leonard & Norma could almost be the prototypes for The Famous Five.

Chatterbox, a popular English publication for children, was published between 1866 and 1955. Its creator was Rev John Erskine Clarke of Derby who served as the Editor until 1902. It was designed to appeal to both boys and girls, unlike the gender specific 'Boy's Own' or 'Girl's Own' annuals. The 1923 annual had more articles more appealing to boys than girls but *Louisa* as first illustration and first story made up for this. There were short articles, puzzles, poems, two educational serials 'The toy that never grows old' and 'The history of our Sports' and many illustrations. Originally a weekly paper, the cost of *Chatterbox* was a halfpenny. There were also special penny editions with the added attraction of a loose colour plate. The 1923 annual has a number of colour plates unrelated to the rest of the contents. The price of a basic *Chatterbox Annual* was three shillings and a more expensive cloth-bound edition with gilt edges cost five shillings. Most of the books that survived from my mother's childhood are still in good condition. They take up feet of space in bookshelves, inches thick with lovely bindings. All the school stories which both Mum and I loved a generation apart, are intact but the binding of *Chatterbox* which was the cheaper fancy board version, was falling to bits. On one page I have the initials of one of Mum's younger cousins, the book must have done the rounds of the extended family. I had it rebound a few years ago and the book-binder was able to keep the Pears Soap advertisement on the back of the old board cover. It shows a little naked child of indeterminate sex hopping out of a steaming tub searching for the missing cake of soap.

The advertisements which apparently did not appear in the gilt-edged superior version are interesting, aimed just as much if not more at the parents of the family as the children. There are nine of which strangely two are for bread, Hovis of Macclesfield—'the reward of appetite' and Bermaline of Glasgow—'children love it' and 'a treat to eat'. The others are Red White & Blue French coffee; Rowland's Macassar Oil; Humber cycles and the Blackbird Self-filler pen with Swan Ink. Joyful children dance in a circle on a sandy beach anticipating Huntley & Palmers Happy Time Mixed Biscuits and another circular dance is taking place at a party where Green's Sponge Mixture is the important ingredient of the cake about to be devoured. As an antidote for all these agents of tooth decay, another page has an elfin person promising 'a new fairy book for everyone' called *The Fort Ivory Castles* where the baddies are 'the ugly old Giant Decay and his wicked Imps'. The book which promises wonderful pictures will be sent free of charge with 'a dear little box of Gibbs Dentifrice' when Mother has written to D & W Gibbs Ltd. in London.

Mothers in far-flung corners of the Empire may not have been able to write letters to London in pursuit of the dear little box of Gibbs Dentifrice, disappointing to the small overseas children. They probably imagined nothing more heavenly than the cake and biscuits which were inspiring such delight in the dancing children of the advertisements. This yearning for the unknown desirable food continued to tantalise English-speaking children for generations.

Trying to find details of Mrs Hobart-Hampden has been difficult. The only details in *Chatterbox* are that she is also author of *The Secret Valley* and *Chinna*. The story of *Louisa* and its Indian setting, especially with the help of the illustrations, is convincing enough but there are few small details that would give it an undeniable ring of truth. Perhaps it could have been written by someone who had a second-hand familiarity with India? Louisa and Kadru, her servant, are given chicken curry and rice in a little village where it might be expected the inhabitants were vegetarian and Louisa's note, written in an Indian language, is left for a villager who could well have been illiterate. I found a list from an antiquarian book shop describing the author in another story as having 'drawn a most lifelike picture of the squalid splendour' of India.

Eventually I discovered Mrs Hobart-Hampden did live in India for many years and a number of her popular children's serials and novels are set there. *The Little Rajah—a tale of hidden treasure in India*, *The Secret Valley*, *Little Prince Tota* and *Louisa* are all tales of English children and their Indian friends who come from all levels of society from child rajah to 'famine child' and manage to have complicated hair-raising adventures sometimes in a very short space of time. So much actually happens in *Louisa* that it is hard to credit that the action takes place over only five days. Perhaps for the sake of her readership, the background of the story is purposely demystified so children halfway across the empire would not be puzzled by exotic details. Chicken curry, literate natives and a pet cat were familiar in most settings but there is plenty that is intriguing. As for 'squalid splendour', there is absolutely none of that. When Louisa, disguised with ash in her hair and dye applied to her skin, has assumed the guise of a venerated wise woman visitor, she and Kadru are accommodated in a pretty little garden pavilion owned by Surabhi, the wealthy old widow. Fountains play just outside the door and Louisa is rewarded for her successful divination and healing with beautiful embroidered slippers and a fine shawl.

The author seems very much a feminist, creating all the good characters throughout the book as women—not just the heroine Louisa and loyal Kadru who is often the steadying hand, but also wise and generous Surabhi and her fat and faithful servant, Maru. Even her nemesis, Mrs Barrington, proves eventually not quite the shrew of Louisa's imagination and Mangli's brow-beaten wife recovers a certain degree of resolution. In searching for the author I had at first pursued a wrong Mrs Hobart-Hampden, also a writer. Her works included *Heavenward: a collection of hymns and poems of consolation, The Changed Cross and other religious poems* and she edited 'A Handy Book of old and familiar Hymns'. It had been tantalising to think that someone with such an evangelical outlook could have been so restrained about heavenly advice in *Louisa*, a thoroughly secular story.

By midway through re-reading the story I would have been very surprised if there had been any introduction of an obvious Christian message or an improving conclusion. There was nothing of the kind, nor any kind of dismissive reaction to Indian shrines or 'spirits'. Hindu gods were not mentioned at all and refreshingly there is little racial superiority in the story. Louisa certainly has a rather superior attitude but she is little different to the outspoken, bolshy, over-confident girls I encountered in my mother's Angela Brazil school stories, charging at things like a bull at a gate but always scrupulously fair. When calamity strikes on a river crossing Kadru weeps at her 'Miss Sahib's' headstrong behaviour and the author cautions that 'She was too proud. Too proud.' But if Louisa had stopped to explain what had happened on the night of the fire and taken Kadru's sensible advice there would have been no story.

Louisa is impatient with Kadru's timidity and when towards the end of the adventure the poor girl twists her ankle and Dukhi their 'hostage' falls and hurts his head, draws blood and clearly has a bit of mild concussion, little memsahib Louisa feels sorrier for the pony than either of the humans. That's a line from a song from *Oklahoma*—'I sure feel very sorry for the pony!' Chota, the steed, is uninjured and was just a little fatigued. It is a very British reaction, feeling sorrier for the animals than the children. There are no dogs present in the book but Bulbo the black cat is a central character though pet cats are not so commonplace in India. I had a friend in Peshawar, a Canadian married to a Pakistani, who was trying to teach her little boy the English alphabet. A is for apple and b is for boy were easy but when she got to c is for cat she hit resistance because, as far as her son was concerned, c was for *billi*, Urdu for cat.

The only real suggestion of racism is actually an expression of loyalty when Louisa overhears two men plotting to burn down her neighbours' bungalow. One of these despicable characters, who are trying to swindle Surabhi and become inheritors of her fortune, is called Mangli. This might be a veiled connection to the first identified mutineer of the 1857 First War of Independence, Mangal Pandey, a character despised by the British. He is widely recognised as one of the first freedom fighters and revered now in India. The fire is retaliation against Mr Barrington, the Judge, who has ruled against them in court, in their determined attempt to divert Surabhi's estate to themselves. Despite her run-in with Mrs Barrington, Louisa 'could not ally herself with another race against her own people.'

My pursuit of Mrs Hobart-Hampden was helped by a peerage site on the internet, something new to me. It was quite thrilling and I really thought I was on to my mysterious author but it was a false trail leading to yet another Mrs Hobart-Hampden, the Earls of Buckinghamshire and to a familiar place. Blickling Hall in Norfolk was the former home of the Earls of Buckinghamshire. It is a magnificent house which we visited during the year we spent in England. We were on a very tight budget but had taken a family membership of the National Trust. Norfolk was dotted with Trust properties and so visiting them was a cheap form of weekend entertainment. It was the first time in England for all of us so it was education for the entire family. The children aged eight and nine were very good about the visits—there was always something interesting for them to see and something nice to eat somewhere during the day. One Friday Jamie tentatively asked if we were going to any 'stately homes' over the weekend. 'Oh no what a shame, not this weekend darling,' I answered. 'Yippee!' he shouted. He was fed up with doing stately.

Our first visit to Blickling, thought to be the birthplace of Ann

Boleyn, was in the daylight and extended to wandering through the glorious park as well as viewing the house interior. The second was to a beautiful Christmas concert held in the evening in the long Library. On the way home in the dark I preached to the children how lucky they were to go to such an event and how they must remember it until their dying day. 'What was the best thing about it?' I asked. Emily said 'Well I liked it when the fire alarm went off' and Jamie said 'I liked the mince pies.'

Louisa was written by the Marie Hélène Hobart-Hampden, née Langel, an interesting sort of a name for a writer of English children's stories set in India. Known as Hélène rather than Marie, she was the daughter of Reverend Louis Langel and in common with other wives marrying into the peerage, her birth-date is not given on the website. In 1901 she married Ernest Miles Hobart-Hampden, a grandson of the 6th Earl of Buckinghamshire, son of Hon. George Augustus who had been with the Bombay Civil Service. They had two sons, Cyril Langel who was born in Yokohama in 1902 and died in Devon in 1972, and Harold Baldwin, born in 1905–1926. The Earls of Buckinghamshire keep popping into my story and their succession by twists and turns enters Louisa's ambit. The current Earl, 10th Earl of Buckinghamshire, is the grandson of Hélène. His name is George Miles Hobart-Hampden and his father was Cyril Langel, Hélène's elder son. Born in 1944, he succeeded to the title 10th Baron Hobart of Blickling, Norfolk in 1983. Even though she died in 1938 before he was born, there must surely be interesting family stories.

My mother wasn't a great reader until she had time to rediscover books in her 70s. She always had a book on the go but it became much more of a joy as she grew older. She especially liked big, fat books. She lapped up novels by Joanna Trollope and others but really loved to let her offspring know that the latest was 790 pages long or 830 or more. She didn't like borrowing from the Library much and if she took a library book to bed, she wore gloves. She made some funny mistakes when making orders at a bookshop in her neighbourhood shopping centre. Once she was trying to remember the best-seller *The Shellseekers* by Rosamund Pilcher but somehow managed instead to buy *The Pebbled Shore* by Lady Longford which was quite a different kettle of fish. Realising her mistake though she read on and loved the book, passing it on to me when I was living in Pakistan.

She was a great Anglophile and delighted in the subscription to a very patriotic, magazine called *Our England* sent her by an English cousin. When I started to read *The Pebbled Shore*, I did a bit of initial yawning and thought, oh here we go, it's another I love England book. But it improved and when I discovered that the last of the Longford children and I were born on the same day that was fun. His name was Kevin Toussaint because the day of our birth is All Saints Day. More interesting than that is it was the day of the Gilgit Mutiny, when just months after Partition, the Gilgit Agency, then part of the disputed territory of Kashmir, revolted and seceded to Pakistan. This I discovered while typing out the copy of an article written by a man from the BBC Pashtu Service. He had gone up to Gilgit to cover the celebrations marking the 40th anniversary of the Mutiny, but an immediate appendicitis had landed him in the Gilgit Hospital and he missed most of the show.

We had visited Gilgit at the same time without quite realising the remarkable confluence of dates. An annual polo carnival takes place at this time of year but it was an especially big gathering for the anniversary. The polo ground is long and much narrower than grounds elsewhere in the world. The perimeter of the ground was bounded by walls more than a metre higher than the ground. On one of the long sides sat a small orchestra, playing enthusiastic tunes as the horses galloped up and down, the music sympathetically supporting ebbs and flows in the game and adding greatly to the whole excitement of the atmosphere.

Whether Mum read and enjoyed *Louisa* or not, I will never know as she has gone to her heavenly abode, but I think my childhood reading of it started my lifelong fascination with India. I'm sure I didn't grasp much of the story's Indian character except to be somehow thrilled by the exotic. Like most children in the 1950s I had been reminded when attempting to leave food on my plate of the plight of 'the poor starving Indians' who didn't have enough to eat and in the season of Lent each year at Sunday School we were given missionary boxes—little cardboard boxes made to look like an altar. Pennies were pushed through the slot to help the poor unfortunate starving and being a very keen child, I managed to dislodge a wobbly tooth and deposited in the box the silver sixpence left by the fairies. Fairies and angels were interchangeable in my pantheon, fairies having the advantage. My tooth was not nearly ready to come out and I had a gap for almost a year.

The only Indian I can recall ever seeing by that stage in my life was a handsome young chemist dispensing at a pharmacy near my childhood home. Why did I notice him? I suppose because he looked so different although children don't always notice such things. He was tall and thin and wore his hair parted down the middle and Mum said he was a Fijian Indian—she must have pointed him out to us because we didn't go shopping much except in school holidays. Perhaps she thought he was handsome too. He was, like my story, exotically different.

Louisa Lumsdale is aged fourteen but already a confident and bossy young woman, 'Mother, brothers or sisters, she had none'. She seems to run the household inhabited only by her vague, academic father who 'was too absorbed in the study of Indian folk-lore' to even notice her absence over the five day period when the action of the story takes place. The time and location are vague. A 'motor' is sent from 'the city' for the rescue which is the only modern reference in the text and the only two place-names are given—a small village called Faridpur and a mention of the River Ganges. Faridpur is an easily imagined name—there is at least one in India and one in Bangladesh, both probably too large to have been the remote little habitation of the book. We read of women wearing *saris* but also full skirts so it is possible that the setting is somewhere in Rajputana where a many-panelled skirt called a *gagra* is worn with a blouse and *odhni* or veil rather than a *sari*.

The illustrations were really what I found so thrilling when I was ten when many books had very few. There are thirty-eight full page illustrations for *Louisa* and eventually almost at the end of the athletic journey through the book—it's a bit like hurdling—

the artist is identified as being Harold Wright. The black and white line drawings are very appealing and keep a young reader interested but now I see quite a few cultural inaccuracies. The 'natives' are all extremely robust and are drawn in the same way as the earliest depictions of Indigenous Australians—rather too European and classical. Kadru looks just like a darker Louisa. There are lapses in the continuity of the drawings but who wants to be critical now especially after acknowledging the source of my love affair with India. Louisa's dress as an English child and that of Mr & Mrs Barrington look exactly like the photographs of my mother and grandparents in Sydney in the 1920s so it was very much a contemporary tale.

Conversations between Indians and also Kadru's mode of address to Louisa are full of thees, thines and thous, hadst, didst and dost, perchance and moreover. The dialogue sounds Biblical or Shakespearean and somewhat patronising when Louisa answers Kadru not with thee and thine but you and yours. I guess it was a matter of class. Kipling's *The Jungle Book* has the elevated animals addressing each other as ye and thee and thou but it is quite oratorical and used when they are gathered together for important conferences at Council Rock. One phrase I had never read before was 'a bump of locality'. Both Louise and Kadru 'had a bump of locality and had never yet been lost.' It means a good sense of direction and has an earlier connection with phrenology. This gift was fortunate indeed as getting lost might have spelled the end for Louisa and Kadru.

The story is in some ways preposterous, not the discovery of the perpetrators of the crime of burning of the bungalow nor the motive, but the passing off of Louisa as a 'wise woman' of considerable years and her ability to cure all manner of ailments, mostly it seems by a dose of something like Eno's Fruit Salts. She has great confidence and says 'Very likely a real doctor often guesses what's wrong with people.' It also reinforces the belief in British superiority over the innocent and simple native, but Louisa obviously reads, writes and speaks beautiful Hindi which is a great asset. Most of the dialogue must be in an Indian language and her credibility is never questioned. The other admirable thing about Louisa is that she wants to help everyone in any way she can—finding the truth and healing the sick.

A great deal more is known about Mary Martha Sherwood, the author of more than 400 books, tracts and articles. One of her most well-known publications was *The History of Little Henry and his Bearer*, written in 1814 and continuously in print for 70 years. Translated into French, German, Spanish, Hindustani, Chinese, Marathi, Tamil and Sinhalese, it is the story of little British Henry who on his deathbed, converts his loyal servant, Boosy. The imperialistic and evangelical messages are not guaranteed to enchant but thinking it would be truly tedious I was surprised at its charm which was satisfying as an interesting path led me to it.

With three friends I set off by train from Calcutta to Murshidabad on an early morning train. Our departure was particularly easy with scarcely anyone at the station, most unusual for Indian rail journeys. Our journey through green Bengali countryside took four hours or so. The carriage was full with a great variety of people. There were several army officers, one with extraordinary facial hair, a well-dressed family group was travelling to a wedding, and the father of a small baby was fascinatingly like an Edwardian dandy from a Kalighat painting—pudgy cheeks, almond-shaped eyes and hair that fell from his central parting in two curves on his forehead.

Throughout the journey a constant stream of vendors and people performing useful services passed up and down the aisle. Chai and coffee were dispensed from huge pots and all kinds of delicious savoury snacks were sold from multi-sectioned trays. One man had a pole from which hung hair-clips, shoe-laces, toys, handkerchiefs and other useful things to buy for the journey including moth-balls. Were we entering a realm of huge and ferocious moths? A man with pitiful polio-ravaged spider-thin legs crawled along the aisle seeking shoes to shine and a solemn little boy swept masses of rubbish out from the initially clean carriage more than once, coming back to be tipped for the service. Just before we scrambled out at our destination a smart-looking girl came up boldly to each row of seats and clapping her hands commandingly, demanded money.

She was a *hijra* and we declined to pay her, hoping she wouldn't expose herself in the crowded carriage which is what sometimes happens and is a sight to be avoided. Much more entertaining was a Baul singer with a crippled hand whose song, accompanied by tambourine, was haunting and rhythmic.

The destination printed on our tickets was Murshidabad but we had to hurriedly bundle out at Berhampore Court, the station for the neighbouring town. A car was waiting for us and there were two or three other private vehicles but apart from those, the local transport was dozens of cycle-rickshaws. They were small, rustic versions with bamboo hood-struts and a cramped bench seat where two people of our size could hardly squash together. The scene reminded me of hopping out of trains on my first trip to India in the late 1960s to a reception committee of cycle-rickshaws and *tongas* or horse-drawn carriages. What fun it had been. *Tongas* were an everyday form of transport as late as 1987 when living in Peshawar in Pakistan but now there are few to be seen anywhere. It was the favourite means of travel for my little children in 1976. In Udaipur a white horse called Snowy became our friend for a day. We rediscovered him in the television series of *Jewel in the Crown* which was very exciting. 'Oh look there's Snowy' we shrieked when we saw him with his driver. They took Daphne to meet Hari and so Paul Scott's wonderful story became familiar and merged almost into part of our own Indian experience.

Places less visited which lie off the beaten tourist track are sometimes rather dull which explains the lack of visitors. But often they are little gems and this was one of them. The countryside was lush and green with crops of vegetables, rice in many stages of cultivation, jute sticks stacked after harvest and healthy grazing animals. It was time for the Saraswati *puja* and images of the goddess similar to those we had seen being created in Kumartuli, the potters' village in Calcutta, were installed in *pandals* or temporary temples in neat towns and villages, the streets around them neatly swept and clean.

Saraswati, the wife of Brahma, is the goddess of learning, science and all the creative arts, in particular of poetry and music. Brahma, known also as Prajapati, is the original being in Hinduism, in existence before even the foundation of the universe. The potters or *kumahars* we saw at work in Calcutta, may be addressed as Prajapati because they like Brahma, fashion humankind. So it always is in India, not just a craft or a craftsman but a continued tradition stretching back to the gods before time began.

Kumartuli had been a scene of frenetic activity. Here and there potters were starting the creation of an image but while they fashioned faces, resting a nonchalant wrist on a breast while modelling an ear, eye or nose, other finished images were being coiffed and dressed. Frequently we had to shrink against the side of the alleyway when a shout announced a completed goddess was being carried out to the road. This was done with haste and hustle, the goddess carried flat as if on a bier, high above the men's heads. It left a feeling of unease as if this was a medical emergency and the lady had urgent need of an ambulance or worse, a hearse.

The images were taken to conveyances of varying degrees of luxury to speed them to their destinations. Some were loaded six at a time into a carrier truck version of a cycle rickshaw. As they set off on their journey standing shoulder to shoulder, they swayed gently together in time with the cyclist's pedalling. Saraswati holds a stringed instrument called a *veena* and so the six of them looked like an all-girl group going off to a gig. Wonderful from the sideview or the front, but because these images are never viewed in the round, there is no particular need to pay the same lavish attention to the lady's back-view as her front and the sight of her naked, grey, clay bottom and the bald back of her head seemed a personal invasion. The scene was of happiness and excitement, something like the annual purchase of a Christmas tree except that these creations were so much more amazing and beautiful. Wide-eyed children watched as their fathers negotiated with shopkeepers and food-stalls at the end of the street did a roaring trade with snacks. I held the hand of Amitabh Bachhan in one little shop specialising in other kinds of images.

We saw one carefully chosen goddess gingerly manoeuvred into the tipped-back front seat of a family sedan. She sat up in dignified splendour like an elegant though rigid great-aunt, post-facelift. She reminded me of Mrs Bedford, a model whom I knew dressed in the habit of a nun of the Order of the Sisters of Mercy. I worked over a period of two years from 2008 on an unexpected project that was one of the most worthwhile in my life. Rather surprised, as a committed Anglican, I was invited to help with a catalogue and travelling exhibition to mark the sesquicentenary of the Irish Order's arrival at Goulburn, Australia's first inland city. I learned a great deal about the Irish and Roman Catholics in New South Wales and the nuns' huge contribution to health, child welfare and education in the communities where they established their foundations in the southern part of New South Wales and beyond.

We thought it would be interesting to have a life-size model dressed in the habit that had been worn until 1968. Efforts to borrow a shop model were unsuccessful and then one of the former nursing sisters had the brainwave of borrowing the anatomical model used for teaching at the Mercy Hospital in Albury. We called her Miss Bedford for a while until we decided it was really more appropriate to call her Mrs with all the obstetric and gynaecological matters that she endured in the 1950s and 60s. I later discovered that at a non-Catholic teaching hospital in Sydney, one of her cloned teaching models was definitely called **Mrs** Bedford. Inside our exhibition, usually located in church or school halls, she welcomed visitors and seemed to change character with each exhibition venue—better tempered at Yass when she rode over from Canberra in a sedan, and less accommodating in the Riverina where she had to endure the front seat of a truck. Her originally ruby lips had been sand-papered back to a paler, more suitably natural colour. Angela Jordan, a Sister herself, made the habit most beautifully and Mrs Bedford fascinated adults and children alike at each of the exhibition venues.

The clay images of Saraswati varied in size from small and doll-like to much larger than life-size. Carrying her *veena*, she is accompanied by her vehicle the swan, often looking more like a duck, peeping out from beneath the edge of her sari. Said to be haughty and disputatious, her gaze though benign is faraway. All the Saraswatis whatever their size that we saw both in production at Kumartuli and installed in *pandals* in villages near Berhampore, had long, lustrous, gorgeously curly, black hair, beautiful garments, jewellery and a look of slight amusement as they presided over a happy time in village life. At Islampur, children dressed in their best clothes strolled from shrine to shrine and danced excitedly to deafening Bollywood music. One little girl with a very smart, short hair-cut knew all the moves for the songs and she and her friends performed with huge energy. In a day or so all the images would be taken to the river, immersed and left to change back to the clay from whence they came. She would disappear and life would resume its normal pace.

Jon & Rumer Godden in the memoir of their Indian childhood, say they loved Saraswati. Hannah, their Thomist Catholic *ayah* greatly disapproved of her charges straying towards idol worship but the children thought Saraswati just as beautiful as Hannah's image of the Virgin Mary in her blue cloak. Years later when involved in the filming of her book *The River* in Bengal, the adult Rumer, by then a very successful writer, was asked to lay the script at Saraswati's feet to seek her blessing.

We had come to a small town called Islampur to see the production of *tussar* silk. Because of the holiday some weavers were not at their looms but many were Muslims and not much interested in the festivities in the street. The weavers were all men and many complained of the difficulty in making a decent living. The region has been famous for fine silk for centuries and sericulture is still an important part of the local economy. The Government Sericulture Research Institute in Berhampore works towards better outcomes but presently most of the silk thread comes from Bangalore in the south and the finished cloth is sold in Mumbai, as far to the west as India stretches.

The next day we were to see the historic sights of Murshidabad, beginning in the morning at a pretty body of water called Moti Jheel or Pearl Lake, an ox-bow lake or what Australians call a billabong, formed by the meandering Bhagirathi River. A splendid palace once stood here, built in the first half of the 18th century by Nawakesh Muhammad who was both nephew and son-in-law of the fourth

Nawab of Bengal. It was called Sang-i-dalan or stone palace, stone being a much more remarkable building material than the usual brick and plaster of the region. Along with a lofty gateway and various other buildings, it fell into ruin and now scarcely a trace remains. A pretty old mosque dating from 1740 stands near a wall where it is believed either treasure was concealed or people bricked in alive. Both could be true, the wall is believed to be cursed. I bought a quaint guide book, more of a pamphlet really, which revealed the nasty death of an Englishman who tried to locate the treasure. Another palace was built in 1758 by Mir Jafar, the sixth Nawab of Bengal. Clive had stayed here and it later became the home of Warren Hastings when he was Political Resident at the Durbar of the Nawab. Like the earlier building, this second palace has completely disappeared. The last remnants were taken by refugees trying to start a new life having fled the awful bloodshed that saw the birth of modern Bangladesh—the border is just ten or so kilometres away. A shy little girl watched us, cuddling her treasure in the form of a beautiful tiny baby goat with the silkiest of ears.

Murshidabad was the last independent capital of Bengal. It was once under Mughul rule and may have been founded by Emperor Akbar. In 1704 Nawab Murshi Quli Khan, Dewan of Bengal, Orissa and Bihar, transferred his administration from Dhaka to the town which he renamed after himself. It became the provincial capital in 1717 and with its ideal location on the Bhagirathi River, trade flourished. It was famous for its luxury goods of textiles, gold and silver embroidery and inlaid ivory furniture which was exported all over the world.

Relations between the British and rulers of Bengal had been far from harmonious and in 1756 Nawab Siraj-ud-daula perpetrated the infamous incident of the Black Hole of Calcutta. The story was embroidered and inflated and rather than 123 deaths out of 146 prisoners, the number of Europeans locked into the horrid cell was somewhere between 39 and 69 resulting in between 18 to 43 deaths. Whatever the numbers, the night was hell and the grim story stirred British passions for centuries. Almost more shocking to contemporary Britons was the abduction of a surviving English lady, Mary Carey, who was taken to the Nawab's harem. The Nawab himself lapsed into a haze of opium and alcohol after successfully trouncing the British. A few days later, recovered from his excesses, he was back in Murshidabad being entertained by elephant fights and tiger hunts. The British could not sit by and let this situation continue and Siraj-ud-daula was defeated by Clive at Plassey in 1757, the year after Calcutta's Black Hole.

Plassey is not far down the road from Murshidabad which Clive described as 'as extensive, populous and rich as the city of London'. Its earlier splendour is hard to imagine in the crumbling ruins of today's peaceful backwater. After Plassey it was eclipsed by Calcutta but the city's decline did not mark the end of grand designs. The vast Hazarduari Palace was not completed until 1837, a huge extravagance for a realm of little political relevance but a cordial and tolerant atmosphere prevailed between the court and the British who were by then well established in Bengal. A cantonment had existed in neighbouring Berhampore since 1763, then the more northerly of the Bengal garrisons. The neo-classical Hazarduari, a monument to opulence, is now a museum housing treasures of all descriptions including some beautiful family portraits.

Our day continued with a visit to the beautiful brick Katra Mosque where we provided a wonderful distraction to a large group of college girls in red and white saris. They found Margaret particularly fascinating and posed with her for each others' cameras over and over again. My guide-book had all kinds of suggestions in a section titled *Tit-bits about conveyance, food and lodging etc. in Murshidabad.* It is comprehensive instruction of what a tourist must do even including 'attending to Nature's call' on detraining. For 150 years scarcely anyone has written anything about Berhampore and Murshidabad but one was Eric Newby in *Slowly down the Ganges.* Near the end of his epic twelve hundred mile journey down the river in the winter of 1963–4, he and his wife Wanda, visited the two towns. He purchased a guide-book which sounds similar to mine. He described his as 'a number of postcards bound together with some eccentric descriptions printed on them.' We found somewhere for lunch and had quite the best stuffed parathas in the world and absolutely the worst, utterly undrinkable, fresh lime soda.

Full of paratha but rather thirsty, we visited an old mansion, the Kathgola Palace. It is described as a 'garden-house' and was built by the Jagat Seths, Marwari bankers whose native place was far away at Nagaur, near Jodhpur. The family amassed great wealth and are famous in Bengali history. In 1757 the house was the scene of meetings after the Battle of Plassey in the presence of Clive. The interior decoration dates now to the late 19th century with some modern, scrappy additions. It has a strange decaying but intriguing atmosphere suitable as a set for a Satyajit Ray film based on a classic Tagore story. The Jagat Seths were Jains and built a fine white temple to the Tirthankara Adinath behind the palace. A secret tunnel is said to run for miles from an entrance in the grounds and there was once a private zoo, the first in Bengal, the predecessor of the Alipur Zoo in Calcutta. When our guide told us about the zoo, Annie looked confused and then tried not to laugh. Bengalis sometimes pronounce z as j and so the early menagerie took on a puzzling religious identity.

As the shadows lengthened and day drew to an end we arrived back in Berhampore where we pulled up at the old Babulbona British cemetery. It is not as enclosed and crowded as the Park Street Cemetery in Calcutta where enormous pyramids, columns, rotundas and obelisks stand as close as small headstones do in modern lawn cemeteries. The effect there is that of a small city of graves, a true necropolis. The uncrowded monuments in Berhampore looked the same vintage and promised to be interesting. We had been told that James Skinner's mortal remains were here. He was a famous army officer whose cavalry regiment, Skinner's Horse, raised in 1803, is still in existence as part of the Indian Army. His grave was located close to the gate but like virtually all the graves, it was nameless. Nearly all the marble plaques have been removed, and the lead picked out of the inscriptions. Only about three remain identifiable. It seemed so sad and ignominious and a signal that it is futile to worry about posterity.

The information about Skinner was correct in part. The famous Colonel James Skinner died in 1841 far away from Bengal at Hansi in what is now the state of Haryana, quite close to Delhi. Buried first at Hansi, after 40 days his grave was opened and, his coffin escorted by 200 men from Skinner's Horse was brought to Delhi. Here he was buried in a vault of white marble below the altar in the church he had built at his own expense and dedicated to his patron, Saint James. He had vowed to become a Christian like his father and to build a church if he survived his wounds sustained on the battlefield of Uniara in 1800. The officer buried in the Berhampore Cemetery is another Captain James Skinner who died in 1773. There's more than one James Skinner as there is Mrs Hobart-Hampden.

I thought vaguely about the small plot of graves which I had seen once or twice when I was working in Jaipur. The plot in the outer grounds of the Raj Mahal Hotel lay across a busy road from my office. The Raj Mahal had been a palace in which the Maharaja of Jaipur had lived for a time with his beautiful wife, Rani Gayatri Devi. Before they had again become the rightful residents, their home had for a long period been the British Agent's Residence, hence the small graveyard. The headstones leaned at drunken angles and some inscriptions were completely illegible. The plot was fenced to keep people out and though it was mown occasionally it looked forlorn. My first thought was that someone should do something about it but I decided it is far better to be helping today's deprived children than worrying about poor old bods long gone.

In Berhampore something else was ticking through my head and from the cemetery we drove onto the old cantonment parade-ground, lined with huge and beautiful trees and still surrounded by neat and well-kept buildings of the colonial era. That's when I remembered hearing an interesting paper given in Canberra at a conference in 2001 by Peter Stanley, a military historian. Surely he had been talking about Berhampore. The parade-ground and its surrounding intact barracks were the light-bulb turned on in my brain but the first faint spark was connected to the lack of inscriptions on the graves in the cemetery. I then imperfectly remembered the connection to Mrs Sherwood but I mixed it up completely, a bit like my mother and *The Shellseekers*. I thought I recalled Peter alluding to the grave of the author of *Little Black Sambo* but I was quite wrong.

The truth is that somewhere in the cemetery lies poor little Henry, the son of Mrs Sherwood, who died in Berhampore in 1807.

Mary Martha Sherwood was born in 1775 in Worcestershire to a clergy family. Her father was Reverend George Butt, chaplain in ordinary to George III. She had an excellent education for a girl of her time and during her teens in Lichfield came under the influence of eminent people, leading thinkers and writers of the time such as the polymath and evolutionist Erasmus Darwin, educational reformer Richard Lovell Edgeworth, his daughter Maria who became a famous writer and Anna Seward the celebrated poet. She was intellectually stimulated but evangelical Mary was distressed by the general lack of Christian faith displayed by these important figures. Still she was determined to become a writer and her first story was published in 1795.

She married her cousin, Captain Henry Sherwood in 1803 and two years later she accompanied him and his regiment, the 53rd Foot, to India. Their first child, Mary Henrietta, remained in England with Mary Martha's mother and sister which must have been a considerable wrench. The four month voyage to India compounded the poor woman's misery at parting with her little one. She was pregnant again and the ship was attacked by French warships. However, eventually they arrived and thus began an eleven year stay. The family was stationed in Calcutta, Dinapore, Berhampore, Cawnpore and Meerut and six children were born in India between 1805 and 1815. Henry was born in 1805 and died agonizingly of whooping cough in 1807 and then Lucy Martha, born in 1807 lived only until 1808. The deaths of these two infants and later those of Lucy Elizabeth and Emily, both in their early 20s, were terrible losses for their grieving mother.

After the death of little Henry Mary Sherwood seriously reconsidered the path of evangelical Christianity which had stirred her soul from earlier days. Her decision was to pursue missionary work in India but first she had to convince the East India Company to change its policy of religious neutrality. With their consent, she established schools for the children of army officers as well as for the Indian children who were attached to English army camps. Her first school began with thirteen children and grew to more than forty. She adopted orphans and neglected children, found homes for others and established an orphanage, setting an example of deeds, not just words.

Not happy with traditional teaching manuals, she wrote her own stories for the children she taught with familiar themes of the army and of India. One was named for her little lost boy, *The History of Little Henry and his Bearer*. Written in India in 1810 and published in England 1814 two years before the family departed India, the book went through 18 printings between 1814 and 1824 alone, after that appearing again almost every three years. The story is of little Henry L---- who was born at Dinapore and orphaned before his first birthday. He was taken in by a fine lady who lived near the River Ganges between Dinapore and Patna in a *puckah* house. She was doubtless well-intentioned but her social life was far more important than her role as guardian. She was superficial, thoughtless and irresponsible and Henry was dreadfully neglected. If it hadn't been for Boosy, his devoted bearer, the little boy would surely have died in infancy.

Bishop Reginald Heber in his *Narrative of a journey through the Upper Provinces of India* writes of visiting Dinapoor (*sic*) at the end of August, 1825. He is very impressed with the appearance of the town which he describes as 'a great English military station'. The cantonment itself was the largest and most handsome he had seen and he glowingly describes the impressive quay and battery at the riverfront, stately houses, shops and barracks for both European and native troops. Everything he saw was on a liberal scale except for anything connected to the Church which presented a great contrast. There was no proper church building and the shabby, small and inconvenient room in the barracks used for services had neither light nor *punkahs* nor even a communion table. In other garrison towns Heber visited on his long, slow trip across the country, he had been heartened by the size and attention of his congregations but here in Dinapoor he found 'gross neglect of Sunday' from military officers and civilians alike. Europeans whether from the Company's regiment or local planters, came only to the clergy for marriage, burial or baptism. As well as neglecting the spiritual side of life, there was no school for either European children or illiterate soldiers and the books for the lending library sent by the Government some months before, had never even been unpacked. Heber felt that the problem stemmed from the lack of a decent church and 'the exceeding bad conduct of the late Chaplain' which had driven worshippers away.

Heber was writing more than ten years after Mrs Sherwood who obliquely described the lax behaviour prevalent in Dinapore which had such a bad affect on little Henry's early years. Perhaps it had always been a station with a rackety reputation. Elsewhere Heber notes that pensioner soldiers have the choice of residing in retirement at Murshidabad, Monghyr, Buxar or Chunar. Reprobates preferred Murshidabad while Monghyr was generally chosen by the more respectable characters. At Monghyr he had met a number of these 'very well-behaved decent old men' who spoke well of India but complained of lack of occupation. They wished for a little more mental stimulation in the form of something like a lending library.

Mrs. Sherwood's story in atmospheric terms is very realistic and rather than viewing it as a contrived situation to illustrate a modern parable, Bishop Heber's observations show how little Henry's neglect could have truly come about. Mrs Sherwood's story is full of Indian words explained in brackets. *Verandah, bangles, pajammahs* and *backshish* are familiar enough to the reader in our times but more esoteric words like *zeemendar* [a landholder], *choota sahib* [little master], *khauna* [food] and *budgerow* [a kind of barge] give the story an exotic reality which in a way *Louisa* did not quite have.

Some dull sections however are like passages from the catechism, questions and answers between Henry and the charming young lady who had come to stay for a time with the negligent protector in the *pukka* house by the river. Henry is then five years old and speaks only Hindoostanee (*sic*), apart from being able to call the dogs and horses and to swear at the servants in English, these words taught him by an officer friend of his adoptive Mamma. She on the other hand was able to scold the servants and swear at them in their own language, observed by Henry on the rare occasions when he ate luncheon with her. At these times conversation was at a minimum because as well as something of a language barrier, she smoked her *hookah* in between mouthfuls.

The young lady was 'the daughter of a worthy clergyman in England and had received from him a religious education.' We do not learn her name until she departed Dinapore and to go down to Berhampore where she married 'a very pious young man'. She became Mrs Baron, assuming an elevated name to match her exemplary nature. Before this happy union took place though she gave Henry the love he has never received before and set about to teach him first to speak English and then to read and write it. Then she convinced him of the truth of Christianity and the falsehood of Hindu gods. It is all very persuasive and 19th century children, whose threshold of boredom must have been far higher than children of today, would surely have taken the goodness to heart. Just like Mr Smith, Henry's later host in Calcutta, they would have been as impressed at his knowledge of the Bible and his dedication in explaining it to Boosy. Their parents may have been amused at the negligent protector's reaction to the god-botherers as being 'downright canting Methodist(s)', as appalling to her as Hinduism was to evangelicals. Mrs Sherwood was vigorously anti-Catholic which became more obvious in her later works of the 1820s and 1830s but despite the didactic tone which is unappealing to modern readers, her books were incredibly popular and some were pirated by multiple publishers.

Mr Smith explained to Henry that in his endeavours to lead Boosy to the light, he should not trust to his own words, but to the Word of God. 'Hold fast to the Scripture, dear boy, and you will be safe.' Returning by river to Dinapore after a year in Calcutta where Mamma had the diversions of 'lively company, many amusements and so many fashionable dresses to purchase', Henry was delighted at the prospect of stopping at Berhampore to see his beloved Mrs Baron. But our poor little hero became very ill and grew weaker by the day. Berhampore was full of Mamma's old acquaintances and soon she was so busy attending balls and dinners and 'deeply engaged in paying and receiving visits' that she forgot Henry all over again, knowing Mrs Baron would take care of him. Towards the end he asked Mrs Baron to sing the verse of the hymn he loved which reminded me of the death of Judy in *Seven Little Australians* when she asks Meg to sing *Abide with me* which would make me cry right now if I read it.

The climax of the story comes when Boosy confesses his sins and speaks of his desire to follow Jesus just before his small master dies. Henry asks Mrs Baron to cut locks of his hair as keepsakes for several of his friends. The poor little fellow thinks of everything and even has an unrecorded conversation with his Mamma, the negligent protector, who leaves his room, greatly perturbed but with 'his little well-worn Bible in her hand'. After his death she arranges for a monument to be built over his grave in the pretty, shaded graveyard of Berhampore. On it is inscribed his name, Henry L----, his age of eight years and seven months and his favourite verse from 1 Thessalonians: 5, altering one word 'Faithful is he that calleth *me.*' Kind Mr Smith takes charge of Boosy who is baptised and given the name of John. A further text is added to Henry's grave from James 5:20 'He which converteth the sinner from the error of his way shall save a soul from death and shall hide a multitude of sins'.

Boosy appeared in a later book by Mrs Sherwood published in 1842 titled *The Last Days of Boosy* as a sequel to *Little Henry* in a tone less evangelistic. This work refers to the Bible less frequently and shows God to be rather more benign although the story is of poor converted Boosy being cast out by his family and community because of his Christianity. It is far more realistic and culturally sensitive than some of her other improving texts which portray Indians as sly, selfish, lazy and dishonest.

The narrator speaks of first visiting Berhampore and going to see Henry's monument 'which was white and fair and inscription very plain' but has been told since 'that the damp of the climate has so defaced the inscription and blackened the whole monument, that it cannot now be distinguished from the tombs which surround it.' Poor Mrs Sherwood, whose real little Henry lay in the cemetery, spoke with prescience. If the tomb was defaced then, it is no different now but the burial ground, despite the anonymity of those who lie there, is a peaceful resting place.

My friend Brigid Keenan has a lovely 1869 edition of the book and its title is *Little Henry and his bearer Boosy: A tale from Dinapore*. It was a 'new edition, illustrated' and at about 14cm by 10cm would have been a lovely size for a child to hold. The frontispiece shows the moustachioed Boosy carrying the infant Henry who seems to be holding a rattle. He is so radiantly blonde and his sun-hat has fallen back behind his head giving the impression that it is a halo and it looks like the Christ Child held aloft by St Christopher. Boosy gazes at the child, his dark hands holding the pale baby secure. The caption says 'All the day long he played with him, sometimes carrying him in his arms or on his shoulder and sometimes letting him walk or roll upon the carpet. Everybody who came to the house noticed the kindness of Boosy to the child.' He was really a miracle of devotion. His name appears in another strange context, in *Love in a Cold Climate* by Nancy Mitford. Re-reading this after forty years, I found the Indian connections fascinating. I hadn't before identified the real characters on whom the Montdore's were based and that was interesting, but also towards the end when Cedric combs Lady Montdore's photograph albums, he finds a snap of Boy Dougdale 'with his bearer Boosee', an alternative spelling for our Boosy who has become the quintessential Indian servant.

A female version of Little Henry, *The History of Little Lucy and her Dhaye* published in 1823, was far less popular and ran to only four printings. Sherwood frequently used her dead children's names for heroes and heroines of her stories, many of whom also die. All too sad but contemporary readers were more closely acquainted with death than we are today and generally had a more convinced belief in ultimate salvation. The reader knows that little Henry will be saved because he was converted by kindly Mrs Baron who not only taught him to read but also to know and love God. Little children reading the story, or having it read to them, are reminded in the last paragraph 'Little children in India remember Henry L----, and 'go and do ... likewise'' This is a quote from The Gospel according to Luke, Chapter 10 verse 37, from the parable of the Good Samaritan, and is clear direction for all readers, child and adult, to convert the idolatrous and follow Henry's example.

Is this story just about God and the Church? The first few decades of the nineteenth century in India were when the earlier broad-minded orientalist attitudes of the British were changing to a narrower view. Part of the reason was that a quick fortune made as an employee of The East India Company was not as easily won as in the past and the ultimate reward for a long period of service might be just a return to Britain with no particular financial gain. This could have encouraged an interest in India culture which earlier Englishmen had found fascinating, but instead a certain philistinism prevailed. In Captain Bellew's *Memoirs of a Griffin* written a little later in 1843, a griffin or new-chum, is viewed with suspicion when caught quoting poetry, a most peculiar habit. Religion, as practised at home in England, established and habitual, was a safer bet than examination of other beliefs and philosophy.

The Hon. Mountstuart Elphinstone, one of the great, enlightened British administrators of India, was Governor of Bombay between 1819 and 1827. He was viewed with cautious mistrust because he slept on the floor and rose at 4 a.m. to read Sophocles. Bishop Heber who visited Bombay in July 1825 during Elphinstone's tenure was asked his opinion of the Governor. A cavalry officer, whom Heber described as amiable though indiscreet and not 'well-judging', had published an account of his Indian travels and had accused Elphinstone as being 'devoid of religion and blinded to all spiritual truth.' Heber broad-minded and fair, had read this account before he met the Governor. He found him an extraordinary man, generous, liberal and wise with an enormous breadth of knowledge, love of scholarship and a huge amount of energy. Though he was 'fond of society', he practiced 'a temperance amounting to rigid abstinence', probably something that did not appeal to the cavalry officer author. Not only that, he was 'always moral and decorous ... regular in his attendance on public worship, and not only well-informed on religious topics, but well-pleased and forward to discuss them'. Heber further said that Elphinstone actually did more for the encouragement of Christianity and the suppression of what the British viewed as horrific practices such as *sati*, than any Indian Governor before him. Heber liked him immensely and found the Governor's kindness, hospitality and agreeable conversation 'the greatest pleasure of the kind which I have ever enjoyed either in India or Europe.' He doesn't mention any discussion of the Governor's partiality for Pontius Pilate on the basis that Pilate's first duty as Governor was to maintain peace but in several letters home he recalled the happy three months which he, his wife and small daughter, spent with Elphinstone. Both men must have enjoyed their far-reaching conversations. Heber, as a churchman, would have enjoyed immunity from criticism on a philosophical level and his remarks should have put an end to the whispers that Elphinstone was a doubter, sceptic and unbeliever.

Life was precarious and as two monsoons was the usual life span of the British in India, prayer perhaps provided the only answer. In her autobiography Mrs Sherwood tells of constant illness in her family. Having lost two small children she must always have been fearful for the health of her family. Religious revival in England was echoed in India where staunch evangelical beliefs replaced even vague forms of scepticism which some had found fashionable. Intolerance became an unfortunate feature amongst church-goers. Evangelicals were growing in political influence in England and the Charter Act of 1813 allowed missionaries freedom to work in India. The important work of converting the heathen strengthened the idea of moral superiority over those who lived in the 'black towns', away from neat cantonments and civil lines. Spiritual and cultural superiority became one and the same thing amounting to imperialism on a grand scale.

A Google Alert for Berhampore brought varied results. Matrimonial advertisements and beautiful photographs of the general area of Berhampore and Murshidabad were followed by an interesting article titled *Unknown Burmese Tombs at Berhampore*. There are five tombs located in the Central Sericulture Institute. The last King of Burma, Thibaw Min, and his family were exiled to Ratnagiri on the west coast of India, south of Bombay after Thibaw's defeat in the Third Anglo-Burmese war in 1855. The story is that the Royal Family were brought to Murshidabad en route to their final destination. They were held in the barracks of the old District Council Building at Berhampore, formerly an indigo processing factory. A recent sleuthing journey to Berhampore finally located the graves of which nobody in town, including our guide, had heard. We had a great tour of the Silk Museum at the Institute, tea with the kind Director who then took us to see the Burmese graves. The King is not there. He died at age 57 in 1916 and was buried in a small walled plot next to a Christian cemetery in Ratnagiri on the coast of Maharashtra, far away. Nobody knows quite who lies at Berhampore but there must be some truth in the story.

The Teller of Tales by Bhaskar Ghose looks back on the friendship of two men who met when they were newly assigned IAS officers to districts in West Bengal. Over decades they meet and reminisce about those good old days, ghosts and wild elephants, eccentric District Commissioners, horses and tea gardens, clubs and *chowkidars*. They had separate stays in the old Circuit House in Berhampore which they described as Clive's residence, and haunted. The famous man actually stayed in it only briefly maybe because he too found the place creepy. The enormously tall ceilings with the skylights placed so high meant that even during the day the upper reaches of the rooms were dark and there was a mysteriously creaking door. The towns have become more and more fascinating.

Mrs Bannerman whom I had incorrectly imagined lying buried in the Berhampore cemetery, wrote *Little Black Sambo* in 1899 while living in South India. The friends with me in Berhampore remembered at least part of the story but one said she had always thought the story was set in Africa. From the time of the book's first appearance, readers have commented on the ambiguous setting but the tigers and the ghee are the keys to India and probably the idea of an African location comes from the half-remembered illustrations from our childhood. The little boy had curls and a very dark complexion, and the inappropriateness now of his name has a link with slavery and the African people taken all over the world against their will by colonial powers.

The word *sambo* may have entered English from a Latin American Spanish word *zambo* which is still in use for a person of mixed African and Amerindian blood. The linguistic origin for this word may be African. A Kongo word, *nzambu*, means monkey which from the start is a pejorative but other kinder sources may be a Hausa word for second son or a Fulani word for uncle. Sambo was a common slave name at least from the 18th century and there are characters in Thackeray's *Vanity Fair* and Harriet Beecher Stowe's *Uncle Tom's Cabin* with this name. At first there seems no intentional racist connotation. It was a stereotypical name like Paddy for an Irishman or Jock for a Scot, but stereotypes have a habit of becoming first patronising then disagreeable and Sambo by the late 19th century had become deeply offensive. Much has been written about terms once considered inoffensive which come to be regarded as highly objectionable. When we lived in Trinidad in the mid-1980s I remember the shock at hearing friends of African origin referring to themselves as Negroes. For them it was ok. At the same time in Surinam a community of people whose ancestors were runaway slaves in the late 17th and early 18th century were still known as Bush Negroes.

Helen Bannerman was a Scot who lived for 32 years in Madras where her husband, William, was an officer in the Indian Medical Service. Born in Edinburgh in 1862 she the daughter of a Scottish minster and had spent much of her childhood abroad as her father had become an army chaplain and was posted overseas. She was well educated with the qualification of LLA which stood for Lady Literate in Arts. This was an external degree granted by St Andrew's University to women who had studied through correspondence or by attending non-university classes. Scottish universities opened their doors to women in 1892 but the LLA remained popular for many years after that and was not discontinued until the 1930s.

The preface to *Little Black Sambo* says that 'once upon a time there was an English lady in India, where black children abound and tigers are everyday affairs, who had two little girls.' During a separation from her elder daughters this 'English' lady—there is no mention of her Scots origin—wrote and illustrated a story of a small boy and his fantastical adventure, originally invented on a long train journey. She bound the book in a format attractive for children and sent it to her daughters. The story was read in her home by a friend who suggested she take it with her to England to offer it for publication. Bannerman agreed but cautioned in a canny Scots way against selling the copyright. The foolish friend was unable to resist the publisher, Richard Grant, and all Mrs Bannerman received for what became a highly successful book, was five pathetic pounds. The book was quickly printed for the Christmas market of 1899 and became an immediate success. Between 1901 and 1909 Bannerman wrote eight more books with titles such as *Little Black Mingo* and *Little Black Quasha* but none would enjoy the success of her first.

It is a great pity that this sweet story should have become so reviled. It is funny, charming and appealing and written as it was originally for family consumption, one can just imagine the laughter of her four children, familiar with terms like *ghee* and *bazaar* which might need explanation to British children at home. They would have been laughing not *at* the little boy but with him. What a lucky fellow he was in the beautiful new clothes his mother, Black Mumbo, had sewn for him. The red coat and blue pants went splendidly with the wonderful green umbrella and enviable purple shoes with crimson soles and linings bought for him in the *bazaar* by his father, Black Jumbo. *Jutis* or slippers made in India today often have superb crimson soles which could possibly lead to regular church attendance so others can admire them as the wearer kneels.

How terrifying it must have been to have been faced by not one fierce tiger but four, and how incredibly smart to outwit them all. The illustrations of the humans are not nearly as appealing as the tigers. Mrs Bannerman was a talented artist but her tigers are far more beautiful and skilful than her people who have crude, almost grotesque cartoon faces. The third tiger who wears the purple *jutis* on his ears is wonderful and how clever of Sambo to tie the green umbrella to the proud tail of the fourth tiger bully. All bullies are alike and the tigers have a terrible fight over who was the grandest of the jungle. They race round and round the base of a palm tree until they turn themselves into a big pool of melted *ghee*. The act of churning connects with the epic story of the churning of the ocean of milk from ancient Hindu scriptures when Vasuki, the king of serpents acts as the churning rope to rotate a mountain and bring forth *amrit*, the nectar of immortality. Images of churning butter may still be seen in Indian folk art and in 1899 it was a familiar task.

Boy triumphs over animal without bloodshed and the ghee forms the basis of a splendid feast—pancakes which were 'as yellow and brown as little tigers' made by Black Mumbo. As well as the racist slur of book's title and its controversial illustrations, complaints have been made by a group called The Central Committee of Teachers against Racism because of what they say is a stereotypical image of African American gluttony. This relates to the feast where although his mother eats 27 pancakes and his father 55, Little Black Sambo manages to devour 169 'because he was so hungry'. Oh dear me, if it was an Australian story the pancakes might have been very small pikelets which some people say originated in Scotland. It does look rather a large mound of food in the drawing, but the poor child is as thin as a pin and deserved them for being so intelligent and his mother who loved him was giving him a wonderful treat.

Initially, *Little Black Sambo* was regarded as a positive portrayal of black characters, indeed a celebration of a black hero. The story was viewed as a delightful adventure in the realm of make-believe where the small, intelligent, successful and heroic protagonist just happens to be black. The child-friendly size of the published book, one in a series called *The Dumpy Books for Children*, its fantasy, action, vivid illustrations and the repetition were quite revolutionary in children's literature. Importantly and refreshingly, there was no hint of a moral or an over-riding signpost to improvement. Sambo is rewarded by his loving mother for his intelligence and bravery.

The story has been in constant publication for more than a century and the butt of criticism since at least the 1940s. Widespread banning began in the 1960s. Much of the censure started in America and the most damning element of the book are the illustrations. Some later versions of the book have been illustrated by other than Helen Bannerman's originals, some far more offensive than hers. Demeaning settings in plantations in the southern states of the USA or African jungles show Sambo clad in typical slave clothing and even a grass skirt. The latest versions of the story are what we now term, politically correct. A Japanese publication in 1997, called *Chibikuro Sampo*, the successor to a 1953 pirated version, has a small boy taking a black Labrador puppy for a stroll in the jungle. The noted American illustrator, Fred Marcellino who felt there were no racist overtones in the story, produced a modified tale with new illustrations called *The Story of Little Babaji*. Babaji and his parents are Indians of wheatish complexion, much paler than many Tamils whose homeland was the Madras Presidency where Mrs Bannerman lived, and they look like a very happy family. It is not too much of stretch to look at illustrations in some children's books of today and wonder what the fuss is all about.

Tulika is an independent publishing house of excellent children's books in India and deals in many important issues of modern life as well as happy fantasy. The editors started their pioneering venture in 1996. Based in Chennai, their focus is on picture books in English and several Indian languages—Hindi, Tamil, Malayalam, Kannada, Telugu, Marathi, Gujarati and Bengali. Their motto is many languages many voices. Subjects have included the decline of forests and pollution of the environment, life and death and reconstruction after the tsunami which affected thousands of people in South India in 2004. There are books about Gandhi, Indian dinosaurs, monkeys and cyberspace, Dr Ambedkar as a boy, work and play, gender, turtles, indigo and weaving, rivers and the sea and the Olympic Games. The age range is for pre-school to mid-teen and some books are published in Braille for visually handicapped children. My friend Zai Whitaker has written *Kanna Panna*, published in 2015 about a different little boy whose visual impairment actually allows him to lead his family to safety. (In India the term differently abled seems kinder than our disabled.)

Children's classics from other languages are translated into Indian languages but familiar locations make sense to small children. While some stories are firmly rooted into a child's own local environment, the modern global world of multi-dimensional India is very apparent as well. I recently visited the Chennai office and would have liked a chat but the receptionist was distracted, the phone rang deafeningly every few minutes and I seemed to be a bit of a nuisance. Never mind, as well as Zai's book I bought four in the *Looking at Art* series, engaging stories about the lives of four important pillars of modern Indian art, Raja Ravi Varma, Amrita Sher-Gil, Jamini Roy and M.F. Husain.

Illustration styles change in every country but some expressions on children's faces in a recent Tulika book could almost qualify for the term grotesque which was used so often in criticism of *Little Black Sambo*. These little faces were fair-skinned, fairer than tens of millions of Indians, so there perhaps lies the difference. What if the story had been written by an African-American mother for her daughters? How would she have told the tale and how would she have illustrated it? Defenders of the book say that Sambo made whites acknowledge the humanity in black people and say the book is a product of its time. Mrs Bannerman's children have said that their mother would be saddened at the accusation of racism and who knows, she like Mr Fielding in *A Passage to India* may have thought that pinko-grey was a more apt description for a white complexion and not at all attractive.

My oldest Indian book is *India: Pictorial, descriptive and historical*. It is a volume from Bohn's Illustrated Library and was published in London in 1854. It was given me by my next-door neighbour in 1962 when I was fourteen. I grew up in an extremely beautiful part of Sydney in a large house with a big garden which ran steeply down through bush which we called The Gully to the shores of a tidal bay on a river. In the 1950s there were few boats at anchor in Woodford Bay and the noises from our river were not of picturesque native craft unloading jute or boatloads of passengers or religious processions. Occasionally rowing crews could be heard early in the morning or brightly-lit ferry boats with a rock band on board might cruise by in the evening on an up-river harbour cruise. We had a tiny sandstone boatshed where we kept our wooden dinghy. She was called Mermaidia, a combination of our names, Meredith, Maitland and Claudia.

Our neighbour was Mrs Emily Broughton MacLeod, the widow Dr Gordon MacLeod, a Scottish ophthalmic surgeon. She lived in a lovely, rather empty late Victorian house called 'Loddington' with a pretty garden full of old-fashioned flowers and huge hydrangeas which flanked the front steps. She was a keen gardener and gave my mother cuttings to plant in our garden. She had pincushion flowers which I found captivating—I was mad on flowers and the first book I ever bought myself with pocket money was *Joan in Flowerland* with lovely illustrations. One thing Mrs MacLeod did not tolerate in her garden were pansies because she said they looked like Hitler. She could do just about everything and was like a benevolent great-aunt to many children of the neighbourhood.

Mrs MacLeod had a ginger cat whose name was Teddy. He was very fat and occasionally stranded himself high in a tree. A fire engine once came to bring him back to earth by way of the extension ladder. Each year Teddy issued hand-painted invitations to Mrs MacLeod's party on Christmas Day. The parties were enormous and I don't remember anything about food for children but the adults drank sherry and ate Christmas cake. My brother when he was tiny went around the room drinking all the dregs until my mother noticed and swept him away.

C'leodie as we called her was very small and was usually dressed in black trousers and a shirt, although occasionally she wore a dress. Her hair was cut as short as a man's, she often wore a beret and she smoked a great deal, her cigarettes in an amber holder which she gripped at an angle between strong teeth. My brother and I often visited her, not in the large reception rooms but in a cosy little room near the kitchen at the back of the house where there was always a jar of barley sugar and a pile of Illustrated London News. We had a craze of asking adults to show us their false teeth. Hideous though we found the sight and knowing it was naughty, still we asked and when the owner of some fake choppers complied (they always did) by somehow dislodging them a bit, we would gaze for a fascinated second and then run away shrieking! Mrs MacLeod never minded and neither I think did Miss Elsie Findlater, known as Nonnie, who was Mrs MacLeod's housekeeper and companion. She had a pet duck who she called each night 'Duck, duck, duck, duck.' She was as small as Mrs MacLeod but thin as a frail little flower. Mrs MacLeod read to her every evening as her eyesight was so poor. I don't remember her teeth as well as C'leodie's but a laundry hint entered our household from Loddington to use Steradent, a denture cleaner, to remove ink stains from our school shirts.

For months each year Mrs MacLeod would work on the Christmas tableau for her party. She would go to town in the bus and walk up to the Museum where one year she sketched reindeer. Then she went home and made them. Extraordinary. She once made a most realistic lamb for my sister and intricately layered and painted paper wings and a halo for me when I was an angel in the Sunday School nativity play. When I went to hospital to have my tonsils out she made me a lizard! What a funny thing to take to hospital, I clearly remember nurses asking me if they could borrow it to frighten people. I have it still, a very realistic Common Garden Skink whose real relatives used to scuttle around our garden. The reindeer tableau party was wonderful, half a dozen deer arranged in front of the fire-place. Santa Claus, really an old man called Bill Dobson who lived down the road, leapt out of the chimney and every child was given a present from Teddy, again with a hand-painted card. I still have a card with a slightly imperious ginger cat sitting against a background of red and green holly saying 'Teddy's choice for Claudia'.

We were always given excellent books but one year Mrs MacLeod did a wonderful thing for me –she **made** me a book. It is called *Christmas Rhymes* and the title page says it is written and pictured by E.B. MacLeod. Her initials are in a round cartouche and then at the bottom it says 'printed and set up by the Loddington Press, Northwood. The dedication is 'To Claudia' and then come six poems and six beautiful paintings. Her technique was to paint the background and then glue in collage form some of the figures, animals, shepherds or the Holy Child in the Manger which had been painted on another sheet of paper. Tiny birds flying in the sky in the painting illustrating a poem called 'The Birds' about the child Jesus in Nazareth, look almost real with the extra skerrick of depth from the collage. I can't imagine why I deserved this most beautiful gift because I wasn't particular good. Perhaps she was amused at the false teeth caper. She did have a very good sense of humour. In one of her guest rooms the light reading by the bed was a colossal Webster's Dictionary.

I know nothing at all of Mrs MacLeod's church-going habits. She was presumed Presbyterian and we were Anglican. Once, my mother took me to see the very beautiful memorial window in St Andrew's Presbyterian Church at Longueville. It stands on the top of the ridge that runs down the small peninsula to the Lane Cove River. From across the bay at Northwood, the window of the church illuminated from within at night, and catching the sunshine on the outside by day, was in clear view from Loddington. The memorial is to C'Leodie's only child, a little boy called Neil, who died from complications of a twisted bowel in 1927 when he was only six years old.

There was a photograph of the window in the Sydney Morning Herald in July 1928 with the caption stating that it had been 'unveiled by the Moderator General on Sunday last'. The glass was designed by Norman Carter with the architectural portion created by Professor Wilkinson. Both men were important figures in art and academic life in Sydney and the memorial, dedicated by the head of the Presbyterian Church, was a highly significant addition to the fabric of the church. The window shows a small boy standing in the central section of the three lancet windows. The expression on the little boy's face is sweet and trusting and was taken from a photograph. I like to think that there might be something of him in the illustration of the blonde-haired child Jesus, making birds of clay, in my book of Christmas Rhymes. In the window Neil's right arm rests trustingly on a huge lion and his left curves around the neck of a sweet calf. The text from Isaiah, Chapter 11, verse 6, the King James Version, says 'The wolf also shall dwell with the lamb, and the leopard shall lie down with the kid; and the calf and the young lion and the fatling together; and a little child shall lead them.' He is surrounded by wild animals doing him no harm and there are some fine buildings which might be Edinburgh University or a Gothic church or something from the artist's imagination.

Even if Mrs MacLeod's faith and her belief in heaven were unshakeable I can imagine that she might not have wanted to attend church regularly—the beauty of the window would have made her achingly sad. I have discovered that her father was an Anglican priest, the Rev. Canon Edward Henley Acton Gwynne, so she must have either decided to accompany Dr MacLeod to his Scottish kirk, or else just kept her faith to herself which her lovely poems show was something very important. Dr MacLeod, whom she married in 1916, died in 1949 and dear Mrs McLeod was left alone and though her heart must have been broken, the gathering up of the neighbouring children must have helped bring joy back into her life.

The image of the St Andrew's window has stayed in my head for the whole of my life and I have returned once or twice to visit it. Once I took photographs after reading Robert Dessaix' *Night Letters*. It starts with the image of himself 'streaking through the jungle on a gaudy leopard' and with a cassowary feather streaming from one side of an extravagant black hat with a drooping brim. In Dessaix' earlier book *A Mother's Disgrace* I found that he had lived in our neighbourhood as a child and had even attended St Andrew's Sunday School before his enquiring mind led him to something he found more satisfying. I wondered if the image from the window had stayed in his subconscious. Once I had to introduce him on the stage of Tilley's Devine Café for the Canberra Word Festival committee. After the talk I told him about the window and I sent him the photographs. He wrote thanking me and said 'I found them very thought-provoking, but can it be true that images such as these could have a passing, profound effect?'

In 1962 Mrs MacLeod left Loddington and went into a nursing home. It didn't seem she needed to go but Nonnie had died and there was nobody to look after her and she had become frail. Family members packed up the lovely house and I was invited to choose a few books. Perhaps it was the *Chatterbox* influence, but one I chose was the Indian number of *Bohn's Illustrated Library*. The title page says there are 'nearly one hundred illustrations' and they are attractive and interesting, especially some of the Initial Letter drawings at the start of each chapter. The very first would surely have gripped anyone's attention with a caparisoned elephant standing on the top of the column that represents the letter *I*, the first word being *It*. Islamic architectural details and a slanting coconut palm form a frame and in a fascinating miscellany there are white bullocks pulling a curtained shrine, two haughty camels, a Jain statue or perhaps he is a meditating priest, a drum and a hookah, a bird, a snake, a lion and a tiger. It was a complete visual immersion into the land that would become the brightest jewel. Mrs MacLeod might have even received some inspiration from the first illustration for the camels in my Christmas book.

More than a century and a half after its publication I find there is a mystery connected with the book, yet another which I will never be able to solve. There is an inscription in fine copperplate writing in the fly-leaf dated 6th July 1857 at Newport, Fife. The book was given as First Prize for an essay written 'On the Principles of the Free Church of Scotland' to Master Hugh Gordon. In brackets the inscription says that 'the prize was competed for, by the young men of the Free Church Congregation of Newport, Fife and awarded by Neil MacLeod, Minister'. How did the book come to be in Sydney? Was Rev. Neil MacLeod, Dr MacLeod's father? Perhaps he was and little Neil who died was named after his grandfather. Whatever happened to Master Hugh Gordon who won the prize? Perhaps some terrible thing befell him before its presentation or perhaps he gave up the church and offended the Minister. Or more happily, as my great friend Lindsay Mackerras, Scottish to the core, suggested, perhaps Dr MacLeod's mother was a Gordon and Master Hugh could have been his uncle.

Clergymen, missionaries and their offspring have figured prominently so far in this essay and even Enid Blyton wrote Bible Stories. Like children all over the English-speaking world in the 1950s, I read Enid Blyton stories but not as many as most. My first school, Woodley, where I started in a class called Transition in 1952 when I was five, was a wonderful place. We wore maroon serge uniforms in the winter and cream tunics in the summer. Our hats with the motto 'Loyal and True' embroidered on the hat-bands were maroon felt in the winter and panama in the summer and our school-bags were leather satchels worn on our backs to improve our posture. Owned and run by Miss Sydney Watson and her sister known as Miss Ngaio, the campus was a series of new, rather flimsy buildings grouped around a big old two storey red brick house built in 1911 and first called St Elmo. The house was in the then popular Federation Arts and Crafts style and originally had four bedrooms. Some had been turned into little dormitories for the small group of boarders. I had one week as a boarder when my little sister was born. It was a happy week with strange things to eat and drink like egg flips—something I had never heard of because I was such a fat little thing not needing building up. The garden was very pretty and the playground had a truly thrilling collection of swings, climbing frames, roundabouts and monkey-bars and most of us turned into little monkeys with hard calluses on our hands and a great capacity for hanging upside-down. After rain the whole school would go into the garden to collect snails which were put into buckets of salt where they fizzed dramatically after which we would demonstrate our love for the school by forming a great ring around the old house, holding hands, to hug Woodley!

Woodley was the only non-denominational private primary school in the Lane Cove area. After a few years as a tenant, Miss Watson bought the house and garden in 1944 and ran a very successful school until her retirement in 1962. It was a glorious start to anyone's education which sadly for some, deteriorated at the next school. Art and music were an enormous part of our lives and this was taught by Miss Constance Monk whom everyone loved. Miss Watson and Miss Ngaio were tall and angular and blue-eyed. They had white hair but perhaps had been blonde and Miss Watson who shouted in a very loud voice though not unpleasantly, always had a white handkerchief tucked into a gold armlet worn above her elbow. Miss Monk smiled all the time and had the kindest brown eyes and rather untidy brown hair in a curly sort of a fringe on her forehead and pinned up somehow at the back. She had painted beautiful murals on all the walls of our class-rooms—characters from nursery rhymes and popular stories for the smallest children in pre-school and elsewhere there were copies of illustrations from classics by Australian writers such as May Gibbs and Ida Rentoul

Outhwaite. Everybody adored *Snugglepot and Cuddlepie* and I have a copy of Outhwaite's *The Little Green Road to Fairyland* which I loved just about more than any other book. I adored fairies. I invented ways to trap them and wrote pleading notes to them when they were expected on a night visit to take away a baby tooth. I was so trusting and throughout my life I think most of the times when I've ended up in hot water are because I've lacked insight because of too much trust. Not such a bad failing I suppose but slightly embarrassing to realise how thick I have been from time to time. When finally it dawned on me that Santa Claus wasn't true, my mother was very relieved as I was then able to help her with purchasing presents for my still-believing younger brother and sister. I still believe in fairies though.

Miss Watson would not have Enid Blyton in the library so our reading was channelled away from her at least at school. We were saved from becoming literary prigs by the fact that everyone had the odd Blyton book at home or had borrowed them from cousins and there was always the Lane Cove Public Library. At the end of the school year prize-winners were asked to choose a book. One friend asked for a Bobbsey Twins books which even not an Enid Blyton was not considered appropriate. I must have been nine by then and I chose *The Crooked Snake* by Patricia Wrightson. It was a terrific adventure story which won the Children's Book Council Book of the Year Award in 1956 and had been read aloud on the ABC children's program 'The Argonauts', to which we were glued every afternoon.

In a poll recently conducted by the Costa Book Awards, Enid Blyton is ranked as Britain's most beloved writer of all time. In her 45 year career she produced more than 700 books and 5,000 short stories. She was a veritable story machine. With some expurgations of racist, sexist or classist passages, the books still sell annually more than eight million copies worldwide and the total of all books sold stands now at more than 600 million copies.

In a very good essay *Into the Enchanted Forest and up the Faraway Tree* published in the Indian magazine *The Caravan*, Amy Rosenberg asks the question, 'Why is there a corner of the Indian Heart that is forever Enid Blyton?' Rosenberg is American and had never heard of Blyton until she married an Indian. Since then she has often seen the alarming excitement which transforms writers from former British colonies when they talk about reading Blyton. She says from first-hand observations and the reading of many blogs she can 'practically see their shining eyes'! Blyton's child characters, despite meeting occasional danger in their pursuit of mystery-solving are always happy and enjoying liberated, glorious fun. The liberation factor is because most of the time the children are without adult supervision. The basis for all these stories could have been the combination of *Louisa* and *Island Adventure* of that 1923 *Chatterbox*. Louisa's father, absorbed with his study of Indian folk-lore, could be a model for George's father in *The Famous Five* series. Mr Lumsdale is far more benign than frowning Uncle Quentin 'who spends all his time studying'. Perhaps anthropology in those days was less taxing than 20th century science. The freedom enjoyed by the Famous Five was enviable for many readers. Occasionally tutors are engaged and homework needs to be done but usually the action takes place in the holidays where a jolly good time was had by all.

At several writers' festivals in Asia and Australia I have heard visitors from former British colonies, where children composed a huge percentage of the Blyton readership, say how fascinated they were by descriptions of food they discovered in the books. Liver was yearned for by one Indian writer who was horribly disappointed when she finally sampled it in England. She thought it so utterly disgusting that she had to race from the table and spit it out in a bathroom. I don't blame her. Offal of any kind has that effect on many, but the additional heartbreak of that overwhelming ruination of a dream must have been frightful! Ham and jelly were two other unobtainable and desirable foods eventually eaten and found disappointing by some non-British writers, Blyton-obsessed as children. Egg sandwiches seem to have been considered exotic by some but for me it was potted meat. Whatever was potted meat and how did it go into a sandwich? It was always something I imagined to be perfectly scrumptious but now I imagine I would have hated it. Bishop Heber in his journals on the first day of 1825 writes of visiting Safdar Jang's tomb in Delhi. He says 'it is very richly inlaid with different kinds of marble, but has too much of the colour of potted meat to please me'. I have found that potted meat could have been something delicious like rillettes but after looking at recipes, I think I can do without it for the rest of my life. I would prefer Peck's most delicious Anchovette on hot-buttered toast if this fishy treat still exists.

Heber did not care for much Indian food in particular three g's — garlic, ghee and grease. In Lucknow he was utterly delighted with some excellent *pillau*. He became tired of lamb and kid and found that Indian fowls were tough and lean. He enjoyed fish greatly and felt that potatoes were 'among the most valueable presents' the populace of India was 'likely to receive from their new masters'. He observed them in the Himalayan foothills and in gardens in Lucknow and heard that they were becoming great favourites, particularly with Muslims who found them 'very useful as absorbents in their greasy messes'. When encamped at Furreedpoor which might be the Faridpur mentioned in *Louisa*, he wrote that 'the milk and butter are generally seasoned with the never-failing condiments of Hindostan, smoke and soot' but he generally did not complain. His frequent tongue in cheek remarks are for himself and his wife whom he missed so much on his travels. With some prescience he noted the Deccan's potential as a wine-growing area.

When I started going down the path of children's food again I asked my daughter if she still had any of her Famous Five books. 'Oh Mum,' she protested 'I have all of them except Number 19!' (I found a copy of 19 to make up the set.) There are 21 in all, written between 1942 and 1963 and Emily's are of the edition first published in 1967 reprinted many times, Em's mostly in 1980. Most were bought during the year in Norfolk when both children watched the series on television. We can all sing the theme song … 'Julian, Dick, George, Anne and Timmie the do-og'! There is a special English way of pronouncing Julian too with rounded, slightly protruding lips — joolian or jewlian.

As children my friends and I all identified with tomboy George and in the drawings Julian & Dick looked much older than do the boys in my daughter's books. Em however, strongly identified with Anne whom she tells me wasn't quite as soppy on television as in the books where she regularly seems to dissolve or burst or subside into tears. I think Em hoped she looked a bit like her heroine, with longish hair held back by a velvet hair-band. Everything had to be organised in fives and I even used to hear her bang her toothbrush five times on the hand-basin each night!

She found the food exciting too and the idea of lashings of whatever it was they were eating was marvellous. She wasn't sure what lashings meant. I skimmed through several of 20 stories looking for food references and find that the pinnacle of provender was when the children stay with Mrs Penruthlan on Tremannon Farm in *Five go down to the Sea*, No. 12 in the series. The good Cornish lady provides a huge ham, 'lashings of hard boiled eggs', 'lashings of peas and new potatoes', home-made salad cream, cream cheese, drop scones, cherry tart and cream, rich creamy milk and fresh fruit salad and cream. There is cream with just about everything and of course when the children are asked if they would like something, the chorus is "Rather!' said everyone at once.'—a peculiarly British reply. Em insists that the Five had shredded wheat for breakfast which I think must be a television addition. In England it became my children's breakfast cereal of choice though Em says now that she really disliked it but persisted because of Anne.

There must have been more changes than shredded wheat for breakfast. Anne is dressed in dungarees, a long-time feminist article of clothing, on the cover of the modern paperbacks which also contributes to her resurrection from sook to heroine. I found the word jeans in the text a number of times which certainly weren't worn by children in wartime England of the 1940s. In Australia we wore jodhpurs as hard-wearing trousers until the late 1950s, something that suited horse-crazed girls very well. Once I went to the cinema to see *Gigi* with my horse-mad friend, Pamela Rushton. We wore our jodhpurs, white shirts and riding ties and of course our riding boots. She had a velvet crash-cap of which I was madly envious and we wore it by turn inside the Crows Nest cinema. Nobody behind us complained about an obscured view of the screen. How could we have thought it was appropriate clothing for *Gigi* of all films? Brigid Keenan spent the first eight years of her life in India was told she was made to pronounce jodhpur as jodepur which of course is correct but when she came home and said it, everyone wearing them thought she was peculiar.

Wearing our jodhpurs we tried to have adventures like the Five. Along with trying to trap a fairy, I was dying to have an adventure. In Northwood we had wondrous bush and even ancient indigenous rock carvings in a park nearby but nothing much seemed to happen of a mysterious nature. My oldest friend, Jill Hartigan, had a bit of a cubby and her father had given her a combination lock for the door which was an excellent start. Another girl gave us some false clues but we picked them up straight away and thought she was something of a cheat. That seemed to be the end to our short-lived mystery club. But Jill initiated me into some more amazing things and one of them was Catholicism. In her bedroom she had a small altar on her dressing-table with a chalice which I confused with the Holy Grail. In her grandmother's bedroom there was a large picture of Jesus Christ of the Sacred Heart which I found terribly confronting. Jill, although almost a year younger than I, told me the facts of life which I could did not believe. How could *that* possibly be true!

In 2002 I was invited to be author-in-residence for a week at an International School in Colombo. Being named as an author was at the same time falsely elevating and extremely terrifying. My oeuvre was more than extremely slim and there was nothing relating to children's literature. I had done far more cooking than writing in the immediate few years so this coupled with my well-known interest in the pineapple was the basis for my week's program. My theme was food in children's literature, appealing to just about everyone. The classes who came to my sessions ranged from Kindergarten to Grade 4 which meant a wide range of literature to be encompassed. I had the use of the school domestic science kitchens and part of my time with each class was doing some basic cooking.

I did not use *Little Black Sambo* as one of my books for obvious reasons though pikelet or pancake manufacture would have had far fewer pitfalls than the chocolate cakes which until we found a bag of imported flour, were a complete and utter flop. There was something really very odd about the school's supply of local flour. Neither did I choose anything by Enid Blyton but J K Rowling was a great resource. As a child she had loved descriptions of food in books so found it natural to include them in her Harry Potter stories. I'm sure some of Rowling's childhood literary food indulgences would have come from the pages of Enid Blyton. She was ranked third behind Blyton and Roald Dahl in the Costa poll. There are 'lashings' of food in many of Dahl's children's books but not so in the work of Jane Austen, William Shakespeare and Charles Dickens who were ranked fourth, fifth and sixth.

My father was a Federal politician, a Liberal member of the House of Representatives from 1949 to 1961 where he was the first sitting member for the electorate of Mitchell. When Parliament was sitting he used to leave home in a Commonwealth car before we got up on Tuesday morning and come home on Friday evening. Once he arrived home with a book for me. It was *Our India—1953* by Minoo Masani and it was I think given him by the author in 1956. Masani was a barrister trained in London but gave up practice at the Bombay Bar to join the freedom fighters in the quest for independence. He admired the Soviet Union, visited Russia during his student days in the late 1920s and was drawn into the Communist Party. However, the horrors of Stalin's brutal leadership in the 1930s repelled him and he came to question Marxist dogma, renounce communism and completely rethink his socialist ideals.

When Gandhi launched his Quit India Movement in 1942, Masani resigned his job and launched himself into the campaign. Like many others he was imprisoned and on his release from jail he entered politics. Having discarded socialism his alternative was a mixed economy in a free and open society. He was elected to the Lok Sabha or Lower House of the Indian Parliament as an Independent in 1957 and in 1959 with C. Rajagopalachari he founded the liberal conservative Swatantra Party which by the 1967 general elections was the single largest party in opposition. In 1971 when the so-called Indira Wave swept all opposition parties aside, Masani, highly principled and insistent on discipline, resigned as president of the party and from party politics as well.

The first *Our India* was published by Oxford University Press before Independence in 1940 and sold over 500,000 copies. It was a prescribed textbook in schools even before independence though the book was withdrawn when the author parted company with Prime Minister Jawaharlal Nehru and the then establishment. The 1953 publication has a preface from Masani saying that there can be few parallels in history for the incredible changes that shaped India in the thirteen years since the first publication. World War II and then Independence and Partition changed the lives of the millions of people whose home was India. He says that *Our India* helped make Indians more 'planning-minded' and that the first book was about the future. The second shows, he says, how 'the present has to a certain extent caught up with the future'. It is essentially the same book with some updates, importantly the maps and the title of Chapter 1 has been altered from *One in Five* to *One in Seven*—one man in every seven is an Indian and the other six are he says, 'an American, a European, a Negro, an Arab, A Russian and a Chinese'.

The cover says 'with many new illustrations by C.H.G. Moorhouse' and these in black and white, are graphic and alluring. Some could have come from *Tales of the Arabian Nights* with overtones of Soviet poster art. A giant with one foot on the Deccan and one in the Arabian Sea is pouring water into the Ganges and breathing storm-clouds over the Himalayas. In the words of the book 'this is the jinn that could be conjured up by Aladdin's lamp ... our familiar friend, the Monsoon.' It is a pleasant way for Indian children to learn about the wealth and the problems facing their country. Nehruvian socialism and its accompanying five year plans were in full swing in India at the time so the author felt children definitely needed to be more 'planning-minded'. Masani believed India's most precious possessions are the sun, the land, the rivers and the mountains and above all the '*crores* upon *crores* of men, women and children who live in it.'

Although there are plenty of pie-charts the tone is kindly and avuncular without being patronising. The author treats his readers as 'good, practical, matter-of-fact young people of the twentieth century' and gives them plenty to think about other than statistics. In a discussion of forest products he tells us that the paper of which the book is made comes from bamboo forests in Mysore. He quotes a Russian poem called *Song of the Forest* which he says comes from a most exciting but inaccurate book *Moscow has a Plan* revealing the doubts he had about some aspects of Soviet plans and collectives. There is also a quote from the famous Bengali verse novel by Jasimuddin, *The Field of the Embroidered Quilt,* which though tragic, brings to life the simplest forms of village life. The stanzas quoted call on the clouds to open and let the soft rain gently fall. He advocates cottage industry and environmental awareness and concludes by suggesting 'let's all sing together a song from one of our great poets, Mohammad Iqbal.' The poem is printed first in Hindi and then while admonishing children that they should understand it, he also gives the English translation which starts with 'The finest country in the world is our India, We are its nightingales, it is our rose-garden.' He was never happier than when amongst children and his first and last books were for them.

Masani has been described as free India's most eminent Liberal and as the 'quintessential dissenter'. I once sat next to the former Prime Minister of Australia, Malcolm Fraser, at a dinner. I listened to what he had to say all night which was very interesting but eventually I politely initiated a topic and told him that my late father had also been a Liberal MP. Mr Fraser asked me his name and when I replied he said 'Oh one of the dissenters.' 'Dissenters?' I queried, to which he replied that in his view debate had been of a much higher quality in 'those days' because of the involvement of this group of committed back-benchers. So if it was Minoo Masani himself who gave Dad the book, then the two dissenters probably had a very interesting conversation.

Dad was a member of the Parliamentary Foreign Affairs Committee and one weekend at home in Sydney we had a special visitor for afternoon tea. It was a spur of the moment thing but Mum, who was a splendid creator of afternoon teas, cooked up a storm and invited a couple of neighbours to meet an eminent

Indian politician then visiting Australia. She was Mrs Lakshmi Menon, an MP from Kerala who later became India's Minister of State for External Affairs. My brother and I were stationed on the bus-seat at the top of our lane to help the Commonwealth Car find our house which was notoriously difficult to locate. We knew what these cars looked like because one came to collect Dad and bring him home when Parliament was sitting. We were perched on the bus-seat when the car came slowly down the hill. Six-year-old Maitland jumped up and put his hand up in a policeman's stop sign which made Mrs Menon chuckle. She was absolutely lovely and I guess that was another positive signal pointing me towards India. She told us how once touring England with a friend, their car had broken down. They walked to the nearest farmhouse where they were aggressively shooed away by the ignorant people who thought they were gypsies! She seemed unbelievably exotic to me.

My first visit to India was in the long university holidays of the Australian summer of 1968/1969. I went in a group of students from all over Australia. I was studying English at night at Macquarie University and working in a secretarial job in Sydney during the day. The group part of the trip only lasted for the first two or three days after our arrival in Madras. Then I went with five others to Mysore where we had been allocated home-stays with Indian families. This was the gentlest and most fortunate introduction to the country and I am still in touch with my hosts. It was the start of the great Indian passion.

After a month in the south I had teamed up in Bombay with Jane Sheaffe, a clever Agricultural Science graduate who went on to study Medicine. Together our travels took us all over northern India and eventually we arrived in Calcutta for our flight home. We stayed at the old Salvation Army Hostel in Sudder Street, now replaced by a new, modern building. The accommodation was very basic but in 1969 we thought it pretty good. We made regular sorties to Park Street for cold coffee and cake at Flury's and into New Market for presents to take home. In New Market I bought a book called *Two under the Indian Sun* by Jon and Rumer Godden. It is a vivid description of the life they led as little English girls in a town called Naryanganj, in the then East Bengal of India. It had become East Pakistan when they wrote the book and I bought it and now it is Bangladesh.

All the extra details left out of *Louisa* are here, magical images conjured up from words to work like a film loop in an art exhibition, making a perfect changing background to the story of the life to which they returned after a year's stay in the greyness in London. They had arrived there when they were five and six and would have stayed in England with their dour grandmother and maiden aunts for all their school years, growing further and further away from their parents and siblings and losing their memories of India. But in November 1914 when danger had intervened in the form of zeppelins over London another, far more amiable aunt from the other side of the family, came to take them away from the peril and back to the loving warmth of their own family circle in India.

The family home was in Narayanganj, a large and commodious square building situated on the banks of what the children called the Lakya River, now called the Shitalakshya, part of the great network of the Brahmaputra. The river was the reason the family lived in Narayangunj as Fa was employed by the Brahmaputra River Steam Navigation Company. When they arrived home by river-boat, all their senses were immediately alert to the sounds, smells, colour and feel of India. It was such a contrast to the narrow, colourless, circumscribed life they had led in London. Their first meal at home sounds like manna—rich chicken pillau followed by an orange mousse. No more 'hateful, sauceless cod', cabbage in water and heavy cabinet pudding. There were laughing people, green lawn, pretty flowers, tall trees and limitless games. Narayanganj is not so far from little Henry's Berhampore on the Bhagirathi River, part of the great network of the Ganges. The Bengali countryside would be much the same then as now, the cycle of rice and jute crops growing and being harvested, busy bazaars and colourful festivals. Even closer, less than 50 kilometres as the crow flies, is a town called Faridpur, the name of the village not far from a river connected to the Ganges mentioned in *Louisa*. All these stories can somehow be nicely connected.

The wonderful thing about a passion for India is that is awakened and enlarged so easily. When I reviewed *The Good Muslim* a gripping book by a young Bangladeshi writer, Tahmima Anam, it drove me back to reading more regional history. Though eventually enlivened by hope, it is a tragic story of the terrible war in 1971 that brought the birth of the People's Republic of Bangladesh, as Anam would say, 'the broken wishbone of a country'. That was the year my baby boy was born and I remember taking him on a showing-off afternoon visit to a friend who backed the Pakistanis and couldn't believe that I thought the Indians with the Mukti Bahini would be the victors. Her husband was in the Department of Foreign Affairs and mine was only a farmer, so how could I possibly know.

Reading more about some of the historical figures in the novel I find that the wonderful Jahanara Imam came originally from Murshidabad. The character only referred to as The Dictator is Ershad and I was shocked all over again at the reaction of Sheik Mujib to the unborn babies of poor women who had been raped by Pakistani soldiers. Their mothers were heroes but the babies were filth and it was considered better to be rid of them. I returned to Faridpur and wondered all over again about Louisa's home in India. The real Faridpur was named after a 12th century Sufi saint, Shah Sheikh Fariduddin. It was known for the fine quality of its jute, its many mostly Hindu zamindari families and it was famous as a focal point for political movements against the British. Several important meetings of the Indian Independence movement were held there and attended by Mahatma Gandhi, Subhash Chandra Bose and Rabindranath Tagore. Whether as a cause or a result of this, the area produced many prominent Bengali politicians and cultural figures, including Sheikh Mujibur Rahman.

One famous literary figure is Jasimuddin, born in Faridpur District in 1903. He is said to be the only pastoral poet of Bangladesh and was a pioneer of the progressive and non-communal cultural movement during the East Pakistan era. He died in 1976, five years after Bangladeshi independence. He collected folk literature including more than 10,000 folk songs and he wrote much on the interpretation and philosophy of Bengali folklore. He studied at

Calcutta University, lectured at the Dhaka University and later joined the Department of Information of Broadcasting where his roles ranged from radio announcer to the post of Deputy Director.

Jasimuddin published more than fifty volumes of poetry alone and with such an enormous oeuvre it is almost sinful to say that I have only read one of his poems. However, *Nakshi Kanthar Math* or *The Field of the Embroidered Quilt*, long enough to be termed a verse novel, is considered to be his masterpiece. His work concentrated on rural life and tradition and his depictions of the Bengali countryside, its people and their traditions are beautiful. Tagore said of his poetry that it has 'a new beauty, a new taste and a new expression'.

On my first visit to Bangladesh I was very keen to look at *nakshi kanthas*, the beautiful needle-worked quilts from Bengal. I had been given an old one and I had seen interesting examples in the collection of the Craft Museum in New Delhi. The word *kantha* comes from the Sanskrit word for rags and originally *kanthas* were old *saris* and *dhotis* stitched into quilts by thrifty housewives. The garments were worn but when sewn together in three or four or more thicknesses, they became wonderfully warm and familiarly comforting quilts. The oldest quilts are usually white in colour with plain borders of red and black. A simple running stitch was used to quilt the layers of cloth together and colourful pictorial designs were filled in with satin and stem stitch using thread drawn from the coloured borders of the original garments.

The name *nakshi kantha* really comes from Jasimuddin's 1939 poem, about passionate love and deep sorrow. With his deep love and awareness of Bengali culture and tradition, he seems to have been the first person to recognise the real significance of the *kantha* and its association with the lives of the women of rural Bengal. His mother embroidered beautiful quilts so he had been aware of them from early childhood. He succeeded so well in immortalising them that the appellation *nakshi*, meaning figured or decorated, prefaces *kantha* whenever people now speak of the quilts. It does in fact distinguish the modern, embroidered and often very sophisticated quilts from the humble, unadorned ones still to be seen in villages which are now much more colourful, made often of machine-printed saris. Jasimuddin's story is about a village love story between the man, Rupa, and the woman, Shuja. They marry but Rupa loses his mind after fighting over stolen land. He abandons poor Shuja who continues to embroider scenes from their life together in her quilt. She dies and the quilt is laid upon her tomb. Rupa returns, wraps himself in the quilt and he too dies to compound the tragedy.

The production of these beautifully decorated quilts had become less vital and interesting until after the liberation of Bangladesh. The revival of the technique is linked to both a sense of national difference which inspired the resurgence of indigenous crafts, and the need to provide for tens of thousands of women left destitute during the war. A start was made in 1972 but the real revival did not get underway for another ten years when several Non-Government Organisations became involved. Important too was the opening in 1981 of a new five star hotel in Dhaka where large and magnificent *kanthas* were a focus of the decor, showing pride in Bangladeshi culture and inspiring visitors to buy one to take home.

Despite the fact that Bangladesh is predominantly Muslim, many Hindu motifs remain and there are many Hindu *kantha* embroiderers. The central image is often a lotus or a mandala and ceremonial *raths* or temple cars used in Hindu religious processions are popular motifs. Images of village life and nature tie in with Jasimuddin's poem. Geometric designs more in keeping with Islam are also popular. *Kanthas* range in size from pieces small enough to be inserted into a greeting card to king-size quilts and are now made from new cloth. I bought quite a collection and showed them in an exhibition in Canberra with a percentage of the sales profits going to a marvellous Bangladeshi NGO.

Surovi is a charity set up in 1979 by Syeda Iqbal Mand Banu aimed at helping underprivileged children, principally by education. Realising how many children have to work to help support their families, some of the schools conducted by Surovi run three sessions daily so a working child could attend a session that fitted into the working day. Some classes I saw were being conducted outdoors in the large compound of the founder's home. Another was located in a crowded building in a place where refugees lived. The school had been established for Bihari children, the grand-children of people who left Bihar in India after Partition in 1947 who were then unable to afford to migrate to Pakistan in 1971. They are a sad group of virtually stateless people, forgotten by most of the world. Other little schools are conducted in unusual settings, in a garage or under shade in an employer's garden. Elsewhere there are more formal primary, secondary and vocational courses for children and adult literacy classes and the organisation has branches all over Bangladesh. In the west many people tend to think that the term NGO essentially means foreign help but it is important to remember that there are thousands of dedicated and successful indigenous organisations everywhere in developing countries.

Narayanganj, home of Jon and Rumer Godden, is the port which serves Dhaka, less than 20 miles away. In the mid-18th century, after the Battle of Plassey, the area was leased to a *thakur* or local chieftan called Lakshmi Narayan. He dedicated property along the river banks for the worship of the god Narayan, another name for Vishnu, which gives the name to the town. It was and remains an important centre for the production of jute.

A completely unrelated fact is that the brothel in the town, established during British rule, was until its closure in the year 2000, the largest in Bangladesh. The Indo-Bangladesh border areas, a stretch of more than 2,000 kilometres, have been defined by a fence since 1986 constructed by the Indian government in an attempt to curb smuggling and illegal migration. Rice, cattle and other goods still find their way through the porous border where many stretches are actually under waterways. 'Other goods' is a euphemism for the tragedy of human trafficking, particularly of young Bangladeshi girls for prostitution, a sad sequel to the old brothel. They are promised a better life across the border in India and become what is known as flying or floating f.s.w.'s, female sex workers. Many are underage and suffer great exploitation by madams, pimps, patrons and even the Border Security Forces. We saw the smartly turned out sentries at the gates of BSF camps—men wearing wonderful cockaded turbans. Members of the Force are alleged to extract bribes and favours. Smuggling and sexual exploitation are intertwined and women are always the losers. On the Indian side of the border human rights organisations and charitable trusts try to help with rehabilitation projects and healthcare but many of these poor unfortunate women and their children find no help at all.

The Godden sisters did not of course describe the brothel or know of the tragic development that has overtaken some women in the place they loved so much as children. But their perceptive eyes took in just about everything else which they presented in fascinating detail. I enjoyed the book so much I handed it over to my mother soon after I returned home. Her enjoyment was very much heightened when she found that the address of the Godden grandmother and the four icy maiden aunts in Maida Vale was almost the same as her own in 1939. They lived at 4 Randolph Gardens and she was at Number 14A, just across the road from a large and impressive church. She was there on the day Great Britain went to war with Germany. She joined a First Aid post but came home on one of the last ships to pass through the Suez Canal. Soon after her arrival back in Sydney she joined the Army Nursing Corps and was assigned as one of the nursing sisters to the Hospital Ship 'Manunda'.

It is a vivid and enchanting book filled with incredible images and my mother twenty years later bought me the first volume of Rumer Godden's autobiography *A Time to Dance, No time to Weep*. It includes photographs which brought the earlier book even more to life — I adore biographies with photographs of the subjects who start to become friends. There is a little piece of paper in the title page with Mum's hand-writing saying 'You will love this.' Re-reading *Two Under the Indian Sun* now more than forty years after I bought it, as well as presenting the never-failing allure of India, there is also within the story a tenuous link with my mother which a generation later grew a little stronger.

My son James was posted to the Australian High Commission in London in 2001 and the next year I went to give grandmotherly help when Amanda, my daughter-in-law, was to have their second baby. By chance they had rented a very nice flat in Maida Vale, on the corner of Edgeware Road and St John's Wood Road and over the six weeks that I spent there, I got to know the neighbourhood quite well, especially the parks where I would take Oscar, then aged two, to play in the summer sunshine. Each Sunday I went to a different church for an early morning service. It was invariably quite discouraging with congregations of three or four ancient and creaky people, usually a somewhat grumpy priest and worst of all, no music. That is until I walked further one week and went to Saint Augustine's, Kilburn.

It was a good twenty minutes brisk walk and I arrived just in time for the Solemn High Mass to start. The congregation was large with many worshippers from the West Indies and the South Asia. When I arrived there were three men in the front pew, two of whom were servers, speaking in sign language. When Mass began there were six or eight servers, looking very fine in their black and white robes. One was a very big Pakistani boy who received a special blessing before going to a Scout Jamboree in the USA. Another was a smaller African boy whose father was also a server. None of those three were the sign language boys.

There were clouds of incense and many bells, not much kneeling for prayers and we sat to sing two of the excellent hymns. At the conclusion of the service, the priest and congregation turned to the statue of the Virgin in the right transept and said the Hail Mary. I had never heard this in an Anglican church before, but I knew it well. When I was three I had been placed by the wireless each night to listen to nice stories and songs while my mother was feeding the baby. It was 2SM, the Catholic radio station in Sydney in the 1950s. At six o-clock each evening the program the program was interrupted by the Angelus which I learned off by heart. When my parents discovered this incipient conversion they were amused but reconverted me by switching over to 2FC and the seduction of The Muddle-headed Wombat of The Children's Hour and the very secular Argonauts to which I became a lifelong devotee.

I bought a few post-cards after the service, a Victorian interior of the church, showing chairs with rush seats similar to those still in use. The church was built between 1871 and 1878 and was designed by John Loughborough Pearson, RA, an architect famous for churches.

175

He also designed the fine murals in 1891. It is considered to be one of the best examples of Victorian Gothic Revival architecture and the ultimate expression of the Catholic Revival of the Church of England. There are many beautiful stained glass windows and it seems much loved. It is known as the Cathedral of North London though it is not a cathedral in the official sense of the word. The interior vaulting and stone sculpture are reminiscent of 13th century Gothic churches and the tower and soaring spire of more than 77 metres give it the cathedral status. The church seems to nestle into a grassy slope and in spite of its grandeur, it is nevertheless approachable.

A nice old man spoke to me and I told him that my mother had worshipped here all those years ago. 'Oh what was her name?' he asked which I thought very touching and sweet, as though he just might have remembered her. The building where she lived had been knocked down and an ugly modern block built in its place. I sent her one of the postcards and later I wrote a poem which then seemed to encompass a lot of what had passed. Funny that Jamie & Amanda should have chosen that part of London in which to make their home and just recently I have visited a couple of lovely new friends who also live there. If I win the lottery I'll buy a flat in Maida Vale.

Saint Augustine's, Kilburn
All hearty and hale in Maida Vale.
My mother lived for a time in 'thirty-nine in a flat
across the road from the parish church
settled like a mighty fortress at the bottom of a grassy slope.
Neo-Gothic, Anglo-Catholic, full of the smell of incense
as the world advanced to war.
Here too in nineteen fourteen lived small Jon and Rumer
Godden come from India
to stay with neo-Gothic, Anglo-Catholic aunts
who entertained neo-Gothic, Anglo-Catholic clergy
whose black clothes were full of the smell of incense
as the world advanced to war.
Solemn High Mass one Sunday morning in the year two

thousand and one.
But for John Wesley I might have been in Rome.
The acolytes were six or eight and two were deaf and dumb.
Smells and bells—the smells intense, the bells were lost on some.
The priest like a cardinal in one of those hats that now we know
are all the go in Uzbekistan.
Ecumenical headgear could be something for world peace
as the world advances to war.
Exchanges in hats and then residencies—gap years for prelates,
an imam for an archdeacon, a muezzin for a precentor.
Saint Augustine of Hippo, for whom the church is named,
should he be blamed?
He who believed just wars avenge injuries?
I bought a post-card afterwards
to send home to my mother—frail, no longer
hale eighty-eight and more than a half a century
away from Maida Vale.

Rikki Tikki Tavi, the story of a pet mongoose from Kipling's *Jungle Book* was included in a red-covered selection of stories we had as a Sixth Class reader. I like mongooses and always feel it is a good omen to see one early in a visit to India. I've seen them in Lodi Gardens in Delhi, so it's not a matter of having to go into the *mofussil*. *Rikki Tikki Tavi* is set in a British cantonment at a place called Segowlee, once an area known for its indigo. It is now generally spelled Sugauli and is a small town in the state of Bihar, close to the border with Nepal. That was the background location given by the author but Rikki-tikki tavi's garden, scene of his brave deeds, is actually that of Belvedere House, a colonial bungalow in which Kipling lived as a paying guest in Allahabad in 1888. In the story Kipling describes the 'large garden, only half-cultivated, with bushes as big as summer-houses of Marshal Niel roses, lime and orange trees, clumps of bamboos, and thickets of high grass'.

The garden he describes was a great contrast to that of his parents in Lahore with whom he had lived while working as Assistant

Editor on the *Civil and Military Gazette*. The senior Kiplings believed that trees and shrubs harboured insects which would bring dread disease to the household. They would be horrified now to see the site of the home in which they lived when Rudyard was born. Within the Sir J.J. Institute of Applied Art close to the great edifice of Victoria Terminus, now more properly known as the Chhatrapati Shivaji Railway Terminus, the Institute was formerly called Sir Jamsetjee Jeejebhoy School of Art. Kipling's father, John Lockwood Kipling, was a professor at the school and became its first Dean. The Kipling's house was destroyed by fire but replaced in 1878 by a pretty building, unoccupied now but still known as the Dean's House. Despite its heritage listing, it is in a very tumbledown state. The jungly garden would have caused the Kiplings nervous despair. In the shady greenness there are tall poincianas, mango and ashoka trees, leggy dracaenas and crotons poking through tangled undergrowth, all a delightful environment for insect vectors creeping towards the pale turquoise two-storey wooden building. The Kipling compound at Lahore was treeless, barren and dusty, known locally as Bikanir House after Bikaner, a princely state located in the desert of Rajputana.

The nick-name would have appealed to Edward Hamilton Aitkin, a humorous naturalist who wrote mostly on India's wildlife under the nom de plume of EHA. Serving in the Customs and Salt Department of the Government of Bombay, he was posted to several places during his career in India. His first station was Kharaghoda, located in the desolate Little Rann of Kutch, where he began writing his charming essays. Kharaghoda became 'Dustypore' in his book *The Tribes on my Frontier* published in 1883. I have an 1887 third edition which once belonged to a lady from Poona.

Kipling had come to Allahabad in 1887, promoted to the more important office of the *Pioneer*, known colloquially as *The Pi*, the most widely-read paper in Northern India at the time. The city was far larger and more Europeanised than Lahore, and Hindu rather than Muslim which did not appeal to the young journalist. At first he lived in the bachelors' quarters of the Allahabad Club but departed for the more pleasant atmosphere of a family home.

The house belonged to Samuel Hill, professor of science at Muir College and his American wife, Edmonia, known as Ted. She was seven years older than Rudyard, and not a particular beauty, but she became his confidante and he her devotee. Teddy, Rikki-tikki tavi's small master, is probably named for Ted Hill.

David Mitford, the father of the famous Mitford sisters, kept a pet mongoose for hunting rats in his office. Lady Pamela Mountbatten also had a pet mongoose given her in Delhi while her father as Viceroy supervised the transfer of power to independent India and Pakistan. Neola, which means simply mongoose, had poor breakfast manners but departed India for first England and then Malta and was introduced to King George VI and other members of the Royal Family. After saving Teddy from the evil Nagaina, Rikki-tikki tavi secured his place in the household for evermore, even accompanying Teddy to bed but he is unlikely to have travelled by air back to England with his family.

Téa Obreht won the Orange Prize in 2011 for her novel, *The Tiger's Wife* which is set in an unnamed Balkan country now and in the immediate past. It's a fascinating story combining myth and fairy tale, the horrors of war and displacement and the joys of a loving family. The grandfather's great treasure which he kept with him for the whole of his life, is a copy of *The Jungle Book* given him as a child by the village apothecary. The stories of the animals and the morals drawn from the law of the jungle, parallel what is happening in the strife-torn country of Obreht's novel. It propelled me into reading the stories all over again, not just *Rikki Tikki Tavi*.

Zoos and what happens to animals caught in the midst of war has been the basis for several novels. The sight of the colossal mound of a poor dead elephant in the midst of a bombed German city is an extraordinary thing. And what of the tigers? The tiger in Obreht's book, escaped from the zoo on the ancient Citadel, learns how to be a wild animal again in the mountains and snow of the country at war. He learns how to love someone who could be seen as a version of Mowgli. Though capable of killing, he seems a far nobler creature than the vengeful Shere Kahn.

Where would Richard Parker from *Life of Pi* sit in the order or tigers? My friend Christiane Lawin and I visited Bithur, a small town on the Ganges twenty-two kilometres from Kanpur, said to be the centre of the earth. In the ancient Puranas, Bithur is referred to as Brahmavarta, the place where Lord Brahma began the creation of the world. A nail embedded in the steps of the *ghat* is said to have been fallen from Brahma's wooden slipper. It is considered to be the place where poor blameless Sita was abandoned by Lord Rama to lead her life in exile and is also said to be where the sage Valmiki wrote the great epic, the Ramayana.

That day it was raining and quite cold. On the *ghats*, to the left of the shrine marking the earth's navel, a marriage ceremony was taking place. The groom stripped down to baggy underpants and a conical, brimmed hat decorated with silvery beads and artificial flowers the whole encased in a plastic bag. Shivering, he steadied himself with the hand of a friend, and descended the steps to immerse himself in the sacred waters of the muddy brown river. As he submerged his hat floated away to the east and he returned without it to his bride waiting on the steps, her face hidden by her pretty red *bandhani* sari. A couple of priests were busy with the business of prayer and ceremony when we heard an utterance which sounded like 'Richard Parker'. 'Did you hear that?' asked an amazed Christiane. 'I sure did!' said I. We asked our guide in a Hinglish accent what 'rricharrdparrka' might mean in Hindi and he answered, somewhat puzzled 'Somebody's name?'

I haven't quite finished with *Rikki Tikki Tavi*. The reason we happened to be in Bithur was an overnight stay in Kanpur en route the next day to Allahabad and the Kumbh Mela. After Kanpur the weather improved — the rainfall one day in Lucknow was the highest ever recorded, and most unusually, in February. Once in Allahabad we first visited All Saints Cathedral, unfortunately closed and then the Swaraj Museum and Anand Bhavan, both former residences of the Nehru family and very interesting indeed and full of Indian tourists. The next stop was to find Belvedere House, Kipling's home for a year and that of the real Rikki-tikki tavi.

I've had some unsuccessful sleuthing attempts when looking for sites linked to famous writers. Even with information from her daughter, Jane Murray-Flutter, I found the wrong house for Rumer Godden's childhood in Narayanganj near Dhaka. It was still an interesting hunt and the wrong house was a wonderful old wreck. But in Allahabad the search was highly successful. Arvind Krishna Mehrotra is one of India's finest contemporary poets and an esteemed academic in the field of English literature. His book *Partial Recall* is a collection of brilliant essays on literature and literary history, scrutinising works by Indian writers either written in English or translated from Indian languages into English. Among Mehrotra's particular interests are the poems of the medieval mystic Kabir which his translations approach in a modern voice. In this context of Kabir, information about Kipling's home was revealed.

Mehrotra lives in Allahabad where he is Head of the Department of English and Modern European Languages at the University of Allahabad. In his essay *Translating Kabir* he tells of the complex ways Kabir's songs have been transmitted relatively recently, even five hundred years after his death. He described two tall crumbling red-brick gateposts across the road from Allahabad University's senate house. They mark the entrance to Belvedere Printing Works. It was easy to find and we walked up a lane and turned left at a corner where an unsmiling man was solemnly ironing a great pile of washing on a concrete bench. As we continued towards an old colonial house, a small car drove past us through the gateway. The driver was a friendly and polite gentleman who was the great, great grandson of the man who founded the Belvedere Press in 1903. Anupam Agarwal is the fifth generation of the family to run the Belvedere Printing Works and whilst some of his ancestors' details are hazy, he did know that the house was purchased from a Mr Hill by his great-great grandfather, Baleshwar Prasad. He had been a teacher in Benares, a journalist writing in Hindi and had translated Shakespeare into Urdu. He moved to Allahabad where he became a publisher, specialising in the works of North Indian poet saints such as Kabir and Mirabhai. His first selection of Kabir's poems came out in 1907 followed by 8 more and now, more than a hundred years later, they remain in print in Hindi in the Santabani Series.

Anupam invited us into his home which still houses the printing works and has been divided into more than one dwelling with modern extensions to various parts of the building. We sat in a foyer with small sky-light windows located close to the high ceilings, a way in which the British fought the blazing heat of the summer. In a partitioned room next door, stocks of books were neatly stacked and the scene was dominated by a full-length portrait of Baleshwar Prasad. He has a neat white beard and is dressed in a black hat and coat and grey trousers. He holds a scrolled paper and looks benignly over the scene, pleased that his legacy remains.

Anupam well knew that Kipling had resided in his family home but he was unfamiliar with *The Jungle Book* and *Rikki Tikki Tavi*. I asked him if he had ever seen a mongoose in the garden and he said oh yes, from time to time. Perhaps they are the descendants of the Rikki-tikki. The compound is much sub-divided but there is a pretty garden attached to the house with a tangle of tulsi, neat marigolds, dahlias, roses and chrysanthemums growing in pots, a row of ashoka trees against a wall, pomegranate and guava bushes and a lime tree.

These investigations really prove not a thing but they are fun and put life and context into the smallest tale. I had wanted to visit Anand Bhavan, the mansion built by Motilal Nehru, for ten years since my last visit to Allahabad which happened to be on a Monday when it is closed. It was certainly worth the wait and ten years ago I certainly did not know that only minutes away, on Motilal Nehru Road itself I would find Rikki-tikki tavi's garden.

It's a strange little collection of stories which I have remembered or discovered. Perhaps there are no really ripping yarns but I did find *Louisa* pretty exciting when I was ten. Certainly the description of cautionary tale fits *Little Henry and his Bearer* but the small group of stories that influenced or interested me as a child have all been charming to rediscover.

With Mrs Lakshmi Menon, MP at Northwood, 1957

CHATTERBOX. 177

"'Twill keep thy old bones warm on a winter's night, wise woman,' she said."

From *Louisa* by Mrs Hobart Hampton, Chatterbox Annual, 1923. Illustration by Harold White

The family on New Year's Day 2007 at Udaipur, Rajasthan

Being Carsick

It's not so much an Indian affliction but it can be all too obvious while travelling there. On my first visit to India as the naive first-time-to-anywhere traveller in a mini-skirt, I set off by myself from the kind and nurturing bosom of my lovely home-stay family in Malgudi, I mean Mysore, to the tea garden town of Munnar in the neighbouring state of Kerala. Travelling by bus I had no idea of the route we took in the 200 kilometre six-hour journey to Coimbatore where I spent a night. Mysore is located on the southern part of the Deccan Plateau and for the first few hours we travelled through flat or undulating country, sometimes through dense forests.

The first part of the journey didn't seem to take too long but then we arrived at the Dhimbam Ghat Road section and the edge of quite a hair-raising descent. There were 27 hairpin bends to negotiate as we wound our way down through spectacular scenery in this section of the Western Ghats, on the edge of the Nilgiris. After a while I realised the bus had become totally silent as we roared around each bend. I can clearly see the bus driver in my mind's eye, a big, muscular man in a khaki shirt, longish hair flopping on his pudgy face which was fixed in concentration as we rounded bend after bend, his strong arms almost wrestling the steering wheel. I think I was too frightened to feel sick but some poor people did and when someone rushed to the window there was a general rapid scrabbling by the passengers closest to the windows to pull down the canvas blinds to prevent the poor traveller's undigested breakfast come flying back inside. A far worse re-entry would be a stray head and in her novel *The Tailor of Giripul,* the author, Bulbul Sharma has a bus conductor say 'If you get sick in the bus, then sit by the hillside or else your head will be lopped off by an oncoming bus' which encouraged conversations among the passengers about the possibility or incidences of decapitation.

We didn't seem to slacken speed but at last we reached the bottom and as we rattled up to the first village on the plain, the driver took both hands off the wheel and clasping them together, he aimed a fast prayer at a shrine under a bodhi tree encircled by a stone seat and we hurtled on. Eventually in the late afternoon we arrived in the city of Coimbatore. I had been told of a safe place in which to stay and I walked from the bus station to the Woodlands Hotel. I had never before stayed in a hotel by myself, and I don't know how I knew what to do! My father or the parent of a friend had always done the needful at a hotel desk whenever I had stayed away from my home. I suppose innocence is enabling and I took a basic room, ordered dinner to be brought on a tray and I asked for information about how to travel on to Munnar the next day.

After half an hour or so, a small man with a face much marked by smallpox scars knocked on my door. He told me he knew how I could travel to Munnar and asked for the money to buy a train ticket. He returned with the ticket and the change and told me he would come to collect me at 5.00 the next morning to take me to the railway station. I was too completely out of my element to be the slightest bit hungry so after a shower I went to bed wrapped in the sheet which came folded in a square on top of the bed, with my handbag rolled up with me. I hardly slept and was ready for my protector when he arrived with a cycle rickshaw promptly at 5.00.

Coimbatore was a city of factories and textile mills and I remember seeing white wraith-like shapes walking in the poorly lit streets, I guess people going to work on the next shift. It was still pitch dark when we reached the station. We sat down on a platform bench to wait for the train. Carriages were being shunted, somewhere an engine was busily puffing and there just a few yards away in our direct line of sight, on the edge of the platform, a man was masturbating in time with the engine's sounds. Oh Lord, this sort of thing didn't happen in Sydney, we didn't even live near a train-line! I looked away but my protector took the situation in hand and hustled me into the Lady's Only Waiting Room where I stayed until my train arrived. The ticket he had bought me was for first class which was quite a good thing for my first solo train trip and that kind man ushered me to my seat, I suppose quite relieved that his good deed had come to a safe conclusion. 'Whatever can I give you for all your help?' I asked him to which he replied in the wonderful phrase which I would often hear again and which I now use sometimes myself. 'Madam' he said 'that is your will and pleasure.' So I gave him some money which pleased him very much and off he went into the still dark morning.

That first epic solo journey continued for the whole of that day. My seat was in a four berth compartment and when I entered, a fine-looking gentleman was lowering himself from an upper berth where he must have spent the night—I suppose the train had come from Bangalore or Madras, now Bengaluru or Chennai. He managed to change from his night attire into trousers without any immodest exposure though by now, the station at Coimbatore had taught me to turn my gaze anywhere else at the slightest prompt. He and I were bound for the same destination, the small town of Alwaye, now known as Aluva. Here, my earlier protector had told me I should get off the train and catch the bus for Munnar. The journey by train from Coimbatore took five hours or so and now I know that I travelled in quite a long westerly, then southerly direction towards the coast and almost to Cochin. In fact Alwaye is now part of Greater Cochin and a very busy station though it did not seem so then. The first person I saw when the train pulled into Alwaye was a lady suffering from leprosy stomping determinedly down the platform. Far from begging or looking destitute, she looked incredibly purposeful. Minus her nose and several fingers, she walked in the strange gait of those whose feet are also afflicted by this horrible disease. That whole flashed vision of her out of the train window as we steamed in must have taken only been of a few seconds but it is as clear now as if I had taken a photograph.

My new protector helped me out of the train and into a waiting room and he went to see when the Munnar bus would arrive. Forty years ago waiting rooms often housed pieces of very nice furniture and here in Alwaye there was a pretty davenport stuck in a corner. Everything always had a ghastly white serial number painted in an obvious place but even that couldn't quite spoil this charming out of place piece of the past. My friend came back to tell me the time of departure and invited me to go to his house to wait. 'Oh no thank you,' I said 'that's so kind of you but I think I will just wait here.' He gave me a sideways nod and disappeared, to return in time to escort me to the bus. The second act of kindness and wasn't I just so lucky?

That journey made people car-sick too, winding 120 kilometres up hills into gorgeous tea country. With nothing in my stomach again I felt ok and I had the constant, nervous, jabbing preoccupation of how I was going to manage when I got to the end of the journey — the bus terminated at Munnar. I had been told to go to the High Range Club where someone would ring the Grahamsland Tea Estate, my final destination. The journey took about four hours and all the way up the hill there were confusing milestones, sometimes we seemed to be further away from Munnar rather than closer. I think some were miles and some were kilometres. I kept hoping the higher number of whatever the linear measurement was the correct one and that by the time we reached Munnar the bus would have miraculously emptied and I wouldn't be so noticeable. No such luck, whenever any passengers departed, more climbed aboard but all journeys do eventually come to an end. My suitcase was on top of the bus, packed in amongst baskets and boxes and extra passengers. When we all clambered out of the bus I found the man in charge of the luggage. I pointed to my bag and looked up just in time to also get a full view straight up the porter's dhoti and I can vouch for the fact that just like the kilt, underpants are an optional extra.

The sky-blue Plymouth with chrome tailfins which was the family car in *The God of Small Things* was bought from an old English tea planter from Munnar. This wonderful book by Arundhati Roy which won the Booker Prize in 1997 is set in Kerala and partly in 1968 exactly when I visited. There are descriptions of 'evenly spaced vomit streaks' on buses but car-sickness is not something from which that family suffered. Shock and fear is what churns Estha's stomach and makes the poor little boy say to his mother 'Feeling vomity Ammu'. I think when he says this to his mother as he is sent away from home is one of the most wrenching scenes in any book I have ever read.

Another brilliant Indian novel to win the Booker Prize — in 2006 —

is Kiran Desai's *The Inheritance of Loss*. Returning to Kalimpong from an excursion to the library at Darjeeling and a Chinese lunch, poor Sai turns green. Father Booty urges her to look at the horizon which he says always helps. If you think about it, gazing at any philosophical horizon is a very sensible direction in any kind of adversity. But gazing at the tall ridges of the Himalayas doesn't help Sai's stomach at all, the car comes to an abrupt halt and as Desai writes, Sai gives them all 'another unfortunate look at their lunch now so much the worse for wear'. She is given a cup of icy cold water and sits in the sunshine. A little way down the hill buses are lined up at a road-block, their flanks splashed with streaks of vomit. Those mountain roads are a test to the strongest constitutions.

When I arrived in Jaipur at the start of six months' work for the Jaipur Virasat Foundation in 2006 I was on the point of being sick after a journey by road from Delhi. Normally it isn't such a bad journey with no hills at all and scarcely a bend in the road but some drivers are prone to swinging back and forth which is hopeless for feeble stomachs. Whatever it was, I felt totally wretched and had to be revived with soda water.

Weeks later on the first visit to India I travelled up to Simla and further on to Kufri where, with two other Australian students, I had a day or two of winter sports. For me it was just one day as I became a bit sick and spent the next in bed, weeping with homesickness and self-pity but looked after by the kindly man who was the manager of the tiny guesthouse in which we stayed. They had skis for hire which had once either belonged to or been donated by the German Embassy. A day on the slopes was very exhausting as we had to walk all the way up the mountain in order to ski down on a terrifying track, steep, icy and twisting. I had little possibility of stopping until I got to the bottom but at least I had skied once or twice in Australia and was capable of dependable snow-plough turns or even a mean stem christie though there was room for neither on this switchback slope. My two friends had never strapped on a ski in their lives before. One was a very fit bush-walker who bounded up the hill like a mountain goat on our first ascent. The other was quite stout and unathletic and she brought up the rear moaning softly. Was it fun? Yes it was but even though I was ill the next day I can't say I was devastated at missing out on another's days frolicking on the mountain. Perhaps I had delayed carsickness. The road was winding and narrow and coming back down by bus from Simla we saw a car over the edge of the road after a horrible accident. All this was too much and I have tried to avoid mountain roads at all costs ever since, not always successfully.

My childhood memories are punctuated by awful car journeys. As the firstborn in my family I set a poor standard by always being sick on even the short journeys across the Harbour to see my maternal grandparents. Later accompanied by a younger brother and sister, we were all sick in relay when we visited our father's family at Gosford, up that winding, dreadful road. Nothing could distract us from this anti-social behaviour and the journeys were misery with a stiff breeze blowing through the windows to make us feel better but which just made us feel cold as well as sick. I don't think we even asked much 'are we there yet?' as being car-sick first makes children very quiet and then leads to faint moans. Even Dad's recitation of Henry Kendall's *Bellbirds* at a certain point just before we came through the bush didn't distract us. Henry Kendall was part of family history. On my grandmother's front veranda there stood a wooden bench on which the famous poet is said once to have sat—some claim to fame! Finally we would see the Margin's Soft Drinks sign at the outskirts of Gosford which meant at last we were almost there.

The journeys were so unpleasant that after several years of them, if the visit was just for the day, we would drive to Hornsby, leave the car in the station car-park and make the rest of the journey by train. We loved those trains with their green leather seats and sepia photographs of famous New South Wales beauty spots, Katoomba's Three Sisters, the Megalong Valley and the Bridal Veil Falls. It was far more exciting and even cinders in the eye if we craned our heads out the windows were preferable to those terrible road-induced churning stomachs.

I've recently been on the same train journey on the streamlined, silver Tangara, rocketing through the dense vegetation on either side of the line. There are no rattles or smells but the view is still as spectacular as the line emerges from the bush and swoops down to the Hawkesbury River. There are many more houses along the line in old settlements that have existed there since the 19th century. Viewed from the train it is quite extraordinary to see number of sheds in their back-yards. Shed-making must really be a growth industry, some people own three or four. The tibouchinas were flowering and their bright purple flowers splashed many gardens with colour. Near Woy Woy mangroves in thickets grow close to the line, the prongs of new shoots punching through the mud. In the 1950s vendors used stand on the platform selling thin tall jars of oysters to train passengers. There are oyster farms in the river, little old wooden houses on the far shore and occasional glimpses of the old road winding its nauseating way through the forest. My brother met me at Gosford Station and I told him I was writing a memorial to our feeble stomachs. As we circled the roundabout at the station he enquired anxiously if I was about to do a re-enactment.

Dad knew all the stations off by heart from Central onwards and I remember the last few—Wondabyne, Woy Woy, Koolewong, Tascott, Point Clare, Gosford. Lovely names and they were something of a mantra. Tascott Dad said was named after T.A. Scott, a pioneer in the Australian sugar industry. My father's feat of memory was puny in comparison with the famous Mackerras family who knew all the stations between Sydney and Bourke. Malcolm who can still recite the list, says his elder brothers Neil and Alastair taught him this very valuable skill. Sir Charles once pacified a bolshy Australian in a London pub with such a recitation.

As we spent many of our childhood weekends travelling around 'The Parish' as Dad called his Federal Electorate, it was absolutely necessary to try and ward off the dreaded mal de Holden. It wasn't such a good look to have us arriving at fete, foundation-stone laying, naturalisation ceremony or church service, listless and with pale green complexions. This was the era of the Sunday afternoon drive and all over Australia family sedans were crammed with kids, Dad with his elbow out the open window and Mum often wearing a hat with a child or two in between them on the bench seat in the front, the rest seated in the back. My father was a careful driver and it wasn't his fault we were so hopelessly sick. I know very well the kind of driving which induces the churning. It's the swinging around corners style and the racing car take-offs from traffic lights which push the poor passengers back in their seats as though it was a rocket launch. I endured that the other day in the so-called courtesy car from a garage and thought that throwing up all over their expensive upholstery might give them the hint their standard of driving could be improved.

Many cars in the 1950s had been fitted with a trailing strip of black rubber like a licorice strap hanging down from under the rear bumper bar. A friend of mine thought they were to stop the car being struck by lightning but they were actually supposed to stop car-sickness. The theory might have been comforting but it was probably purely psychological. We didn't have one anyhow. My parents experimented with travel sickness pills. One brand just sent us straight to sleep and a clutch of comatose children was also not the image of the interested, happy family our parents hoped to project. Finally wonderful Kwells came to our rescue and we arrived, suffering from terrible thirst but otherwise ok. Mum would turn around before we reached the destination and aim her terrible, hard hairbrush at our heads making sure we were a credit to the Liberal Party. I still take Kwells. There were years of incident-free travel when I sat in the front of a car or even better, in the driver's seat, and I'm never sick in trains or even buses as long as I don't read. But now in the back seat of a van or a car it all returns, especially on mountain roads where I have dared to venture again.

I passed these unfortunate genes on to my children. As infants they suffered badly. At first Jamie sat up in his car-seat and seemed ok but then Emily, a year younger, seated in another good old 'safe n sound' side by side in the back seat, always seemed to surprise me when I had no change of clothes for her. Once I scrambled down an embankment to a creek and washed her little dress and then drove into town holding it out the window to dry. Of course it didn't dry and so then and at other times, I would carry her into a rather grotty store in Queanbeyan and buy the least offensive pair of pyjamas available. She always had plenty of pretty dresses and pyjamas were the cheapest option. I think she seemed to infect Jamie with the vomiting tendency because they did it regularly for years. Judicious removal of milk from pre-trip breakfasts sometimes helped. They became practised at recognising the signals and the plastic boxes which had become standard equipment in the back seat at least helped with the results.

When we had a year living in England, our old bomb of a Renault was terribly fumey in the back seat and travelling in the winding country lanes was purgatory for them. Travelling on some of those roads with high hedges is like being on a switchback with no escape. Jamie seemed to suffer more than Em in that generally difficult year. The poor child had to exit the car fast in the far west of Cumbria on a freezing November day where the gale-force wind on the coast of the Irish Sea quickly taught us which direction to face when being sick. There was nothing funny at all about that at the time but the next memorable occurrence really did have a rather amusing side.

The children and I were going to leave England behind for a few weeks and the first stage of our journey was to travel by overnight ferry from Harwich to a western point of Denmark and then on to Copenhagen by train where we were to stay with dear friends. We were living in East Anglia in a town we called East Drearham. The ferry departed late in the afternoon but there was quite a full day's worth of events to get through before we would wave goodbye in the gloaming. First my husband had to drive into Norwich to feed pages of figures into the university computer there to be collected later that day in Cambridge, then drive to London and catch a plane to Port Moresby. That was *his* agenda but meanwhile one of Emily's only pair of shoes had come apart and he insisted on fixing it himself. It was a little damp so he put it in the oven and then forgot about it. The shoe melted, Em sobbed but what to do! She had a pair of despised black school plimsolls so she unwillingly set off in those.

We drove in a southerly direction and somehow I misdirected us onto secondary roads. To make matters worse we were caught in the midst of a convoy of Army vehicles and the road was hardly wide enough to overtake. We were already running late when the warning signs suddenly were upon Jamie. 'We can't stop darling. Just stick your head out the window.' At that very moment we were travelling through a town called Long Sutton. It is so called because it is a linear town with habitation strung along the long road and Jamie was sick out the window for the entire length of the town. We looked straight ahead and told ourselves that nobody saw, we would never revisit the town and we weren't tough and heartless at all, we just couldn't miss that ferry. What a nightmare. By the time we reached Harwich, in silence, it was well after the ferry's departure time but there it still was, sitting tied up to the wharf almost it seemed on the edge of the green fields. We could hardly believe it. The children and I leapt from the car and started to run. I had the passports and my purse but I didn't care two pins about the rest of our stuff, it was a matter of getting to the barrier. Black spots were flashing in front of my eyes and we were steaming like race-horses but we tore over railway tracks and up a flight of steps to arrive in front of a man seated at a desk. 'Oh madam, do compose yourself.' he said phlegmatically. We made it. My husband panted up with our bags and despite the fact that the children were sea-sick all the way to Denmark, we arrived happily and the next day went to a smart shop in Copenhagen and bought Em a gorgeous new pair of shoes.

Em once vomited spectacularly all over the trouser-leg of a young man on the deck of the ferry taking us from Rameswaram in South India to Talaimannar in the north of Sri Lanka. That was the result of several most delicious fish-cakes ingested before too many turns on a razzle-dazzle roundabout sort of a thing on the boat. But I think that was the only injury to anyone outside the family circle. The young man was extremely polite and unfussed about it—saintly really.

My brother was once sick into his cap in the back seat of a neighbour's car returning home from the beach. He was such a good little polite boy he didn't like to ask to stop. His daughter, my niece, was taken as a special treat for a ride in a Rolls Royce owned by a neighbour's father. Unfortunately she had had a few too many footy franks shortly before the journey and had a very unfortunate episode in the glorious interior of the car. A friend of mine as a child once timed his need to be sick while crossing Sydney's Harbour Bridge where stopping is not permitted. He was told to stick his head out the window and did so but his aim was poor and it all dribbled down inside the door. The smell was so vile that the whole door of the family car had to be replaced. This is a true story. Another was told me by a friend travelling in Turkey with her mother-in-law. 'Don't look' she said but of course when anyone says that you generally do have to peep — oh revolting — there was a plastic bag passed around for communal random vomiting.

Indians used to be terrible vomiters on planes and render the washrooms unfit to enter by dumping full sick bags down the sink. Too frightful but true. They are still bad on buses and coming down from Mussoorie behind a bus this year our driver had to turn on the wipers several times to wash the windscreen. As airline passengers they have improved greatly over the decades with genes surely modified by the millions of diasporic South Asians, travelling all over the world, too smart to feel sick. There is however a new incarnation of Indian bus drivers in the South Asians who drive taxis all over Australia, who are maintaining the tradition of making their passengers feel frightful.

If fear is a contributing factor to being sick then one should definitely not travel in the buses owned by a well-known company in north India called Panicker's Travels. It is a very reputable company I hasten to add, pioneers in the field of package tours in India with almost fifty years of experience. Starting with one bus in 1967, now they have a huge fleet and claim to be a household word for tourists. Fortunately Mr Panicker's given name is not Manik which would be too much for the nervous traveller.

Penny and Ernst Tideman are friends who loved living in Delhi for more than twelve years. With their three children they travelled far and wide and had many intrepid adventures. Their youngest, Alexander, was not a good traveller and one trip on twisting mountain roads resulted in regurgitated *poori baji* in the map pocket behind the driver's seat which was very difficult to remove. The combination of mountain roads and altitude was a bad one for poor Alexander and his parents suggested when he was eight that perhaps he might like to stay with friends in Delhi rather than join the family on a trip to Ladakh. The road from Manali over the Rotang Pass and then along the Lahaul Valley towards the Spiti Valley was winding and long. The Kuzum La Pass between the two valleys on the way to Kaza is the third highest pass in the region at 4551 metres above sea level. The road had been completely deserted for hours as the car wound its way steadily up to the pass, poor Alexander who had insisted on coming, becoming more miserable with every bend in the road. At the top were some *chortens* and prayer flags so Ernst decided to stop. Alexander opened the door and promptly threw up—a good aim this time, not in the map pocket. There was no visible sign of habitation anywhere but within minutes two dogs arrived to dine on the remains of this second-hand breakfast. It was not Alexander's record for high altitude vomiting—that was on the way to Leh on the Chang La Pass which is 5360 metres above sea level. I have seen the photograph of the *chortens* at the top of the Kuzum La Pass but Penny does not have one of the dogs.

This is getting too disgusting for anyone to read but I may as well press on. I felt appalling in Sulawesi, seated in the back of a mini-bus going up to Rantepao in Torajaland from Ujung Pandang. So on my next journey in Indonesia I sat in the front of a crowded mini-bus on a journey from Solo to Jogjakarta. Unfortunately the 'seat' on which I sat must have been directly connected to the engine because it was blisteringly hot and there was absolutely nowhere to move. They weren't great journeys.

When we lived in Port-of-Spain we went to Maracas Beach every weekend. The road there was winding and frightful and on arrival I would have to lie quietly on the sand for twenty minutes before I felt all right again—the children too when they were there on holidays. We stayed long enough though to enjoy the beach, watching the little dusty brown pelicans diving into the waves beyond the breakers and lunch of shark and bake which we all adored. Strangely, the return journey from anywhere is never as bad as the outward. Why is this I wonder? Anticipation? Nerves? Whatever the psychological reason, I have resorted again to the use of Kwells. They were highly effective recently on winding roads in Uttarakhand in India and in the Chittagong Hill Tracts of Bangladesh.

Many bus-drivers in Bangladesh drive as though possessed by the devil. It is a terrifying enough experience just travelling on the same road, I can't imagine what it must be like imprisoned as a passenger. Cavalier cowboy conductors stand on the bottom step, hanging half out of the bus yelling abuse at anyone they pass as they roar along the road. So bad are they that even the ever intrepid *Lonely Planet* advises that to get out of such a flying death-wish is not a cowardly thing to do. Sushmita, one of the sisters in Philip Hensher's beautiful book about Bangladesh, *Scenes from Early Life* is very prone to car-sickness. After a journey that crosses seven rivers by three ferries and four bridges, the family arrives for their holidays at father's family home. Sushmita goes straight to bed to lie in the dark for the whole of the next day cosseted by her sympathetic country aunts.

If I was smart I would take a pill before I set off but I always optimistically imagine I'll be ok. I therefore have to wait until I actually feel frightful before I suck one which is pretty stupid but hope springs eternal. I think it is actually much better to vomit rather than stop and hope that awful feeling will disappear. It never goes away and being sick is usually a huge relief. Unfortunately for me, it's not as easily done as said so that's why I'm eternally grateful to the chemist who invented Kwells. It's a great name too. Perhaps the company will give me a lifetime's supply now I have given them such brilliant publicity. I bought some the other day for my next trip to India at my wonderful local chemist. This generous business gave me a super donation in the form of 30 jars of children's vitamins, 3000 pills, to take to a school project at Kempty Falls near Mussoorie. They also gave me a letter just in case Customs thought I was running drugs.

A very similar sensation to car-sickness can unfortunately strike in the cinema if there is a lot of hand-held camera footage of running about and jerky movements. In a supreme effort of will I managed to sit out a French film, *The Secret of the Grain,* where the camerawork was compounded by subject matter which dealt with food and a terrible rancid smell of popcorn wafting into the cinema from the foyer. That one I managed but there was nothing for it but to leave Banksy after twenty gruelling stomach-churning minutes in *Exit through the Gift Shop*. Not so long ago my daughter and her boys and I went to see *Beasts of the Southern Wild*. My reputation as a responsible grandma is now on the line as far as films with the children go. We all emerged from *Red Dog* in tears and after my latest effort with *Beasts,* not only was one boy sobbing but also feeling horribly nauseated. *Red Dog* also involved hand-held camera — actually they are usually supported on the shoulder — but that one didn't actually make us feel sick. *Beasts* though certainly did and I found if I closed one eye and put my head on the side it was slightly more endurable. It's an awful trend which some producers dismiss as being an age thing and only worrisome to elderly film-goers. If a ten-year-old feels sick as a result of the 'shakycam' technique then I think the ageist response is completely wrong. Colours can contribute badly to efforts to control a churning stomach. Lime green and some sickly shades of pink do not help, but this is getting into another realm of feeling sick.

Surprisingly there is one good thing to be said in defence of people who are susceptible to being car-sick. I have been told that they probably have very good hearing and a great sensitivity for musical sounds due to a delicate inner ear. We are clearly people of great sensibility, even if we aren't always the greatest of travel companions.

In a coracle with Jane Sheaffe, Ranganathittu Bird Sanctuary near Mysore, 1968

Riding with the Mounted Police Unit, Mysore, Karnataka, 1968

Jamie & Emily in the bath in Calcutta, West Bengal, 1976

From Greenland's Icy Mountains

Church attendance in Australia in the 1950s was much higher than it is now. For many small children, Sunday School was their first form of socialising with unknown children of their own age. Cousins, neighbourhood children and the offspring of parents' friends were the start of our social circles, the latter not always turning out as well as the parents might have hoped. Most children didn't start school until they had turned five but Sunday Schools enrolled smaller children and I guess that was the start of how many of us learned to get on with each other.

My introduction to the kindergarten section at St Aidan's Church of England Sunday School at Longueville was at the age of only three. I went with my friends Susie and Nettie who lived next door. My mother took our photograph as we set out on the first morning, in our best summer dresses and starched sunbonnets, looking innocent, sweet and slightly bewildered. We had been recruited by an older boy, the son of our parents' friends. He is also in the photograph too holding hands with Susie and Nettie and looking older and responsible as a six- or seven-year-old might, pleased with the merit he had earned by finding three new little girls.

Once there, I have little recollection of anything other than the most ghastly smell of fart in the little fibro building where the kindergarten gathered. It was horrible and something I hadn't come across before. We didn't do that sort of thing at my home! How weird that I can still recall it, I can almost summon up the unpleasant smell of the room. I know we used to sing *You in your small corner and I in mine* every week but apart from that I remember virtually nothing of Sundays until I was much older. I suppose we may have been driven by car when we were very small but later we joined the trails of children walking towards the church from all directions of Longueville and Northwood every Sunday morning. On Saturday mornings, similar trails with the angelic host clad this day in white could be seen heading towards tennis courts in Lane Cove and Longueville for induction into those skills. Tennis and Sunday School, fitness and godliness, were the pillars for our training for the future and we were perfectly safe walking everywhere throughout the whole of our childhood.

I was destined to remain at Sunday School for an awfully long time. The Superintendent's wife telephoned my mother soon after I had been confirmed and suggested that because I was such a well-behaved girl at church, they thought I should become a Sunday School teacher. Mum thought this was a wonderful honour—they were obviously just short of teachers. Anyhow, I said yes I'd do it. My first class was really awful as my sister, seven years younger than I, was one of the group and she and some her friends, their minds unfocused on the spiritual, were extremely unruly for their thirteen-year-old teacher.

This could have been a good grounding for class control but it was probably an indication of a worse situation a few years later. After taking up a Teachers' College Scholarship on leaving school, I had a month's practise teaching at Willoughby Girls High School at the end of First Term. My first year class was a dream but the 2E5 second year class was a total nightmare. I was seventeen and only out of school myself for a few months and they were big worldly girls of fourteen. I was so naïve, a babe in the woods in comparison with those cheeky creatures who ran rings around me.

A ghastly thing happened after I had set them a test on the topic of irrigation in their Social Studies syllabus. Several of those girls had decided to substitute the word erection for irrigation and later in the prac teachers' staff room I read this out thinking they were just being stupid! Everyone else howled with laughter and I didn't know why. Oh how humiliating. That month was the finish of a profession in teaching as far as I was concerned. However, I continued to teach at Sunday School for years until it became too hard to get up on Sunday morning after late parties.

I had been discovered as a pianist and I often played the hymns in the church hall where the older children sat in rows with their teachers, boys on one side and girls on the other. Hymns became a regular part of my life and by the time I was in my final year of school, I used to play one every morning at Assembly. Wenona School for Girls at North Sydney was independent and non-denominational and for the time, very broad-minded about religion. Jewish girls and others, whose parents did not wish it, were not compelled to attend Assembly, but for everyone else the routine at the start of the school day was to sing a hymn, read the Bible and pray. More fun than playing the hymns was belting out a march to accompany the girls as they marched into our ramshackle old Assembly Hall. We adapted John Philip Sousa marches arranged for one pair of hands into duets. My usual duet partner had learned jazz piano rather than classical and set a terrific pace. We folded back the lid of the upright piano and made quite a noise. My great friend, Lindsay Ryan, in order to avoid lining up in the playground, offered her services for turning the pages. She was a great help but somewhat uninformed as she didn't read music. We had to hiss 'Now Dig, now' as we all tried not to laugh. Playing hymns for an audience which always sniggered at mistakes was probably my undoing for a lifetime of performance anxiety. I've never enjoyed playing in public but for someone of limited talent, I have sure had to do a great deal of it. In many places where I would live as an adult, I seemed to be the only person who could play, or at least the only one honest or silly enough to admit to it. Despite hideous nerves, which it must be admitted contributed over extended weeks or months of rehearsals to beneficial weight loss, I have had some absolutely brilliant fun with all the different performances I have done.

 The hymns that we sang at Sunday School were those suitable for children like *All things bright and beautiful*. Some that we loved have disappeared from the Australian hymnal. *There's a friend for little children above the bright blue sky* is one which has been deemed unsuitable. Bad theology, a Catholic friend told me, but it had a rollicking tune. When my brother Maitland started at Shore, we occasionally went to school chapel services and there I became aware of a far greater wealth of hymn tunes. At Saint Aidan's we seemed to sing a lot of whingeing, whining tunes which at Shore were replaced by splendid, rousing ones suitable for boys' voices. Muscular Christianity accompanied by an exceptional organist. It was a revelation to hear, for instance the tune Thornbury for *Your hand, O God, has guided* or Duke Street for *Fight the good fight* instead of whatever we had been singing. I heard of a wedding once where *Fight the good fight* was one of the chosen hymns—perhaps they are still fighting. Now my grandsons attend an Anglican school it's delightful to discover new and wonderful boy hymns. In one, *Shine on me*, the boys clap their hands between lines in wonderful rhythm.

When I came to live in the Canberra-Goulburn Diocese the tunes were similar to the ones used at Shore. Our baby daughter's baptism was held in the little country church of St Edmund at Tharwa where regular services were held fortnightly. We had moved into the area just a few weeks before and I went to church the next Sunday to wave the flag and not be seen as a breeze-in rites of passage convenience user. I was sitting quietly waiting for the service to begin when the curate bustled up to me, a complete stranger to the congregation, and said 'Don't suppose you can play the organ can you?' I was so caught off guard I said, 'Well yes I can.' The elderly organist was absent that day and actually didn't ever play again as she had been waiting years for a replacement. The instrument was an old American harmonium from Brattleboro, Vermont and playing it was really quite an exhausting experience. I hadn't been taught to play the organ but apart from sustaining the notes it's not so different from playing a piano after all. I had learned the basic rudiments on childhood visits to my grandmother's parlour at Gosford where a piano occupied one corner and a tall harmonium the other. She lived in extraordinary place, a sub-tropical version of Miss Havisham's house and when we went to visit her and my maiden aunt, we had a wonderfully mad time playing hide and seek with cousins in the overgrown garden and roaming around the crowded house.

For my elderly predecessor at Tharwa, the exercise of pedalling to open the bellows, pushing the wooden knee flaps out for extra volume and sustaining the notes with strong fingers, was a real work-out. Nerves add determination to muscle power and I used to find myself pedalling hell for leather as though I was sprinting in a 100 metres dash, far faster than was necessary. My legs like furies kept pace with the pounding of my heart.

The hymnbook is full of marvellous music—melodies from English and Irish folk-songs arranged by Ralph Vaughan Williams, Bach's 17th century arrangements of 16th century melodies, old French airs, Woodlands by Greatorex is a setting of the Magnificat, and the beautiful tune Repton by Parry which was used as the theme tune for a television serial called *To Serve them all my Days*. As well there are tunes called Sri Lanka and Urdu and a couple of hymns translated from Hindi and Urdu. I bought my first copy of *The Australian Hymn Book* before we went to live in Laos in 1989. It has been superseded by a revised version, *Together in Song* which I have bought to keep up with the grandsons' hand-clapping efforts. I've had to surrender it however to one of the boys who has inherited my hymn gene and is dying to learn the organ.

I was the useful provider of music for many events in the years we lived in Laos, even playing for the only funeral—well really a memorial service—that took place while we were there. The departed was a bit of a rough diamond who had, somewhat the worse for wear through drink, carelessly fallen from an upstairs window, thinking he was in a bathroom. Professing no current faith, his exit from this world coincided with the pastoral visit from the Anglican Vicar of Bangkok. Vientiane was a far-flung colony of the church in Thailand. The service was to be held in a place called The Stockade, in the grounds of the Australian Embassy. It boasted a white grand piano and while others arranged flowers, I practised my hymns. One of the departed's infamous cries to all the girls he saw while running in the Hash House Harriers, was 'show us your tits'. Disgusting really and very unpleasant. But if that was so well-known I thought, 'in life in death O Lord', perhaps I would have a private joke with God and play *Jesu lover of my soul, let me to thy bosom fly*. The Ambassador's wife entered and boomed 'That's not a funeral hymn, I think you should find something else.' So I dutifully played *Abide with me* but managed to include my small joke in the music before the service began. I told it to a Catholic friend, unfamiliar with Anglican hymns and she thought it very appropriate. The offending word 'bosom' has been changed for modern usage to 'refuge' it should be noted. Usually the Ambassador had to bribe the congregation with the promise of drinks after the Vicar's pastoral visits but this service attracted Buddhists and Calathumpians and we barely fitted into the room. The Vicar was so delighted with the numbers and the bonus of a potential resident church musician that he decided there and then it was the time to re-establish the parish in Vientiane, closed since the Revolution.

I have played for weddings and services in a couple of other New South Wales country churches and also at my parish church in the city where the element of surprise has probably been a good thing. Forewarned might have meant avoided. One Sunday when it was my turn to read the lessons, I was also suddenly asked to play the hymns a minute before the service began when the organist's absence was discovered. So it was quite a busy service for me and several people later asked me if I was to preach the sermon next week as well! I played the piano in the sanctuary, the excellent organ located in the loft at my church being quite beyond my capabilities. I had to sight-read two of the hymns but I did know the other two. One was a 17th century tune with harmony by Bach and words by Bishop Heber, second Anglican bishop of Calcutta. It starts *Brightest and best are the sons of the morning* and it has been the target of feminists who have tried to change 'sons' to 'stars'.

On his arduous journey across the Upper Provinces of India, Heber was delighted to hear this Epiphany hymn sung at his consecration of the church of St John at Meerut on 19 December 1824. He found the church one of the largest and most handsome in India and equipped with one of the best organs. He estimated the church would hold at least 3000 people. It is salutary to consider such an architectural episode in history today when a great fuss is made by some alleged Christians when they discover a mosque or a temple is about to be constructed near their homes. The first savage outbreak of what the British call The Indian Mutiny, took place at

Meerut on 10 May 1857, a Sunday when evensong was about to begin at St John's.

Meerut today is a large sprawling city with the second largest cantonment in India. St John's is one of several churches in the cantonment and these days, like elsewhere in the former almost Anglican Empire, has a far smaller congregation than the Catholic church. The Scottish church in the Cantonment is now a private home with a small steeple erupting from an encroaching newer roof-line. It has been thus for as long as anyone in Meerut can remember.

My first visit to Meerut was in 1977 on the epic Indian odyssey with the two little children aged 4 and 5. On a long train journey from Calcutta we met a most charming man, who reluctant to speak to us directly, had chatted first to the children. He lectured in physical education in Meerut and was a champion tennis player. 'Come and visit,' he said. So one day during our Delhi sojourn we caught a bus and travelled north into the countryside for a couple of hours. We caught a cycle rickshaw from the bus station to our friend's home and found him meditating. He was happy for the interruption and said 'Well, we must go and see my friends.' His friends were brothers who ran the Greenlands sporting goods company.

We spent a fascinating afternoon watching cricketing equipment being made by hand. Most wondrous was the construction of six-stitcher cricket balls. It was winter and the light was pale in the factory. Lengths of brilliant, bright crimson leather hung from lines near the ceiling and sitting on the floor were men making the balls. Thin slices of corkwood were wound about by strands of wool and then buried in a pod of leather inside the hard red casing, a strange amalgamation of elements to go into a ball. It was all so interesting and after viewing the factory, little Jamie to his utter joy was given a complete cricket set—bat, ball, stumps, gloves and pads. My plans to see anything to do with 1857 had gone completely out the window and that is just an example of the fascinating deviations that travelling in India can bring.

Coming back from a visit to Mussoorie and Landour at the beginning of 2012 my friend Jennie and I stopped in Meerut in order to see St John's Church. It took some finding as our driver was unfamiliar with the town. We stopped at the Catholic Church and I went to the Presbytery to enquire about the Church of North India. The priest was a little grumpy at disturbance to his afternoon but he kindly pointed the way to St John's. The next delay was in locating the custodian of the key. He came on a bicycle and then had to check with the priest to see if it was ok to allow two foreign ladies to enter. It is a very handsome building, small wonder Bishop Heber was impressed with it.

Large and rectangular, the church has pilasters and columns supporting pediments over doors on three sides. The western front is very grand and above a classical pediment a tall, square-tiered steeple and spire soars to a height of 174 feet. There are variations of this charming style in many cities and towns in India and throughout all the former British Empire. Two important Chennai churches, St George's Cathedral and St Andrew's Kirk built between 1816 and 1819, St John's and St Andrew's in Kolkata and St John's in Meerut, were all based on the English Baroque style of St Martin-in-the-fields, designed by James Gibbs and built in London between 1722 and 1726. The plans were reproduced in Gibbs' *Book of Architecture* published in 1728 and so were available to colonial engineers in far-flung corners of the world. St Martin-in-the-fields, located on the edge of Trafalgar Square was impressive, beautiful and grand with added great symbolic and philosophical importance of being located at the heart of Empire. The attractive copies built throughout the Empire reflected the power and superiority of church and state.

The Meerut church is painted a warm buttery yellow with columns, pilasters, dentils and all other architectural details in white. The woodwork of the many doors on the ground floor and the arched fanlight windows on the upper storey is dark green. As Heber noted, the interior could accommodate 3000 people which these days is a colossal congregation anywhere other than St Peter's in Rome. The large airy interior space has a long nave with three aisles and a simple chancel at the east end. Tall white Ionic columns punctuate the nave, rising through the upper story where tiered step seating is no longer in use. The vertical emphasis of the columns and the lofty ceiling is heightened by lights and electric fans hanging from long extensions from the ceiling. Walls are yellow and details white, though window frames, the borders of memorials and of the large, arched marble plaques of the Ten Commandments in Hindi and Urdu are lavender. The colours are very pretty and somehow rather un-Indian in their restraint. The pulpit, railings and pews are dark wood, the pews with wicker seats which are so much cooler in the long, hot summers. The church after the merger of several Protestant denominations in 1970 is no longer called Anglican but is a Church of North India. It looks well-loved and is in fine condition apart from the poor old pipe organ, probably younger than the church, which has certainly seen better days. The keyboard was made in Calcutta by Hurry Brothers who built many of India's organs. Their parts were mostly imported and many still exist in playable condition.

Heber arrived in Meerut on 18 December 1824 and was met a little distance from the town by a group of soldiers and citizens including the chaplain, Mr Fisher whom he had once heard preach years before in England. The welcoming party somewhat unsettled his horse, Cabul, who leapt about as though possessed by a *djinn*. Once settled in tented accommodation within Mr Fisher's compound, Heber had time to absorb Meerut. He found that geographically at least, situated on a wide, dry plain, it looked a little like the steppes of Russia.

On 19 December Bishop Heber continued in his narrative 'The Church, which I have described, was consecrated this day with the usual forms.' The congregation he said was 'very numerous and attentive, the singing considerably better than at Calcutta and the appearance of every thing highly honourable both to the Chaplain and military officers of this important station.' He was pleased with the inclusion of *Brightest and best*, particularly the way it was sung by the superior Meerut voices. At that time the tune was the Scottish melody *Wandering Willie* which no longer appears in the hymn-book. More's the pity with such a wonderful name though the current tune is splendid. It is called *Liebster Immanuel* which has a harmony by Bach taken from a tune dating from 1679. The hymn was first published in 1811, long before Heber was consecrated

Bishop and posted to India.

Time erases details in a haphazard way. Scraps of history are remembered imperfectly and often details of no apparent importance to the present inhabitants are lost completely. Piecing things together is sometimes difficult. I expected there would be many monuments in St John's to the British who died when the rebellion broke out on the evening of Sunday 10th May 1857, but the only one easily visible was in memory of Lieutenant Colonel Gerrard who died near Delhie (*sic*) in November 1857. In the footsteps of Heber, it's hard to work out even the facts of the consecration. Over the west door there is a somewhat confusing marble plaque reads 'This church, the first erected in the Upper Provinces of India was founded AD 1819 and completed AD 1822. The Most Noble the Marquis of Hastings the Governor General of India. The Rt. Revd. Thomas Fanshaw Middleton D D Lord Bishop of Calcutta; The Revd. Henry Fisher, Chaplain of Meerut; Captain George Hutchinson, of the Engineers Architect.' These days some parishioners think the church was consecrated by Middleton, the first Bishop of Calcutta. There is no mention of consecration in the inscription and why would Heber say he had 'consecrated this day' the church if in fact he hadn't? In some contemporary accounts the word *constructed* is sometimes confused with *consecrated*. The plaque seems therefore to be more likely the foundation stone or at least a commemoration of the foundation. There is also nothing to say that either The Marquis of Hastings or Bishop Middleton were in attendance at any stage, rather they were the current incumbents.

The Marquis of Hastings, 10th Governor-General of India from 1812–1823, visited Meerut in January 1815. He was not particularly impressed and in his private journal he said 'The approach to it, over a waste plain, is not calculated to impress one with a favourable prepossession.' However, he had a pleasant stay and was happy with all he saw, except for one thing. He attended Divine Service which was held, there being no church in 'one of the barrack bungalows' a 'building quite unfit for the purpose' and he noted the sermon sounded somewhat fierce. Perhaps the lack of a suitable building lodged in his mind and he therefore happily endorsed the proposal for constructing a more suitable house of worship. He stayed in Meerut for several days, reviewing the troops who impressed him and visiting hospitals and regimental schools where he found 'many striking instances of proficiency' among the children. He held a levée for the Europeans, civil and military, a durbar for 'respectable natives of the neighbourhood' and then he resumed his journey.

It seems that Bishop Middleton unlike the Marquis did not visit Meerut. He must have been extremely busy as first Bishop and Metropolitan of all India, formally establishing the church in all the territory of the East India Company. With the rise of Britain as a power in India, evangelical Christians had agitated for some time for the creation of an Indian diocese. Middleton, with his preference for the more authoritarian forms and hierarchy of the high Church of England rather than the more democratic and evangelical low choice was considered a safe choice and both his arrival and consecration were restrained. The work of unlicensed missionaries in North India often met with his disapproval but the church prospered under his administration.

Bishop Middleton's tenure in Calcutta is covered thoroughly in *The Bengal Obituary*, published in 1851. It is 'a record to perpetuate the memory of departed worth', a 'compilation of tablets and monumental inscriptions from various parts of the Bengal and Agra Presidencies to which is added Biographical Sketches and Memoirs of such as have pre-eminently distinguished themselves in the History of British India since the formation of the European settlement to the present time.' Middleton travelled quite extensively, primarily by sea. After a year of establishment in Calcutta, in December 1815 he sailed to Madras and visited many settlements in the South then continued by sea around the coast to Bombay, south to Colombo and back to Calcutta. In 1819 he voyaged again to Madras returning to Calcutta via Penang and in 1821 he sailed to Bombay, visiting Cochin en route. He died in Calcutta of sunstroke on 8 July 1822 and is buried in St John's churchyard.

Topics of an amusing nature might not be expected in such a serious tome as *The Bengal Obituary* but there had been quite an exchange between Bishop Middleton and Dr Bryce of St Andrew's

Kirk, the Church of Scotland in Calcutta. Bishop Middleton's church was St John's, the Cathedral Church until St Paul's was completed in 1847. Its foundation was laid in 1784, designed by Lieutenant James Agg, inspired by St Martin-in-the-fields but with several deletions and later additions. One of the omissions was the fourth tier of the steeple and spire which give it a somewhat compressed look. Dr Bryce's Kirk was constructed decades later, between 1815 and 1818. It also referred to St Martin-in-the-fields, or at least by one remove to the neighbouring St John's. Dr Bryce and the Bishop were rivals and had travelled to India from England together. Bryce found the Bishop more trying than his other great foe which was prickly heat! He was determined to have his steeple higher than St John's and despite government opposition and lack of finance, he succeeded.

Since my January 2012 visit to Meerut I had been trying to unravel the story of St John's. It seemed to me that the 1905 photograph that appears on several on-line sites is actually St John's church, Calcutta and not Meerut. A side veranda and a porte cochère, plus the compressed steeple and spire indicate Calcutta. I then had an unexpected opportunity to revisit Meerut in June 2012. It was incredibly hot and the temperature outside the car was 47° on our journey from Delhi. It was only five months since my winter visit but my great luck on this journey was that I had made contact with another charming Meerut inhabitant. The city has a reputation for rebellions, conspiracy, strikes, trickery and *badmashes* but my experience of the people of Meerut is the opposite.

Anil Bhattacharji writes a history site about his home town and lives with Susan, his wife, and their elderly parents in an old house in the Cantonment which dates back to before the Mutiny. Anil's mother founded a primary school more than thirty years ago and during term time, 800 children are accommodated each day in classrooms in the large and shady compound. I had come in a taxi from Delhi with Yogi, the driver, who knew Meerut a little. As a student he kept caged birds and Meerut's bird market was where he sometimes bought them. This was quite a different journey for him and he was as keen as I to see new sights.

The interior of Anil's house was dark and cool. It is an example of how the British managed to cope with the blazing heat of an Indian summer. The ceilings are enormously tall and placed very high on the walls there are small windows, almost skylights. It was an ingenious British method of keeping the heat outside and may be seen all over the country in circuit houses, dak bungalows and barracks. Hot air rose and exited via the skylights while cooler air came in through the open doors at night. I have a similar strategy in my flat in Canberra but not to the exclusion of light which would drive me nuts. Burglar-proof mesh doors mean I can open the place up entirely at night when the glorious cool air enters. By day, with the place closed up before the sun strikes, even when the temperatures are in the 40s my flat is always quite comfortable.

After a cold drink in the cool interior of his old house, Anil hopped into the car and we drove around the empty roads of the neat and spacious Cantonment for an hour. We visited the St John's Cemetery where some of those who died on 10 May 1857 were buried. The extensive graveyard, about a mile from the church is overgrown with trees and shrubs, the undergrowth looking a nice habitat for multitudes of snakes. The Mutiny graves, were in an area partially cleared of vegetation, located in the north-west corner of the 1835 first extension to the cemetery. This burial ground was founded in 1807, an earlier one near the race-course was used between 1803 and 1814. There are surprisingly few Mutiny graves recorded, eleven to be exact. Some fifty British men, women and children, including soldiers, are said to have been killed. More graves could be concealed in the overwhelming vegetation or perhaps the poor souls were never buried.

In the gatehouse a marble plaque reads 'placed here by private subscription 1904' with the scale carefully shown as '32 ft to an inch'. It shows the ground plan of the rectangular cemetery which was extended thrice 1835, 1855 and 1881–2. A few graves are marked with an alphabetical key—the eleven 'victims of the Mutiny' are A. Mrs C. Chambers, B. Mr J. Phillips, C-D nine others. It is odd that only two of the graves are identified for several still have legible inscriptions. There is Captain John Taylor, 'killed during the mutiny', Colonel John Finniss 'who fell while endeavouring to quell the mutiny' and Lieutenant William Pattle 'killed in the mutiny'. Others who died on 10 May were Captain Donald McDonald 'who was killed by his own men and of his wife Louisa Sophia, barbarously murdered on the same night while trying to make her escape with her 3 infants from her burning house to the European Lines'. Another grave is that of a Surgeon, William Boyle Chavasse MRCSE, Assistant Surgeon 2nd European Bengal Fusiliers, who died later in the year, his death 'greatly accelerated from excessive fatigue during the whole of the siege of Delhie'.

These old British cemeteries are fascinating, telling a strand of the stories of the Raj. There are two million European graves scattered all over India but apart from keen family historians who know where their ancestors rest, they must be slipping further and further into oblivion. The Berhampore cemetery in West Bengal is such a place where almost all of the inscriptions have been removed and nobody knows who is where. Anil's father used to hold the Registry of graves for Meerut but he is now 97 and someone else is doing the job.

When rebellion broke out, the first concern of the mutinous troopers had been to liberate their comrades from gaol into which they had been cast the day before. Members of the 3rd Bengal Light Cavalry, they had been court-martialled after refusing to use the cartridges for their new Enfield rifles. Greased it was said with pig or beef fat repulsive to both Muslims and Hindus, the sepoys were required to tear off the cartridge paper with their teeth. The soldiers were soon released by the mutineers but so too were more than 700 civil prisoners also housed in the gaol. Many of these men who mingled with the sepoys were hardened criminals, on the lookout for any opportunity. No attempt was made by the British to stop the troops who rode towards Delhi and the Emperor. 10 May is celebrated as a local holiday in Meerut.

Indians do not choose to use the name Mutiny for the great rebellion of 1857 which is more correctly called the First War of Independence. At the last major anniversary of the conflict in 2007, the observances of several tour groups from the United Kingdom were not welcomed. In Lucknow, site of the famous siege which for the British was one of the most heroic struggles of its Imperial history, the tourists met hostile crowds who halted their progress. Sir Mark Havelock, descendant of Sir Henry Havelock and a member of the group which had planned a remembrance ceremony to take place within the Residency, was eventually able to visit his great, great grandfather's grave undetected. The grave is situated at Alambagh, miles away from the Residency which Sir Henry had relieved, only to have it besieged again for almost 8 weeks before the final relief by Sir Colin Campbell and his Highlanders. Havelock was a highly respected officer and loved by his men who brought his body from Dilkusha where he had died of sickness soon after the final relief of Lucknow.

Anil told me there were also some scenes of minor protest in Meerut when a British group visited the city in 2007. Some retired British soldiers had sought permission to place a memorial plaque in St John's commemorating the 150th anniversary of the uprising and extolling the bravery and distinguished service of men of the 60th Queen's Royal Rifles, the earlier name for their regiment. The Bishop and the District Magistrate both denied the insensitive request.

The Cantonment was virtually deserted in the baking summer sun as we drove around in air-conditioned comfort. We saw a regimental mess in which local legend holds that Bahadur Shah, the last Mughul Emperor, spent some time imprisoned before his exile to Burma. This seems unlikely but it is true that the Duke of Connaught, one of Queen Victoria's sons, lived in Meerut in the 1880s. His home at 55 The Mall, is now the Allahabad Bank. The once handsome Cantonment railway station was built in 1865 but has acquired some unfortunate architectural accretions in the recent past. It is a busy station with many travellers commuting daily to Delhi. It was just too hot to walk in Company Bagh, the garden known now as Gandhi Bagh, where in the evenings there is a musical fountain show. We drove around the Sadar Bazaar where some crumbling shops date from before Independence. London House, Drapers and Tailors, established 1920 looked like some of the shops in Peshawar in Pakistan when I lived there in the late 1980s. These crumbling vestiges still undertake tailoring for Army officers but are surely not going to last for much longer. Vendors were selling marvellous mangoes from carts—one very good reason for visiting India in the summer. We looked at quite an amazingly realistic monument to the Army Veterinary Corps and the Wheler Club. Sometimes spelled Wheeler which is my maiden name, the connection is a little intriguing. There used to be bookstalls on Indian railway platforms run by a family called Wheeler who published some of Kipling's first editions. There's a Wheeler Senate House in Patna and General Wheeler was the commander of the garrison at Cawnpore (now Kanpur) and died, with his family, in the fighting. But there's nothing in a name such as Wheeler, our ancestors were people who usefully made wheels and we therefore don't have to be related except in the collective subconscious.

I somehow lost Bishop Heber during the day at Meerut but my connection with Anil and his family was worth far more than any historic excavation. Back in the cool, old house I shared a wonderful lunch with them and I really hope we will meet again. Now anyhow, I'm stuck on finding out more about Meerut and what happened after the British pulled themselves together in the aftermath of 10 May. It seems that quick fortifications were constructed and the remaining officers defended the garrison for the duration of hostilities as well as making sporadic efforts to help relieve the siege of Delhi and other threatened towns nearby.

It was too hot to go to see Jain temples at Hastinapur, 40 km away but after farewelling Anil and Susan, I did go into the old part of the town to see the Jama Masjid. Built by Hasan Mahdi, the chief minister of Sultan Mahmud Ghaznavi in 1019 and restored by Emperor Humayun, it is said to be the oldest mosque in Northern India. Yogi, ever vigilant about my welfare, asked if I would like him to come with me. No need I said and set off down a lane towards the large dome rising behind stout walls. It was Friday and throngs of men and boys were flooding past in both directions. Worship had just finished and apart from some Muslim beggar-women, entirely obscured in black *burqas*, I was the only female in sight. I had no thought of entering the mosque so I just stood on an elevated footpath and watched. Everyone smiled and nodded and some wanted me to take photographs. So it was a quick and uninformed visit and that was fine. Meerut has 32% Muslim population, making it the highest percentage of any major city in the state of Uttar Pradesh.

On the way out of the city there is another monument in the centre of a roundabout. It says 'HRS Chowk welcomes you to Meerut, the sports city of India'. The inscription is flanked by two sculptured cricket bats and crowned by a soccer ball. It is wonderful! The journey back to Delhi took about two hours. Ghaziabad on the way is full of faceless clusters of housing estates. Plantations of tower-blocks have sprung from the plain and hoardings exhorting purchasers to buy, buy, buy stand one after the other. Excel Heights, Fortune Residency, Highend Paradise II, Quantam Residency, VVIP Addresses, La Royale and Satya Ville de are possibilities for a lifestyle change. There are no trees because the plots used to be fields of waving wheat and mustard. I am lucky to have seen the fields that so reminded Heber of Europe.

Now, in a post-script to Meerut, I have made contact again with the family who ran the sporting goods factory which we visited in 1977. Sadly the kind brother who gave Jamie his kit, was killed in a car accident but the other brothers are fit and well and the small factory has grown into a sporting empire now called Sanspareils Greenlands. I thought I had 'done' Meerut but now Jamie and I will definitely have to return and a third family member will have to be my daughter's son, Maitland, a cricket tragic. He discovered how famous SG is now and was almost overcome by the three SG cricket balls I gave him for Christmas which my friend Gia Metherell was able to buy for me in Mumbai last year.

I went to Holy Eucharist at the Cathedral Church of the Redemption on my first Sunday on that Meerut investigation visit to India. The Cathedral Church is the former Viceroy's Church and was designed by Henry Medd after a grander design by Lutyens had been abandoned through lack of funds. When the project finally started, Lord Irwin was Viceroy. He was an ardent Anglo-Catholic of such high moral integrity that even Gandhi was impressed. Because of his personal interest in the project, generous funds for the building's construction came from Britain. Irwin laid the foundation stone in 1927, the Bishop of Lahore consecrated the church on 15 February 1931 and it was finally completed in 1935.

It is a very handsome building which references Palladio's Il Redentore Church in Venice and Lutyens' St Jude's in Hampstead Garden Suburb. Massive from the outside, the interior is somehow quite intimate despite the length of the nave. Yogi had a little mishap with the time and I arrived during the Lessons but when these concluded it was delightful to find the next hymn was one of Heber's. The bishop must have been far more thrilled to find *Brightest and best* was sung in Meerut in 1824, but I was very happy to sing *Holy, holy, holy* in Delhi in 2012. It was very hard to hear the sermon because of the buzz of standard fans in the aisles, I counted at least 24. In his book on British Architecture in India *Splendours of the Raj*, Philip Davies comments how the cool, shaded interior is so perfectly adapted for the heat of India's summer. I think winter in the church might be hard to handle and there is a certain psychological coldness to the lofty interiors. In Peshawar in the winter, coal braziers were placed inside the pews of St John's, the former garrison church, perhaps the Delhi Cathedral has a similar solution.

Three Heber hymns appear in my *Australian Hymn Book*, now superseded by *Together in Song*. As well as *Brightest and best* there is *Holy, holy, holy! Lord God Almighty* which is sung to a great tune by John Bacchus Dykes which bears resemblance to Bach's tune for 'Wachet auf!' or 'Sleepers Awake'. The third is *Bread of the world in mercy broken*, sung to a 16th century tune from the Genevan Psalter called 'Rendez à Dieu' which I have never heard sung. Another Heber hymn which we sang with gusto at school did not make the grade into the new hymnal, sharing the fate of the friend for little children above the bright blue sky.

From Greenland's icy mountains, to India's coral strand is the opening line of one of Heber's best known hymns, usually sung to the tune of 'Aurelia' by Samuel Wesley. In the early 19th century the singing of hymns in churches other than metrical psalms was not officially approved by the Anglican hierarchy. There was considerable informal hymn-singing and Heber was one of the first High Church Anglicans to write his own. He was a prolific writer of hymns and by 1820 he had compiled a collection of ninety-nine, of which fifty-seven were his own compositions. This collection would eventually be published posthumously by his widow in 1827.

In 1819, the Society for the Propagation of the Gospel had raised the enormous sum of £60,000 for missionary work in India. Three-quarters of the sum came from a collection made throughout England in response to an appeal authorised by royal letter. Heber had been invited to deliver a series of sermons to coincide with the launch of the appeal and thus inspired, he wrote the hymn at great speed the day before the appeal was officially launched. It surely helped motivate congregations to donate so generously.

A century later, Mahatma Gandhi, although intensely interested in all matters spiritual, would not be the first person we might associate with Heber. He personally, though not politically, believed that all religions were equal before God and was very fond of certain Christian hymns. His favourite was *Abide with me*, words by Henry Francis Lyte and sung to the tune 'Eventide' by Monk. It is played every year at the end of the Beating of the Retreat ceremony, held in New Delhi at the end of the Republic Day celebrations. He admired the historical figure of the intellectual, even-handed Heber but at a meeting of missionaries at the YMCA in Calcutta in 1925 he expressed his negative feelings on aspects of missionary work. It is amazing to think that the missionaries themselves were so oblivious to criticism that they invited the Great Soul to speak. Did they not realise there was much criticism of their evangelising and proselytising in this perhaps the most deeply religious country in the world and home of the most ancient of living faiths—Hinduism, Jainism and Buddhism? The East India Company had initially banned missionary work. The Company believed conversions caused riots, riots affected trade and trade was of foremost importance. But by the early 19th century missionaries of all persuasions were living in India.

To his YMCA audience Gandhi said, 'You, the missionaries come to India thinking that you come to a land of heathens, of idolators, of men who do not know God. One of the greatest of Christian divines, Bishop Heber, wrote the two lines which have always left a sting with me: "Where every prospect pleases, and man alone is vile." I wish he had not written them. My own experience in my travels throughout India has been to the contrary. I have gone from one end of the country to the other, without any prejudice, in a relentless search after truth, and I am not able to say that here in this fair land, watered by the great Ganges, the Brahmaputra and the Jumna, man is vile. He is not vile. He is as much a seeker after truth as you and I are, possibly more so.' Gandhi did admire the gracious Heber who was seen by all as conciliatory and always accepting of undeniable faith.

Some years later while serving a prison sentence during the fight for freedom, the Mahatma was given some literature by well-meaning missionaries. He found them to be 'written as if merely to belittle Hinduism'. He mentioned *From Greenland's icy mountains* again which he felt 'is a clear libel on Indian humanity.' Those lines which had earlier appalled Gandhi were followed in the same verse by 'In vain with lavish kindness the gifts of God are strown; the heathen in his blindness bows down to wood and stone.' How frightful and short-sighted this seems now and surely it can be said that Christians of many persuasions all over the world are just as prone to bowing down to wood and stone as any of Heber's so-called heathens. The old missionary hymn was omitted from Anglican hymnals thirty years ago so it will be forgotten like most of the others from Heber's original collection.

While travelling in the Himalayas he wrote in a way that immediately recalls *From Greenland's icy mountains*. 'My attention was completely strained, and my eyes filled with tears, every thing around was so wild and magnificent that man appeared as nothing, and I felt myself as if climbing the steps of the altar of God's great temple.' Describing man's appearance as 'nothing', perhaps his use of the offensive word vile in the hymn was meant to mean merely ignominious. It is an awful word but it did rhyme with isle, two lines earlier in the verse. In truth Heber was very reasonable and his words on the vileness of man probably included himself.

Although I had known Heber's name for a long time, when I discovered the Indian connection his whole history became much more interesting. Born in 1783 into a comfortable, clerical family in Shropshire, he showed great intellectual promise from early childhood. His father had taught him Latin and Greek and at the age of only seven he translated the fables of Phaedrus into verse. Later his Oxford career was predictably highly distinguished. He won a prize for an essay on *The Sense of Honour* and the Newdigate Prize for his poem *Palestine* which was set to music and described as the 'first English Oratorio of real note for forty years'. He was interested in both landscape and architectural drawing and his talent for writing spontaneous verse was frequently encouraged by others. His father for instance once requested some verses which were to be sung the following morning by recruits for a volunteer corps to defend England against a threatened French invasion in 1803. He was a poet of great facility and convenience. John Betjeman described Heber's style as consciously literary, with careful choices of adjectives and vivid figures of speech: 'poetic imagery was as important as didactic truth'. Greenland is certainly that.

After a Northern Grand Tour he took holy orders in 1807 and was appointed rector of the family parish at Hodnet in Shropshire. In 1809 he married Emily Shipley, daughter of a Dean and granddaughter of a Bishop. Heber designed a new rectory which would become their home at Hodnet. At this time he started to learn much about India from the Clive family, descendants of Robert Clive, who lived nearby. An aunt had married Sir William Jones, the great orientalist and founder of the Asiatic Society of Bengal, who might not have exactly approved of his nephew's Christian endeavours. Heber's interest in India was deep but he twice resisted offers to become Bishop of Calcutta. By the time his first little daughter was two years old, his concerns about her health in the notoriously unhealthy city were allayed by a Bengal medical expert and in 1823 he accepted the post which had become vacant at the death of Bishop Middleton.

At the time of Heber's arrival in India there were Church of England priests, but no ordained missionaries teaching or preaching in Indian languages and not a single ordained Indian priest. His time in India was marked by devotion, energy and tact and he was one of the first churchmen to try to integrate the Scripture readings, prayers and sermon with the hymns—something taken for granted these days. It was not practised much I recall at school where favourites from the season of Lent might be sung at any time of the year with no connection at all with prayer or Bible reading. This lacked a certain logical continuity but wasn't such a bad thing if we sang, read and absorbed.

I learned something of Heber from entries in *Songs of the people of God*, a companion book to the *Australian Hymn Book*. The author, Professor Wesley Milgate, formerly the Challis Professor of English Literature at the University of Sydney, had a warm sense of humour which pervaded what could have been a dry old book. He was a specialist on John Donne and while studying at Oxford soon after World War II, having been awarded the first Nuffield Dominion Fellowship in the Humanities, he collaborated on the new Oxford edition of Donne. Further publications on Donne appeared in 1967 from Oxford and from Australia in 1970. After his retirement, Milgate, who was a fine pianist and organist, worked on the publication of the new Australian hymnals. For many years he had played the organ in churches of various denominations without, he said, any noticeable signs of improvement but congregations begged to differ with his modesty about his considerable talents.

As well as painstaking entries for every hymn and biographical notes for every hymn-writer and composer, there is an introduction which in the preface he says will for some 'seem unnecessary and avuncular'. His aim though was 'to be as helpful as possible to the less experienced—for instance, to the possibly conscripted amateur organist of a small country church, or to clergy and musicians confronted (as they are all fairly certain to be) for the first time with texts and tunes of which they wish to make the best use.' He might have written that precisely for me! There are separate sections on the obligations of the clergy, of organists and choirmasters and of the congregation which are gently humorous. He is also amusing about the names of tunes, likening them to a farmer naming his cows 'for quick reference in conversation and to distinguish them from other similar-looking cows'. Tunes have been named for friends of the composer, for saints or even the less saintly composer himself. Others have been named for a favourite fishing stream—Spean; a character in a novel—Mrs. Miniver; a motor vehicle—Birabus; a composer's birthplace—Down Ampney or the place of a composer's honeymoon—Little Cornard!

I was loaned the Companion by Rev. Robert Willson who had studied under Milgate at Sydney University. Robert, who was once Chaplain at my daughter's school, is a tall, kind man with a booming voice who writes interesting articles about church history and entertaining reviews about historical books of great variety.

Heber is interesting to us, not only as a hymn-writer but because he was at one time Bishop of Australia. While on tour of the already vast episcopate in India in 1825, the whole of Australasia was added without his foreknowledge. Quite a parish! It already included what are now the modern states of Pakistan, Bangladesh, Burma and Sri Lanka as well as India and was probably the largest diocese in Christendom. The largest Anglican diocese in the world today is located in North West Australia with Holy Cross Cathedral in Geraldton at its centre, large in area but with a very small population.

India in Heber's time had a population of 100,000,000 in a country of 1,500,000 square miles. He learned of the additional southern reaches of his parish on his return to Calcutta after an arduous 2500 miles journey of Episcopal visitation across northern India which lasted more than 18 months. His wife and elder daughter joined him in Bombay after nine months and following an enjoyable stay of some months with Governor Elphinstone, they sailed onto Ceylon before returning to Calcutta. As an energetic and enthusiastic traveller, had he lived longer he may well have come to Australia on a pastoral visit and it would have been a healthy holiday for his small family.

Heber has left a legacy of observations of his delight in India in the three volumes of his *Narrative of a Journey through the Upper Provinces of India* which was published after his death, edited by his devoted wife, Emily. The story he tells is eloquent and thoroughly enjoyable and Emily's footnote additions in the last volume are also written in a similar agreeable style. The bishop, as she refers to him, could have remained in the comfort of Calcutta but set off on arduous journeys to acquaint himself with India and its inhabitants, native and introduced. Like the famous diarist, William Hickey (1749–1830) another Calcutta resident, he had a keen eye for detail and was curious about the exotic flowers, trees, animals, people and buildings he saw in his new home. Fitting for churchman, his writing is not gossipy like Hickey's, but his vivid narrative, combined with his own illustrations, give a valuable picture of India of the early 19th century. Despite occasional yearnings for home, he expresses joy and pleasure at what he finds in India and rarely complains. He is constantly amazed at the mere sight of people in the crowded streets, their faces, dress and ornaments. He describes domestic features such as *punkahs* and hard beds and when travelling preferably by boat or horse rather than uncomfortable palanquins, he records 'villainous' smells, 'stinking fogs' on the river—the Ganga sometimes nine miles wide, beautiful rural vistas, fields of opium poppy, cotton and 'silkmulberries', monkeys, fireflies and nightingales, the scene of a *sati* and the strange sight of workmen dyed blue from their work in an indigo factory.

He has the eye of a farmer in his judgement of crops and livestock and quickly learns the names of the exotic trees and bushes he sees for the first time. Throughout his travels he notes glorious botanical specimens and in the correspondence which is attached to Volume III of the Narrative, he positively exults in a letter to his cousin, Harriet Douglas. He declares 'the peepul, the teak and other larger round-topped trees will bear no disadvantageous comparison with our oaks, elms, and limes; the mangoe and tamarind greatly surpass in beauty our walnut and cherry-trees, and we have nothing at all answerable to the banyan, the bamboo, the different species of palms, or the plantains, aloes, cactus, and ananas'. He particularly loved coconut palms and several times he is reminded of illustrations seen in the publications of the voyages of Captain Cook, obviously also familiar to his friends and family. He knew of Alexander von Humboldt's *Geography of Plants in Tropical countries* published in 1807. Of all his theories on the harmonious, interrelated unity of nature, Humboldt stressed the subject of plants more than any other. He also singled out the palm as 'the loftiest and most stately of all vegetable forms', something with which Heber must have agreed. They would have loved Pradip Krishen's *Trees of Delhi*, a beautiful little book full of fascinating information and excellent illustrations.

He is reminded of Scottish airs in some of the tunes of Bengali songs, the language which he finds soft and liquid in comparison with that spoken in Hindoostan. His interest in architecture, both the contemporary buildings of the British and monuments of antiquity, is evident and informed. Usually inclined to damn with faint praise, he did express horror at the vulgarity and 'vile' (there's that word again!) taste of some of the Government House complex in Madras and wrote eloquently of how even the grandest buildings decayed in the harsh climate of Calcutta. The construction was of brick plastered with chunam, a form of stucco made from lime extracted from burned seashells and polished to resemble marble. Buildings of classical grandeur built for upstart merchants revealed a disfigured base core when the chunam fell off and the exposed common brick seemed a symbolic visual metaphor. Elsewhere in India, river frontages and esplanades remind him of St Petersburg, fortifications are similar to the Kremlin, mountain scenery of Norway, vistas recall Egypt and mountains and rivers are compared to the scenery of Wales, Scotland and England. He is often homesick for his native land but his curiosity is ever piqued by the exotic and his comparisons of scenes in India with familiar places at home, create a clear word picture for not only himself but readers of his letters.

His visual memory is marvellous and he uses recalled images and literary allusions to describe the unfamiliar by which he is surrounded. In picturesque vocabulary he recalls Poussin and Cuyp, the model of an Egyptian tomb by Belzoni and portraits by Wouverman and Rubens. When he sees the troops of the King of Lucknow's guard he is reminded of the way British sepoys were dressed twenty years ago as they were represented in Kerr Porter's

Storming of Seringapatam. The wars in the south against Tipu Sultan were well known through these paintings and engravings and just mentioning them presented a clear image of the soldiers he observed.

While in Lucknow, the capital of the Kingdom of Oudh, he learns of the anarchical situation in the state. Assaults, robberies and murders were commonplace, Europeans and Christians were said to be hated and local advice was not to trust the people of Oudh. He personally experienced 'invariable civility and good nature' doubtless reflecting his own character but here and elsewhere he observes that while the British are not guilty of injustice, they 'shut out the natives from our society' and very often assumed a bullying and insolent manner when dealing with them. His descriptions are prophetic when considering what happened in Lucknow during the 1857 rebellion. The British Residency, which the bishop visited many times during his visit, was the scene of the infamous siege. Heber was convinced however, that despite the arrogance and even connivance of some Britishers, the arrival of the English in India had to be considered a blessing.

Tempering the fascinations of his new home were regular reminders of how tenuous the hold on life could be. Two monsoons was a common lifespan for the British in India and during Heber's stay in Calcutta, two chief justices died, one after the other, each after only six weeks in office. The second had been an old friend so his loss was felt keenly. The heat must have been intolerable without the modern comforts we take for granted today, and Heber notes that houses in the west of the sub-continent seem not to be designed as well as those in Bengal to combat the furnace of summer.

Many of his observations are as amusingly pertinent to India now as then. It is a great place for surveys with invitations to fill in forms at the end of a drive in a car, a meal or even a visit to a shop. Each morning at breakfast at a stay in a Calcutta hotel my friends and I were asked to complete a survey. One day I gave appreciative remarks about food, cleanliness and service but when I came to the box about the music I said it was dreadful. It was—far too loud, horrible, canned, nebulous, ghastly Muzak noise. The waiter took it to his superior who rushed over to me seriously perturbed.

An entry in Heber's journal in October 1824 as he nears Cawnpoor tells of the Jemautdar of the 'village who came to ask for the usual certificate of his having rendered us assistance'. The Bishop did this, leaning on the top of his palanquin, using 'Sir Thomas Ackland's inkstand'. The man was grateful for the good words, but he had a brother, clearly a fine young man, who was anxious to join the East India Company. Could Huzoor have the goodness to give a recommendation for his brother to the judge Sahib of Betourah? The bishop said he didn't know the judge sahib and the man said, never mind, 'Huzoor is Malik of the land and your Firmaun will be obeyed.' Then the Bishop protests that he also didn't know the brother. 'Huzoor may believe me when I tell him that my brother is one of the best men in the world!' And so it went on with Heber remarking that 'the natives of India seem to attach very great importance to a written recommendation by a European, or person in a public station, in which, as in many other points, they strongly resemble the Russians.' He said the whole scene, mutatis mutandis, might have taken place at a ferry on the Don or the Dnieper.

Are many of these surveys ever read? My breakfast music remark was at least momentarily taken to heart. Foreigners' hand writing is often difficult for others to decipher. On the old immigration forms that were in use when we lived in Laos much personal information was required including the answer to a question about race. As my children often went across the Mekong to Thailand for the afternoon and usually leaving only minutes to spare before taking the last boat across the river, they had the filling out of forms down to a fine art. They used to vary the 'race' section from 50 m freestyle, 100 m breast-stroke, or even women's relay!

Home in Calcutta for only three months, Heber set off again for another Episcopal journey to Madras and the southern provinces, despite the hot season being already underway. He departed Madras on 13th March, 1826, in his own words 'almost worn out', having presided over confirmations—one for 478 people and another for 120, and preached eleven times in little over a fortnight. After consultations with the local clergy, he saw there was an enormous amount to be done in the southern outposts of his episcopate where far more ecclesiastical complications existed than elsewhere in his vast domain. These were to be Heber's last few days of life and we know much of them from a letter written after his death by a missionary from Tanjore who had journeyed to Trichy, arriving a little later than the Bishop. The days in Tanjore had been very busy with Easter services, confirmations and meetings with priests and missionaries from the Tanjore and Tinnevelly Missions. Often travelling in the cool of night, he arrived in the city of Trichinopoly or Tiruchirappalli or as it is familiarly known, Trichy, in the early hours of the morning of 31st March. His party included two whom he intended to station there and his chaplain who was sick. The surgeon who had accompanied the group had been left behind at Tanjore where he died of an abscess in the liver.

Again time was taken up with meetings and services and a confirmation of seventy persons at St John's one evening. Heber decided to confirm the young people of the Tamil congregation the next morning, 3rd April, at the Mission Church in the Fort and this took place at sun-rise in a 'solemn and affecting' service with the Bishop pronouncing the final blessing in Tamil. The day grew hot — it was usually about 100°F in the shade at this time of the year. He visited schools and the mission house, called on his sick chaplain and then went to cool off with a swim at the home of his host, the English Circuit Judge, something he had enjoyed on the two previous days. And there he was later found, lifeless in the swimming bath or as the later publication of his *Life* put it, in the water which was 'the destined agent of his removal to Paradise'. More prosaically the cause of his death was recorded as heat apoplexy.

He is buried near the altar of St John's Church in Trichy. There is an error in the memorial slab which lies in the floor, engraved marble inlaid with brass and enamel. The words 'Here rest the remains of Reginald Heber DD, third Bishop of Calcutta' appear on a scroll held by crossed crosiers and surmounted by a bishop's mitre. In fact he was the second Bishop of Calcutta. The engraver might have been confused by the succession of deaths of incumbents in Calcutta, Heber's successor who was the third in Calcutta, Bishop

John James, died after only nine months in India. This memorial cannot be seen by the congregation from the nave but in 1885 some fine stained glass windows were dedicated as a second memorial. He is remembered then, unlike so many British who left their bones all over the sprawling empire.

Today St John's has a thriving congregation and is a most attractive Georgian church with fluted columns and a series of arched louvred doors which deflect the sun's rays and improve cross-ventilation, essential in the hot climate of the south. The interior walls are white and the church furniture is dark wood, the pews with caned backs and seats for coolness. The fine condition of the church reflects the congregation's devotion. Music is supplied by an old reed organ with guitars at some services appealing to younger members of the parish. Whether Heber's hymns sound good or not with guitar accompaniment, song must keep pace with the times. Bishop Heber College in Trichy is named for him.

There are two statues by Chantrey—one in St Paul's Cathedral in Calcutta and another in St Paul's Cathedral in London. He was quite hard to locate in London. First, having forgotten his location, I enquired at Westminster Abbey. A charming elderly volunteer said he liked questions he couldn't answer. He took me to the Library which looked quite wonderful but having telephoned ahead, a rather bossy Librarian opened her door at the top of a narrow staircase and shouted 'No need to come up here. No need. He's at St Paul's.' I went to the Cathedral on a Friday afternoon to find the entire building was closed for a special Bicentennial service of a school so I returned early on Saturday morning before the multitude of visitors. I asked at the information desk and nobody had heard of Bishop Heber. The guide book was elsewhere so after conferring with two colleagues at another desk, a helpful volunteer led me towards the crypt. We passed Bishop Middleton in a heroic attitude, right hand outstretched and at his left two Indian children kneeling. 'Was this not him?' 'No not him?' I said. In the crypt we found a map of the Cathedral and Heber's monument which presented another problem. He was within the OBE Chapel and it was closed for a wedding. This was just too bad. Tickets for overseas visitors are good for one day only and having come 12,000 miles to see him, would that mean another £14 on Monday? We went back to the desk where the situation was explained to the person on duty who said that the wedding was later than they had thought so it would be ok for me to be taken in to view the sculpture. I hadn't thought I would feel so moved but finally to come face to face with him but it was unexpectedly touching. At last here was the kindly, clever man about whom I had read so much.

Heber's widow wrote that when they learnt of his death, his friends in Oxford opened a subscription for a monument to perpetuate his memory, describing him in their advertisement as a man 'distinguished in this university by his genius and learning, ... virtuous and amiable in private life, and ... thoroughly devoted to the great cause in which his life was lost.' His friends felt such a monument would 'transmit to posterity a record of his eminent services in the propagation of Christianity in India.' Funds soon accumulated. The subscription was then opened in London as well, and extended to include 'the endowment of an oriental scholarship.' At length, the plan bore fruit: 'The monument is the work of Mr Chantrey,' his widow explained. 'It is that of a colossal figure of the bishop, kneeling on a pedestal, in the attitude of devotion, with one hand on his bosom and the other resting on the Bible'. In the *Gentleman's Magazine & Historical Chronicle for the Year 1833* in the section on Fine Arts, the statue which was about to be installed in London was described as having 'an air of sincere devotion on the brow, and a natural elegance about the drapery, which make it one of the finest works of the eminent sculptor' and a worthy companion to Lough's statue of Bishop Middleton.

The inscription says 'This monument was erected by those who loved and admired him. His character exhibited a rare union of fervent zeal with universal tolerance of brilliant talent with sober judgment which no applause could disturb, no success abate. He cheerfully resigned prospects of eminence at home in order to become chief missionary of Christianity in the east and in the short space of three years visited the greater part of India and conciliated the affection and veneration of men of every class of religion was therefore summoned to receive the reward of his labours in the XLII year of his age MDCCXXVI.' Heber is shown in a far more humble attitude than Middleton and it seems to suit his character, his lack of self-importance, patience and kindness. The statue was once located in the south aisle of the choir but was moved to the crypt which probably suits him better.

Far away in a tiny rural hamlet in the colony of New South Wales, once a corner of his vast diocese, there is another memorial to him. The Heber Chapel was built by Rev Thomas Hassall, the first Minister of the parish of St Paul, Cobbitty and dedicated by Rev Samuel Marsden, Senior Chaplain of the colony, in 1828, two years after Heber's death. The little brick building which was used as a school and a hall as well as a church, is still very much a part of the active life of St Paul's, Cobbitty. I went to an Easter service and enjoyed a hot cross bun in the chapel-hall afterwards. A white picket fence surrounds the church-yard where generations of parishioners are buried beneath the lush green turf. The honey-coloured stone of the church is in harmony with the pale brick of the chapel. The palm trees at the gate would have pleased Bishop Heber, and bell-birds piped from tall gum trees beyond in a scene of peace and tranquillity.

The city of Trichy where Heber died is close to the great temple of Sri Ranganathaswamy at Srirangam, probably the largest in India and the biggest active Hindu temple in the world. The contrast between this pulsing hub of devotion and worship and the quiet peace of Cobbitty is hard to imagine. The location of this colossal house of worship is on the Sri Rangam Island, which lies in the middle of the sacred Kaveri River. River confluences or *sangams* are extremely holy places for Hindus and whilst this is not actually a junction of two rivers, the two clasping arms of the Kaveri at either end of the island form auspicious places for bathing. There are railed areas on the edge of the banks where many pilgrims take their holy dips. Others, able to swim and comfortable in deeper water, wade out further into the limpid blue-grey river which at this point is at least half a kilometre wide. On the banks Brahmin priests conduct *pujas* for worshippers. Some sat cross-legged holding black umbrellas or under shady trees, while others sat in the hot sun close to their hearths of sacred fire, banana leaves forming a barrier between the earth and the offerings and other ceremonial paraphernalia. Some pilgrims who have had their heads shaved, offered the hair to the gods. Women were dressed in their most gorgeous saris and many had falls of scented white flowers pinned to their glossy dark hair. A man in a bright orange *dhoti* paraded an elephant with a painted face around the perimeter of the crowd. People gave coins to the enormous creature which held its trunk out in what is taken as a blessing. Everywhere there was colour and movement and away on the southern horizon, out of the plain is the great rock fort of Trichy which has been a strategic lookout and a temple site itself since at least the seventh century.

More than four kilometres of dark red-coloured walls run around the compound, painted in wide, white, vertical stripes. Within are six more walls, one within the next and crowned by the tall South Indian gateway towers or *gopurams* crowded with figures of gods and men. The Hall of a Thousand Pillars houses in fact 953, but who would bother to count? Some pillars are splendid rearing horses dwarfing their human attendants, so lively they appear to be snorting and stamping. People are everywhere—groups of village women dressed in matching saris, some a brilliant orange, devoutly completed their *parikrama* or circumambulation. Men sat threading fragrant, waxy white flowers on strings to offer to a deity, sometimes almost obscured with vermilion. Blessed food can be bought from a temple kitchen and everywhere groups of people sit patiently. After *darshan* with the god in the sanctum sanctorum they can sit and ponder the extraordinary experience. It all flashes past so fast and feelings are heightened by clashing cymbals, loud trumpets and the ringing of bells. Maybe they are waiting again for the moment when they can exchange glances with the god and this time remember what it was they meant to ask. It is very different from the kind of worship Bishop Heber knew but no less meaningful.

PS I didn't expect to encounter Bishop Heber in the Auckland Art Gallery, Toi o Tamaki, but Auckland like Sydney or Calcutta was another outpost of Empire and Church. The Gallery which houses New Zealand's largest art collection, opened in 1888 in a fine Victorian building. It has had a brilliant modern extension and renovation, filling some areas with natural light and allowing views of the adjacent Albert Park with its long awning of sheltering trees.

In an upstairs gallery hang late 19th century portraits by Goldie and Lindauer of Maori chiefs and other important people. Their gaze is level and proud, some tinged with sadness and the almost photographic attention to the detail of *moko* and tattoos, traditional dress and weapons is compelling. On another wall hangs a large painting titled The *New Zealand Chiefs in Wesley's Home* (1863) by James Smetham (1821–89). The work belongs to the Hockens Collections, University of Otago, Dunedin.

Two groups of people frame the central section of the painting. Ten Maori on the left, three Maori and three British on the right. The Maori men are dressed in English suits and the women look demure in full-skirted Victorian gowns but men and women all wear traditional cloaks, flax, feather or dog-skin. One man carries a staff and men and women wear ear-rings, head-bands or *heitiki*. In the centre an upright piano is flanked by a tall Maori and a shorter Englishman. The Maori chief gestures nobly towards a painting on the wall of John Wesley, founder of the Methodist church. The Englishman, one hand on hip, one on the keyboard of the piano, looks fairly pleased with himself.

The informative caption states that William Jenkins, a Wesleyan missionary, organised a trip to London in 1863 for a group of *rangatira* or chiefs to enliven with dance and song a proposed lecture tour on the topic of New Zealand. While Jenkins travelled First Class, the Maori travelled miserably in steerage. *Rangatira,* a novel by Paula Morris published in 2011 tells the story from the point of view of one of Maori men. Much is imagined but fact remains that the relationship between Jenkins and the group deteriorated until Jenkins' final abandonment of the Maori. They were rescued by good Christian people and most returned to New Zealand. During their stay in England they were received by Queen Victoria at Osborne House on the Isle of Wight and by the Prince and Princess of Wales at Marlborough House.

The artist, James Smetham was a follower of the Pre-Raphaelite Dante Gabriel Rossetti. He was a writer, a devout Methodist and as a painter worked in a range of genres—religious and literary themes as well as portraits and landscapes. His religious devotion became manic and he suffered several breakdowns. At the time he painted the Maori group he was in the grip of religious mania though this is not evident in the painting. The story was interesting but what a strange thing, as I peered at the painting I discovered the hymn-book on the piano was open at the page bearing *From Greenland's icy mountains* by BP Heber.

And further, with cricket in mind, how could I have not noticed earlier the connection with the famous sporting goods factory in Meerut—Greenlands with those faraway icy mountains?

Bishop Reginald Heber

Jamie and Emily with the engine driver, near Mysore, Karnataka, 1977

St John's Church, Meerut, Uttar Pradesh

Birds and Cosmic Eggs

Today's domestic fowl probably dates back to ancestors in many regions of Asia about 8,000 years ago. The Indian subcontinent was certainly one origin site and beautiful wild Red Jungle Fowl still roam a wide sweep of territory in forests and national parks. By 2000 BC the fowl had been domesticated by the people of the Harappan Civilisation in the Indus Valley and from there it spread to Europe and Africa. It seems that domestication was achieved first for sport rather than nutrition, cock-fighting found to be more exciting than the joys of roast chicken or a boiled egg. The question must have been the same then as now, what came first the chicken or the egg?

A *Swayambhu Lingam* has been in the collection of the National Gallery of Australia since 1977. I remember talking about it in guided tours of the 1995 *The Vision of Kings* exhibition but it's only really dawned on me twenty years later that it comes from the sacred Narmada River which I have visited a number of times. I have swum in it, diving blithely off a boat into a current that was deceptively strong, and I have taken a dip from the *ghats* in Maheshwar.

Narmada in Sanskrit means 'the Giver of Pleasure'. The river is also called the Rewa, referring to its leaping motion through its rocky bed, from the word *rev* which means swift. Located in Central India, it is the country's fifth longest river and third longest of those which flow entirely within the sub-continent. It forms the traditional boundary between north and south India, flowing westwards 1,312 km from its source to where it meets the Arabian Sea at the Gulf of Cambay on India's west coast, near Baruch in the state of Gujarat. The river is said to have sprung from the body of Shiva, created in the form of a lovely damsel with whom the gods fell in love, hence the name 'the giver of pleasure'. It rises in the mountains at Amarkantak at an altitude of 1057 metres above sea level where the Vindhya and Satpura Ranges meet the Maikal Hills. For hundreds of kilometres the river passes in a rift valley between rocky cliffs. It leaps over chasms and flows through deep narrow ravines before entering a series of fertile basins and finally meandering through rich coastal plains to the sea.

Several holy sites are located on its banks or within its waters. One is the Omkareshwar Temple situated on the island of Mandhata. The island is shaped in the form of the sacred syllable *Om* which gives its name to the famous temple. A huge dam now forms a glowering backdrop to the island. It is part of a controversial hydro-electric scheme which threatens to change the face of the river and its passage through the country.

The Narmada is one of the five holy rivers of Hindu India, along with the Ganges and the Yamuna in the north and the Godavari and Kaveri in the south. The Indus, now in Pakistan, and the vanished Saraswati at Allahabad would make the total seven and other rivers are locally important. To bathe in these rivers, or 'take holy dip' as Indians would say, is to wash one's sins away. A legend says that the Ganga, polluted by the millions of people who bathe in it, takes the form of a black cow and comes to cleanse itself by bathing in the Narmada which is said to be older than the Ganga. In February last year a friend who lives at Maheshwar, met a *sadhu* or holy man from Allahabad who was staying on the *ghats* in one of the little cells let into the base of a temple wall. She asked why he was there when the Mahakumbh Mela, the holiest of Hindu festivals and one which only happens every 144 years, was taking place at his home. 'Too many people.' he said. There were 30,000,000 at the Kumbh! He felt more comfortable at Maheshwar, a small town with a population of only 20,000 people and rather out of the way, 90 km from Indore. This is not to say that it is of no importance, the Baneshwar temple in the middle of the river, *is* said to be the centre of the universe.

A temple at Bithur near Kanpur on the Ganges, several hundred miles away to the east, makes the same claim. In a small shrine at Bithur on the Brahmaghat, a metal bar is said to stretch to the earth's core and Brahma, the Creator, is said to have started his work on the universe here. The lotus, most sacred of flowers in India, is associated with the creation when it arose from the navel of the god Vishnu with Brahma seated on the centre of the bloom. Vishnu is the Preserver and Brahma, who is self-born, is the Creator which presents another chicken and egg situation. Vishnu is equated with Prajapati,* as supreme god and in this manifestation he encompasses Brahma himself as creator and Shiva as destroyer. Vishnu *is* the Cosmic Ocean which spread everywhere before the creation of the universe, in another version of the Great Flood. One of his many names is Narayan or 'moving in the water' and in this role he takes human form, sleeping on the coiled serpent, floating on the cosmic waters. After each destruction of the universe Vishnu resumes this position and the hope is that Brahma will once more recreate the universe.

Nobody need worry at being confused by the distinction between gods and creators because so was Brahma! The teachings from the Jodhpur Court accompanying some of its magnificent early 19th century Nagaur paintings illustrating the ancient texts, describe the moment. While Narayana sleeps, a magnificent lotus with an endless stalk, a pericarp of brilliant hue and the luminosity of ten million suns comes forth from his navel. It quivers into extravagant bloom and Brahma, the four-headed creator god, emerges in a state of utter bewilderment asking the fundamental question of existence, 'Where have I come from? Who is my creator?' The Shiva Purana text says Brahma was 'deluded by illusion' and it took 212 years to find enlightenment. He sought answers to his questions within the lotus, the only thing he knew. It took one hundred years to descend the endless stalk, seeking its base. Receiving no answers, he wandered for another century searching among the petals and stamens. Then began a mental journey of another twelve years of penance, ending when Narayan appeared to reveal that Shiva was the ultimate cause of all creation, the destroyer who destroys in order to create.

Whether or not this happened at Bithur on the Ganga or on the little island temple of Baneshwar in the Narmada, is impossible to say, but holiness is one thing that is not in doubt. There are many stories about the Narmada's origins and two give geographical possibility to Baneshwar's claim. The omnipotent Shiva meditated so hard that he started to sweat—a variation says the sweat came from Shiva Nataraja's body at the time of the cosmic dance. The

---

* Brahma may also be known as Prajapati.

sweat accumulated in a depression and then started to flow as a river. Another story attributes the river's creation to a tear-drop from the eye of Lord Brahma. The river is particularly sacred to Shiva and the stones which roll in the rocky bed of the great lapidary tumbler of the river take the shape of his emblem and become a personification of the God.

These are the *lingam*-shaped stones, *swayambhu* which means self-existent mark or sign of God. Called *Banalinga* or *Banashivalings*, they are cryptocrystalline quartz and are much sought for use in worship at both temples and household shrines. Worshipping a *Banalingam* is considered one thousand times more effective than any other type of lingam. The properties of the rock are believed to have come from a large meteorite which crashed into the Narmada 14 million years ago. The fusion of the meteorite and earthly minerals—religious descriptions label it impregnation rather than fusion—resulted in a new type of rock with extraordinary energetic qualities. The rock is made up of fibrous or granular aggregates of tiny, microscopic quartz crystals and the gemstone chalcedony, with an iron oxide and goethite inclusion, along with basalt and agate. This unique composition coupled with the elliptical shape has a precise resonance in alignment with our energy centres or *chakras*. The hardness on Moe's Scale is 7 and it has one of the highest frequency vibration rates of all stones on the earth. *Shaligrams* from the sacred Gandaki River in Nepal are similar though smaller stones, important for worshippers of Vishnu.

An origin story for self-born lingams is connected with a demonstration of Shiva's destructive nature. In the midst of a huge battle between gods and demons, he shot a fiery dart at the demon, Banasura. It broke the great city of Tripura into tiny pieces which fell on three spots, one on the banks of the Narmada. The pieces multiplied into *crores*, tens of millions, and each became a *lingam*.

Size is not a consideration as far as holiness goes, small is highly meritorious for a self-born lingam. They can be the shape of ripe jambu fruit, lotus seeds, a hen's egg or a swan's egg. Certain families are permitted to collect the stones from the Narmada at Mandhata or Omkareshwar, once a year at a time when the river is low and the stones more safely harvested. They are hand-polished with a secret recipe, a mystic mixture of mud, dung, natural oils, special herbs and wax which bring out the beauty of the natural markings. In the film *Indiana Jones and the Temple of Doom* the sacred stone at the centre of the search is a *swayambhu lingam*.

The construction of dams on the Narmada is affecting exporters of *Shivalinga* who say the stones 'will be submerged by more than a hundred feet of raging water and the chances of future harvests are extremely slim'. These businessmen say they are becoming rare and valuable, and therefore more expensive. It is possible to buy one off the net for $63 and 'big size is available' from one company called Occult Treasures. Another company called Divine Energy Tools sell divine energy wands of Narmada rock.

The term *lingam* is perhaps the most misunderstood symbol in Hinduism and for the gallery guide not the greatest thing to have to describe to children who get the giggles if the explanation includes its definition as a phallic symbol. It is the symbol of the energy and potential of Shiva. The word *lingam* means the way in which the divine is understood or approached. The derivation means movement, etymological not physical. Some of the explanations of its meaning are very esoteric but one is that *ling* can mean to dissolve, become merged with or destroy and *ga* can mean to emerge or go out. The conjunction then refers to all beings becoming dissolved in Shiva at the time of cosmic dissolution and emerging again in the creation that follows Shiva's act of destruction. The *Shivaling* therefore represents the cosmos and the transcendent reality of Shiva (paramashiva). Its upright egg shape—they *are* called Cosmic Eggs—represents the pure consciousness of Lord Shiva and the coloured markings, usually reddish tones, represent the interactive aspect of the Goddess Shakti, the female energy or *shakti* which inspires Shiva's urge to create the divine seed, fertilized to manifest the creative power of the cosmic dance. It is wholeness and oneness, the blending of knowledge and wisdom, harmony through duality—everything really!

Swami Vivekananda famously brought Hinduism to the notice of the rest of the world at the Parliament of the World Religions in

Chicago in 1893. At a Paris conference in 1900 Vivekananda refuted statements by Western scholars regarding the *lingam*. He traced the symbol, not to any form of phallicism but to the idea of a sacrificial post in Vedic ritual, the symbol of the Eternal Brahman or the Supreme Cosmic Spirit, the unchanging reality in the midst of and beyond the world. Another famous teacher, Swami Sivananda, explaining why equating the Shiva *lingam* with the phallus was incorrect, said that the *lingam* become symbolic of the generative power of Lord Shiva and is almost an abstract concept, devoid of smell, colour, taste, hearing and touch and is spoken of as *Prakriti* or Nature.

So perhaps we should describe a *swayambhu lingam* as ovoid rather than phallic. They are considered the most auspicious of all *linga* and because they are naturally occurring or self-born, they do not need to be consecrated before worship. They are one of the most potent of all Hindu sacred images. When installed in some temples they may be set within a circular stone base, the *yoni* or *pitha*, symbolising the female generative organ and female sexual energy which probably makes it harder to be convinced about the absence of phallic symbolism in the lingam.

Many different flowers and leaves are used to worship the god in this form, marigold, lotus, hibiscus, tulsi and neem. In Maheshwar a fascinating form of worship happens each day in a small dark room near shrines and temples in the Ahilya Fort Palace complex. Through a heavy carved door, each morning a group of Brahmins enter to perform an act of devotion called *lingarchan*. They make hundreds of tiny *lingams* from Narmada River clay, the river laps the *ghats* below the walls of the Fort. Older, more experienced priests take about two hours to complete their daily ritual, some younger ones take a little longer. Although the room is quiet it is not an unbreachable silence. The men look up and smile and welcome cameras. The boards on which they place the *linga* are old and smooth from use. There are 365 of these tiny *lingams*, one for each day of the year. Some temples have 365 steps where oblations can be left on any single visit in a substitution for visiting every day of the year. Grains of rice are placed on the top of each small mound and then the whole washed in holy Narmada water.

The bathing of these and any *lingam* has its origin in a story from the Ramayana. Lord Brahma granted a wish to the pious King Bhagirath. He asked for the River Ganga to come down to earth from heaven to wash over the ashes of his ancestors and thus remove a curse which prevented them from entering heaven. Lord Brahma granted the wish but told the king to pray to Shiva for he alone could support the weight of the river's descent. His prayers were answered, Shiva allowed the Ganga to fall on his head and flow through his matted locks until the holy river reached the earth. This moment is re-enacted each time a lingam is bathed. In Maheshwar after the mesmerising creation of the tiny *linga*, the clay will be gathered up again, unceremoniously reformed into a big lump and put in a bucket for the whole procedure to take place the next morning.

There are many other interesting things about Maheshwar. Temples and shrines are found along the *ghats* where each morning worshippers bathe—and wash their clothes. It is close to the largely intact ruins of the medieval city of Mandu where strangely the vegetation includes many introduced baobab trees which give an added layer of the exotic. An ancient archaeological site lies just across the river from the fort and there is a thriving weaving cooperative which produces beautiful handloom textiles of cotton, silk and wool. It is called Rewa, that alternative name for the Narmada.

The fort is named for Ahilya Bhai, a brave, able and virtuous Maharani who, after the death of her husband, father-in-law and son, ruled the Kingdom of the Holkars of Indore from Maheshwar from 1767 to 1795. She is one of India's great women heroes and everywhere in the modern state of Madhya Pradesh things are named after her, the airport in Indore, hospitals, schools and institutions. Her image is found in many places in Maheshwar and in small market stalls specialising in holy pictures, she is almost as prominent as some of the gods. At the gatehouse to the fort a more than double life-size gilded statue of Ahilya Bhai stands as guardian close to the steps that lead down to the *ghats* through a temple forecourt. Each Monday she is symbolically taken, in the form of a garlanded painting, in her *palki* or palanquin down to the town. This recreates the weekly visits she made to her advisors. Musicians accompany her and she is brought back safely to a shrine in the palace, her former home.

Another part of this home is now a wonderful small hotel, one of India's most delightful places to stay. It is owned and run by a charming bon vivant, Richard Holkar, a descendant of Ahilya Bhai. He has an interesting history and in the hotel there is photograph of him as a small boy with his Indian father and American mother.

His father, as a young man, was painted several times by the French artist, Bernard Boutet de Monvel. The first showing an incredibly elegant, tall, thin man in western evening dress, is dated 1929. The second, dated 1934 shows him in Indian dress seated on white cushions and bolsters. He wears a white garment of fine cotton over a pale golden silky undershirt and the distinctive red Maratha *pagri* or turban, boat-shaped with a cockade flipping up on the left hand side. It is called a *shindeshahi*. A long sword in a striped scabbard, red, green, saffron and white lies diagonally on one thigh, resting on gorgeous saffron silk. His hands rest on his knees, his long, artistic-looking fingers looking a little fidgety. His triangular face holds a level gaze but he has the look of a tiger about to spring. He might be a little tired of sitting for this portrait. The gaze and the beautiful composition of colour and whiteness almost distracts from what he is wearing around his neck. It is a double string of large pearls mounted with the Indore Pears, a matched pair of pear-cut diamonds which his father bought from Chaumet in the early 1910s. The portrait graces the cover of *Made for Maharajas: A Design Diary of Princely India*. I bought my copy in Delhi as a reward for finishing six months work for the Jaipur Virasat Foundation. It is a first edition and came in a small saffron-coloured suitcase, about the same size as a portable typewriter.

His name was Yeshwant Rao II Holkar Bahadur who was until his death in 1961, Maharaja of Indore, today part of Madhya Pradesh. Born in 1908, he ascended the throne while still in his teens after the abdication of his father in 1926. He had been educated in England at Cheam, Charterhouse and Oxford and had developed sophisticated western tastes. He loved jazz, fast cars, the casinos at Monte Carlo, modern design and technology and with an annual of income of at least $40,000,000 he could indulge most passions. While at Oxford he met the German architect designer Eckhart Muthesius whom he chose to design a new palace located on the then outskirts of Indore. It must have then been surrounded by fields, but now although still in a large, leafy compound, it lies within a suburban neighbourhood of the city. Built between 1930 and 1932 as a private home, the older Lal Bagh palace was used for formal events and was the administrative headquarters of the state. Muthesius' design for the new palace was realised in close consultation with the Holkar and his wife, Maharani Sanyogita Raje. It was a showplace of avant-garde European style, described as a 'fairy tale palace of modernism'. The building took three years to build with a hundred local workers and a number of elephants on site. Most of the mechanical elements of the palace came from Germany—heating, air conditioning and refrigeration, the water works, laundry and automatic telephone systems. The furniture and fittings were commissioned from Emile-Jacques Ruhlmann, Eileen Gray, Louis Sognot & Charlotte Alix, Johan Eckel, Max Kruger, Muthesius himself, Le Corbusier and other contemporary luminaries. It was called Manik Bagh which means Gem or Jewel Garden, perhaps a connection with the family's astounding collection of magnificent jewellery.

I have visited Indore five times over thirty years in pursuit of this palace. There are at least four former royal residences in and around the city and the last Holkar Maharaja maintained 17 homes run by 200 staff in various parts of the world. Prior to Manik Bagh's construction the most recent was Lal Bagh begun in 1886 with a 'mystifying mix' of baroque and renaissance architecture. The impressive gates were modelled on those of Buckingham Palace, built and shipped from London.

My first search in 1984 was fairly desultory, I was a keen new Gallery Guide on a mission but with only two days in the town and no contacts, I made little progress. I was somewhat better equipped on the last couple of visits but each time I was firmly told that a visit to Manik Bagh was quite out of the question. Indore is not a tourist destination and the person who tried to deter me was an immensely likeable and well-educated man with strong connections to the erstwhile royal family. I was never pushy about it and so it was easy enough for him to say no when I somewhat feebly broached the subject, though he in fact had no actual say in whether I could visit or not. I think his attitude was tinged with regret at what the palace once was and how it is today, occupied by the regional Department of Customs & Excise. The royal family relinquished Manik Bagh in 1971. I thought I really only wanted to put my nose through the gate just to say to myself that I'd seen it because after all, that which I sought, enigmatically, had actually never existed.

At last one November, luck was on my side. I was leading a tour and Sandhya Harendra, a wonderful friend from Bangalore, accompanied us as guide. She is up for a challenge and thought the best thing to do was just turn up at the Customs & Excise office, be perfectly charming and see what would happen. I can get excited over a pin and this was a pretty big pin—Customs & Excise occupy the building in which once rested the National Gallery of Australia's great treasures, a white and a black marble *Bird in space* by the Rumanian sculptor, Constantin Brancusi. We were welcomed in.

The writer, Henri-Pierre Roché, brought the maharaja to visit Brancusi in his Paris studio in 1933. A 1989 NGA publication quotes Roché.

'The visitor looked at every work slowly and quietly as in a dream ... He pulled his little notebook out of his pocket and began careful calculations. Why? He simply wanted to buy the three major and related works which were there: a large Bird in Space in black marble, one in white marble and one in polished bronze. A unique trio. He was counting the money he was able to spend.

He also wanted, later to have a temple built for them by Brancusi, twelve paces by twelve, placed on the lawn near his palace, as if it had fallen from the sky, without doors or windows, with an underground entrance, a temple in which to meditate, open to everybody but to only one person at a time.

Inside there would be a square mirror of water with the three birds on three sides and a tall oak sculpture, The Spirit of Buddha by Brancusi on the fourth side, arranged so that the Golden Bird in polished bronze would be struck by the sun precisely at noon, through a circular hole in the *ceiling, on a particular sacred day of the year.'*

The Spirit of Buddha has been renamed *King of Kings*. The monumental 3 metres tall is now located in the Guggenheim Museum in New York. It is dated 1938 so if this was the work destined for the proposed temple, only the idea could have been discussed at the outset. It was never owned by the maharaja.

The birds arrived at Indore in 1936 and according to an article 'From the Archives' in *The Art Newspaper* of March 2004, the maharaja's first idea was to display them in an architectural 'aviary'. But following the death of his young wife in 1937 at the age of only 22, the Maharaja invited Brancusi to design a Temple of Love and Peace in which her ashes would be interred. The usual Indian form for a royal cenotaph is a stone *chhatri* and in Indore there is a lovely peaceful garden with a cluster of fine *chhatris,* memorials to several members of the Indore royal family. The ashes after cremation would normally be cast into a sacred river so the newspaper's deduction in the newspaper is somewhat inaccurate.

The Art Newspaper's tone and the terms 'Temple of Love and Peace' and 'architectural aviary' sound a little patronising. It is not certain whether the original idea of the temple was that of the maharaja or the sculptor. Roché said it was the Holkar but the prompt could have come from Brancusi. In Michael Lloyd and Michael Desmond's book *European and American Paintings and Sculptures 1870–1970 in the Australian National Gallery* (1992) they quote correspondence between the two using Roché as intermediary. This indicated that the Maharaja first envisaged a 'sacred precinct' open to the air and 'enclosed by a tall, hardy hedge' with the 'Birds sheltering in niches at the sides of a rectangular pool of water'. Brancusi, in his desire to combine sculpture and architecture in a place of spiritual contemplation, suggested a 'small Pantheon-like structure lit by a single opening in a vault or dome'. Another plan was a small building resembling a stupa which appropriately suited the fourth sculpture, *The Spirit of the Buddha,* the stupa originating in India as a Buddhist architectural form. Yet another suggestion was that the temple should be egg-shaped which would have had a great regional and spiritual link to the Narmada *swayambhu lingams.* Considering all the divine ovoid shapes in Brancusi's oeuvre this may have been appealing.

The temple interior too underwent many unrealised changes. Frescoes of birds, such a central theme for Brancusi, might have provided the abstract sculptured birds with a reality as well as a metaphor. Sketches of the Brancusi's temple have survived and it would seem that the project appealed to him greatly. He arrived in India at the end of December 1937 ready to start work.

I read years ago in a book about maharajas, the humorous exasperation of a British resident, endlessly waiting for a decision from *his* prince. Quoting from the 1937 Walt Disney animated film, *Snow White and the Seven Dwarfs*, he sighed, 'Someday my Prince will come'. The song, is ranked as the 19th greatest film song of all time. Snow White sings it to the dwarfs as a bed-time treat. AND it is our 19 gun salute Maharaja for whom Sir Kenneth Fitze, then Resident for Central India, waited.

Brancusi might well have echoed the feeling. A photograph taken in January 1938 by Eckhardt Muthesius, shows him wearing his *sola topi*, sitting perhaps in a temple or a gazebo, gazing into the distance and looking rather pensive. A better description of his mood might have been, fed up. The maharaja was away, apparently on a tiger hunt, having lost interest in the project. A particular distraction may have been his new American wife, previously engaged as nurse for his motherless daughter. Brancusi cooled his heels at the palace for a month before giving up and returning to Paris. He never lost interest in the temple project however, and spoke of it as late as 1950.

Quoting from the Guggenheim website, the temple 'would have embodied the concerns most essential to Brancusi's art: the idealization of aesthetic form; the integration of architecture, sculpture, and furniture; and the poetic evocation of spiritual thought.' The Temple of Meditation was never built but where would it have been located? Indore's rulers were keen on underground passages. At Lal Bagh, the kitchens were located across a stream reached by tunnel and at Manik Bagh the laundry and bakeries occupied adjacent buildings connected underground to the palace. Another private residence was designed by Muthesius just a few kilometres away from Manik Bagh on the shores of Rajpilia Tank.

The Maharaja had requested a private underground railway linking the two palaces but the Rajpilia building was never constructed.*

Was the temple access to have come from the palace or from steps located in the lawn near the temple? I don't think anyone knows. There are still extensive lawns in the flat garden behind the palace which might have been a likely location for temple. Photographs taken in the 1930s show this part of the garden has undergone some fiddling and suffered a bit of Mughulisation to turn it into a pseudo *charbagh,* the Persian fourfold garden plan though there had been some small reference to the Mughuls in the original plans for the inner colonnaded courtyard where a narrow glass-covered channel flowed along the middle of the central path, continuing down four shallow steps and on for a yard or so. The plan may have been to locate the temple in the large lawn at the front of the palace, beyond the porte cochere. It is impossible to say.

When we saw the U-shaped building, the roof was covered in bright blue tarpaulins and I wondered if that meant that renovation work was underway. The answer was that the tiles were European and of heritage value and for this reason were being protected. The bright blue distorted our perception of the building which had originally been a contrast of whitewashed roughcast walls and rusty red awnings sheltering the many windows and verandas. On a large pediment set into the central roof overlooking the courtyard, the coat of arms of Indore looked a little weather-beaten. It shows a field of poppy and wheat, the state's principal crops, and over them are crossed broadsword and spear. A rearing saddled horse appears on the left and on the right is Nandi, the sacred bull, the vehicle of Lord Shiva, seated as he always is in a temple, facing his Lord. The horse and the sword refer to Khande Rao, a warrior-god and tutelary deity of the Holkars whose chief temple is to be found at Jejuri near Pune. Above all a radiant sun refers to the Holkars' descent from Udaipur, the paramount state of Rajasthan, which has the sun as its emblem. Above that again is a *chhatri* or royal umbrella which, as well as being an emblem of state, refers to the story of a hooded

---

* In *Treasures of Canberra* by Betty Churcher and Lucy Quinn, the idea of the temple and its subterranean access is linked beautifully with the Turell SkySpace *Within Without*.

cobra sheltering from the sun the sleeping founder of the dynasty. The motto is written in Hindi within a ribbon and translated says 'Umesh (i.e. Shiva) has said, success attends him who strives.'

We were asked not to take photographs inside the building but the Director of Customs & Excise invited us into his office and more than happily posed for a photograph with me in front of an original 1930s decoration, a silver map of India inlaid into the wall. Several gentlemen showed us into some of the first floor offices where we were greeted by clerks who looked pleased at the variation in a normal day's work. The offices in former bedrooms were furnished with bashed old Indian public service tables, chairs and filing cabinets. Odd moulded forms graced the ceilings. It was pure art deco but functionally they related to mosquito nets. Photographs taken of the finished 1930s interiors show net curtains which could be pulled all the way around the moulding. The air conditioning unit, one of the earliest installed on the subcontinent, might have meant that windows need not be opened for cooling but mosquitoes must have been a continuing nuisance. The clerks were keen that we look into the en suite bathrooms which they said were not in use. They were gloomy and dark with great clunking chrome fittings and actually quite repellent though in the 1933 photographs they look streamlined and smart.

The Maharani's bedroom was not in use as an office and the door was locked with a sealed padlock. Inside there were vestiges of the greens of the original décor, eau de nil and emerald, but the room was bare. The original spare interior with its chrome, glass and tubular steel furniture looks cold in photographs and one of Muthesius' briefs was to safeguard the inhabitants from the ferocious summer heat. Light was regulated by awnings and smoked glass, indirect lighting, verandas and covered walkways. Small silver-coloured metal particles were added to the paint to reflect light on both exterior walls and interior ceilings, applied by the new technique of spray painting. The shimmering effect must have been beautiful, adding to the palace's name of Jewel Garden.

The theatre ballroom was marvellous and in very good condition, located on the ground floor at the end of the right hand wing, close to the garden. So perhaps the site for the contemplative temple might have been more sensitively placed further away from a place of potential riotous fun. The gentlemen from Customs & Excise were keen to tell us that the floor was sprung. Muthesius' original plan specified a marble floor but as the Maharaja and Maharani were enthusiastic dancers a sprung floor was provided. The mural at the end of the long, slim room is by Luigi Parisio, a sculptor who worked for the Atelier André Hunebelle in Paris. The subject is an Amazon in a half-crouching position, about to fire an arrow from a taut bow, sandblasted on a black roughcast glass plate from Saint-Gobain. The work has an affinity with Bakst's Ballets Russes designs which is another oblique link to Brancusi and his theme of birds. He completed 27 bird sculptures over 30 years in marble and bronze. The magic bird in Romanian folklore with its glorious song and brilliant plumage which inspired the creation of his first bird *Maiastra*, comes from the same legend which in its Russian form was the inspiration for *L'Oiseau de feu (Firebird)* commissioned by Diaghilev in 1910 with music by Stravinsky and costume and set design by Bakst. *Maiastra* was created in the same year *Firebird* had its Paris premiere. The National Gallery's *Birds in Space* are dated 1931–36.

The baby grand piano and orchestra's music stands and chairs have gone from the stage. The original cantilevered chairs which look very agreeable for the audience and almost too comfortable for the orchestra, were designed by the German architect designer Hans Luckhardt. Made in Berlin of tubular steel and black lacquered wood, examples may be found in collections such as MOMA in New York. The music stands and the lights fixtures were also manufactured in Berlin to Muthesius' design—the lovely triple saucer lights are intact.

The metal and glass light fixtures throughout Manik Bagh were, like everything else in the palace, very avant garde. The lights in the ballroom are a similar saucer shape to the supported wall lamps found in the banqueting hall. They are bronze and nickel silver, designed by Muthesius and made in the Berlin workshop of Max Kruger. Photographs taken in 1933 and then again in 1968, show the addition of a rather nasty central chandelier quite out of keeping with the sleek art deco lighting. The table also contributed to the illumination as recesses in its thick glass top accommodated both sunken lighting fixtures and flower arrangements.

The later photograph taken by New York art dealer, Richard Feigen, is interesting because the spaces on either side of lamps flanking a black stained American walnut sideboard designed by Muthesius and made in Berlin by Johann Eckel, are where the National Gallery's *Birds in Space,* the last of Brancusi's marble birds, came to roost. The black bird on the left and the white on the right, rested on pale limestone bases. The bronze bird was placed in a corner of the maharaja's sitting room. The photograph is not only interesting but historically important as it was all that members of the Gallery's Acquisitions Committee had to examine at their meeting in November 1973.

That year the Tate in London had wanted to buy the black *Bird in space* but the trustees decided against the idea because of what they perceived as problems regarding its export from India. It had left India not as a work of art but as a 'marble stand and a limestone table'. It was a curious repetition in reverse of an event which happened in 1926 when crates of Brancusi's works, escorted by Marcel Duchamp, arrived in New York for an exhibition. US Customs officials opened the crates to find discs, eggs and elongated forms which they refused to recognise as art and thus exempt from customs duties which were very stiff. A bronze *Bird in Space*, already purchased by photographer, Edward Steichen, was particularly dumbfounding to the customs officers. Under pressure from the indignant Duchamp, Brancusi and Steichen, Customs agreed to reconsider and released the *Bird in Space* and other works on bond, classified as 'Kitchen Utensils and Hospital Supplies'.

Something similar happened again in 1938, when Peggy Guggenheim planned a sculpture exhibition at her London Gallery with works by Arp, Brancusi, Moore, Calder and others. A 1932 law had been passed in Great Britain to discourage the import of gravestones made on the Continent. Such materials entering Britain were treated as stone and wood carvings and were subject to heavy import duty unless held to be works of art. In doubtful cases, the director of the Tate Gallery became the arbiter. J B Manson, the director at the time, was no fan of modern art, and ruled that the sculptures destined for Guggenheim Jeune were not art and should be kept out of Britain. In an interview Manson contemptuously said this 'sort of stuff' had 'played havoc' with young art students and that on being told that 'an ostrich egg in marble represents the birth of the world, something must be wrong.' This was a Brancusi work—and there's that egg again. Debate about the case went as far as the House of Commons which ruled that the works could be imported as art and thus the show could be staged, buoyed along by the huge publicity. Manson was humiliated and resigned his position.

Peggy Guggenheim owned several Brancusi sculptures. She had also had quite a lengthy affair with him. She was a tight-fisted negotiator and was shocked at the $4000 price he asked for a bronze *Bird in Space*. For a time she gave up on both creator and bird but meanwhile bought a 1912 version of *Maiastra* from the sister of the famous dress designer, Paul Poiret. She described *Maiastra* as 'a beautiful bird with an enormous stomach' but hankered still after the bronze *Bird in Space*. A mutual friend patched up the rift and Peggy determinedly renegotiated the sale, buying francs in New York so saving $1000 on the purchase price. These negotiations took place during her rather cold-blooded amassing of art works in Paris in 1940 as the Germans were actually attacking the city. She wrote to a friend that of everything she owned she loved this bronze the most.

Richard Holkar, son of the Maharaja, remembers the birds as 'just being there'. I've stayed now several times at Ahilya Fort part of which he turned into a boutique hotel in 2000. In 2009 I took with me some photocopies of new acquisitions in the National Gallery of Australia's photography collection which Gael Newton, Curator of Photography, hoped he might identify. I also took a copy of a truly beautiful photo of his father and his aunt as children now in the Gallery collection. He'd never seen it before and found it very touching. Gael then kindly sent him a good copy.

Richard's American mother was the Maharaja's third wife. His half-sister, Usha Devi, inherited their father's title. In 1950 she was chosen to inherit by her father. It was unprecedented that a ruler be succeeded by a female when male issue existed, but the Maharaja made application to the Indian Government who issued a gazette extraordinary, approving the decision. The Maharaja expressed his pleasure at the Indian government's consent by giving £3,000 for women's education in India. His privy purse from the Indian government at the time was £131,000.* Why this all happened it is hard to say, though some sources say Richard, who was only six years old at the time, was ineligible because his mother was American. If this was the basis for the decision it would seem a continuation of the harsh and heartless British practice of not allowing Indian princes to marry foreigners. There are many interesting stories about *that* and three Indian princes married Australian women. One even has a connection in Canberra—Joan Falkiner who married the Nawab of Palanpur. It is her parents who are shown in the National Gallery's painting by George Lambert, *Weighing the fleece*.

Yeshwant Rao Holkar Bahadur II, 14th Maharaja of Indore, departed for his heavenly abode on 5 December 1961 aged only 56, and Usha Devi Malhotra as successor assumed the title of Maharanidhiraja, 15th Maharani of Indore. The family was faced with frightful death duties as little financial planning had been done. The tax bill was Rupees 100 *crores* i.e. 100 x 10,000,000 a shocking amount. The two marble birds from Manik Bagh palace were inherited by Maharani Usha Devi, who had in 1956 married Mr Satish Chandra Malhotra.

The Tate's decision was the National Gallery of Australia's good luck. Director James Mollison consulted with the Indian High Commission in Canberra and was reassured that Indian export prohibitions regarding art did not extend to modern works by foreign artists. So the 1973 Acquisitions Committee decided to go ahead with the purchase of the black bird, insisting at the same time on first option to purchase the white bird which Richard Feigen felt he would secure. Decades later Feigen told *The Art Newspaper* that he refused to take delivery of the white bird in India and that ownership

---

* The Government of India withdrew official recognition of all the symbols of princely India in 1971. Their titles, privileges and remuneration by privy purses were abolished.

took place at sea once the ship was out of Indian waters. When *The Art Newspaper* questioned Satish Malhotra about the matter he said 'no, we never had them.' Like George Washington, he probably 'cannot tell a lie' and they probably never *did* have them *in their own home*.

There are many contradictions in the whole story, from Roché's description of the Maharaja's visit to Brancusi's studio to their final dispersal. *The Art Newspaper* stated that Richard Holkar's mother was Marguerite Branyan (known as Peg), his father's second wife. In fact his mother was Euphemia Crane Watt (known as Faye) who had obtained a Reno divorce on the same day as Yeshwant Rao and they married on the same day, 7 July 1943. It was two divorces and a wedding, not four weddings and a funeral. The ruler was still only 35 so he had packed a lot of life into those years. The second wife actually was given custody of little Princess Usha, aged 9, whom she had legally adopted, and as part of the divorce settlement she was given the bronze *Bird in Space*. *The Art Newspaper* says that on Peg's death it passed to 'her son, Richard' but as we have seen, he was not exactly her son. Richard Feigen sold the bronze bird to the Californian collector Norton Simon in 1972 and it is one of the highlights of the Norton Simon Museum in Pasadena, California. They show the provenance of their works on their website and there it lists the work as going by inheritance from Peg Branyan to both Richard Holkar and Maharani Usha Devi.

Recently I heard an interview with Mark Cocker, the author of a book called *Birds and People*. He said that because they can fly but still have two legs like man, birds have become exalted in symbolism. He calls them the ambassadors for our environment. They figure in numerous coats of arms and symbolise joy, consolation, wisdom, irritation, perseverance and tenacity among other things. I am sure that Brancusi's *Birds in Space* are inspirational. He was fascinated by flight in any form. He said, 'All my life I have only sought the essence of flight. Flight—what bliss!' The first installation of the birds at the National Gallery of Australia in their contemplative and protective pool was homage to the unrealised dream of the temple and the end of a long journey.

Narmada River, central India. *Self born linga (svayambhu linga)* 19th century or earlier, polished stone, 48.25 diameter cm. National Gallery of Australia, Canberra. Gift of Philip Goldman 1977

Devare & Co. Established Bombay c.1900-40s. *Prince Yeshwant Rao Holkar and his sister* c.1920, gelatin silver photograph, water colour, original gilded frame, 36.7 x 26.6 cm. National Gallery of Australia, Canberra. Purchased 2009

Gone for Shopping

My connection to the National Gallery of Australia in Canberra is one of the most important things in my life. For years I was a volunteer guide, starting training in 1983, the first year of the Gallery's physical life in the building on the edge of Lake Burley Griffin. I later worked as a volunteer in Asian Art, usually in jobs connected to the textile collection through the Conservation Department. Because I could sew and iron, skills which are becoming increasingly endangered, I had enjoyable and interesting spells in textile conservation connected first to an Australian folk art exhibition and later work on a big exhibition of Ballets Russes costumes in the 1990s. Later I was lucky enough to join the staff. I could type and take shorthand and the comprehensive year-long Guides Course meant I knew my around the gallery well. I spent very happy years working for terrific men and doing all manner of interesting things—being press liaison for the Vivien Westwood exhibition was exciting and once I made the Indonesian dishes for the Director's morning tea with the wife of the Indonesian Prime Minister who was accompanied by Mrs Howard, the wife of our then Prime Minister, who preferred the scones.

In 2003 I was having a great deal of bother trying to extract money owed me by publishers in New Delhi. They had taken on my pineapple book and had somehow neglected to pay me for copies sold. Instalments were supposed to have come every six months but eighteen had passed without a penny received. It was only the matter of about $1500 but my slim finances at the time meant that was pretty important to me and amounted at least to a fare to India and back after all. Telephone calls, faxes and emails had no effect, I was too far away to consider. But impecuniousness leads to persistence and fortunately I knew the good-natured Indian High Commissioner who brought quiet pressure to bear and the publishers grudgingly paid up. Before this happened I sighed to

Ron Ramsey, my boss at the NGA, and said 'I should go and do the buying for the Indian shop and sort out this scoundrel.' 'Why don't you?' he said. He put it to the Marketing Department and all was agreed. I had to pay my own fare but I was later able to get it back on tax and the Gallery paid for costs for five or six days. The purchases would stock the exhibition shop connected to a wonderful show called *Sari to Sarong* due to open at the Gallery a couple of months later. One of the shop staff members had a business connection to Bali and she went there to do the Indonesian shopping.

A week later at a dinner following a talk by Sir Roy Strong at the National Portrait Gallery, one of my work colleagues said how pleased he was to hear of the shopping expedition. My friend, Annie Poxleitner, was seated beside me and said without a pause 'I'd like to go with you.' I replied like Ron 'Why don't you?' She rang me at about 7.30 the next morning to say she had already organised a dog-sitter, a house-sitter and when would we depart? We set off a few weeks later in half-empty planes because of the Asian bird-flu crisis and arrived in Delhi in fine shape. It was May and very hot but on the first morning, unable to sleep for excitement we went walking in the Lodi Gardens which is a great start to any day.

That is how my epic Indian shopathons began. I have now done quite a few—four for major exhibitions and many smaller sorties for general stock for the main Gallery shop. I've also shopped twice in Jakarta in Indonesia and once in Kuching in Malaysia, a spot in Hong Kong as well as smaller amounts of merchandise for a couple of regional gallery shops. That first time made me very nervous and I did a deal of circling like a hovering hawk before I plunged happily headlong into spending someone else's money. It was great having Annie's company and as she is a very forthright woman of definite views, it made me crystallise my own thoughts and go into action. I had been given a very complicated diagram of how much I was to spend on various types of merchandise. It was a big triangle with a variety of things on the long base, the cheapest range including what they called counter fodder—cheap things to sit on the counter near the cash register. There were prescriptions about how much to spend percentagewise and on what, from baseline through each diminishing division of the triangle ending with expensive jewellery and treasures on the top. It was terribly complicated but I dutifully followed the recommendations. Thank goodness I've never been given such structure again and having proved myself, now the gorgeous trusting people in the shop leave it to me. It *is* quite something to be entrusted with thousands and thousands of dollars to spend on what it is hoped everyone will like. No not just like, *adore* and fight over. Sometimes I have to buy things I don't find madly appealing and in colours I dislike but I've learned how to cope with that.

Sari to Sarong: 500 years of Indian and Indonesian textile exchange was a very beautiful exhibition. Robyn Maxwell, the curator and head of Asian Art, had an international reputation in the field of Asian textiles and the Gallery has one of the best collections of South and South-East Asian textiles in the world. The exhibition showed the historical connections of the textile trade between India and Indonesia and the exchange of ideas resulting from what was far from a one-way process. Some of the 200 textiles on show were designed in India for trade and tailored for the destination market, while others from Indonesia featured motifs and symbols from Hindu, Buddhist and Islamic cultures common to both countries. Sumptuous cloths with much use of gold came from Indonesian royal courts, old Indian patola cloths were reincarnated in Indonesian ikats and whimsical batiks showed the influence of the Chinese Peranakan community.

I've shopped for splendid NGA exhibitions of Indian paintings, Islamic arts in South East Asia, animist art from the same region and twice I have focused on the subject of Krishna, visiting particularly Vrindhavan in the state of Uttar Pradesh and Nathdwara in Rajasthan, two towns which inspire pilgrimage to different forms of the god. Before leaving home I talk with curators and shop managers and I am given a great sheaf of photocopies of works to be included in the show and text explaining the ethos of the exhibition. Sometimes there are themes to pursue like cows or peacocks, spirals or crescents or mandalas and occasionally people have strong views about what not to buy. 'Don't buy thimbles' I was once sternly told!

The first trip taught me an enormous amount though some of the lessons were ghastly to endure. Quite often things go slightly wrong, almost always in connection with freight forwarders. Public holidays are something to be taken very seriously, particularly in South-East Asia. Ramadan and Idul Fitri in Jakarta or the eve of Gawai Dayak in Kuching, Diwali, elections or even a cricket test series in India can wreck the best-laid preparations. There's no point getting agitated with anyone as it will make no difference. Staying as cool, calm and collected as humanly possible is of prime importance, even if it is total pretence and all is a seething terror underneath. Once in Jakarta I was ham-strung by a local day off when nobody answered telephones and finding myself in a bit of a predicament, I rang the National Gallery in Canberra to find exactly the same situation. Nobody was answering the phone there either. I started to feel as though I must be on some other planet until I realised that it was the first Tuesday in November and it was exactly the time of the great horse race!

The freight forwarders in Delhi whom the Gallery had suggested I use on the first trip turned out to be a pack of utter crooks and on the day before I was due to fly home, I was suddenly faced with a room full of goods and nobody to take if off my hands. I called my friend Laila Tyabji, the director of a wonderful craft NGO where I bought a lot of merchandise. She suggested I call her pal, Mr Gupta. It was boiling hot—about 44° outside—and after an enforced and very hurried errand in the burning sun I returned to find Annie calmly organising a cup of tea for Mr Gupta. He took everything in hand and then asked for payment in cash. This was almost too much for my equilibrium. If Laila said I could trust him that was recommendation indeed, but handing a great deal of cash over to a man I had known for an hour? What to do? I know *now* that in certain situations this is what one has to do for freight but I wasn't so sure then. I did have a certain amount of cash plus two credit cards. He took me in his car to the Khan Market where we tried a couple of ATM's which gave me instant heart failure, declaring 'insufficient funds' and other unsettling and incorrect information. At last we found a cooperative machine which disgorged the money but in handing it over I felt as though I was handing over my life. Mr Gupta has an incredible reputation for doing a faultless job. He can pack up a huge terracotta statue of a many-armed god and have it arrive at the Metropolitan Museum in New York with every finger intact. He's the tops, as honest as the day is long and a perfect gentleman. I've used his services many times since. He has a brother who looks exactly like him—two peas in stout little pods.

Before I left home in 2003 I had contacted various organisations and shops on behalf of the Gallery and asked if we might have a discount. I always try to buy where possible from craft NGO's and cooperatives and fair trade businesses known to be kind to workers and suppliers. Laila Tyabji, who suggested Mr Gupta as my rescuer, is the current Chairperson and one of the founders of Dastkar. It was founded in 1981 as a society for crafts and craftspeople with two main aims. It promotes the survival of traditional crafts but also aims to improve the economic status of the craftspeople. It believes that craft has a great social, cultural and economic force which is endangered by urbanisation and the growth of the industrial sector. Workshops and gentle introductions to new ideas and techniques help tradition keep up with contemporary taste and in times of natural disasters Dastkar is there to help wherever possible. They assist craftspeople to become self-reliant and independent enough to avoid the commercial middleman. Several times a year in a number of Indian cities it holds 'Nature Bazaars' where the array of craft is a sight to see. They are not to be missed, drawing the finest craftswomen and men from all over India who display their goods and sell in a convivial atmosphere. We bought beautiful handloom shawls and scarves, sweet lac toys for little children, leather goods and all manner of interesting things in the shop at Shahpur Jat.

The State Emporia on Baba Kharak Singh Marg are a mixed bag but we quickly zipped past less interesting establishments and found wonderful traditional red and white towels from Assam, block-printed table-cloths from Madhya Pradesh and mirrored and embroidered animals from Gujarat. Some years ago part of this area underwent a face-lift and Kamala, the shop run by the Crafts Council of India and located in Rajiv Gandhi Handcrafts Bhawan, is where I make a bee-line these days when I'm in Delhi. They always have something new and fresh and interesting and it has lifted the standard of design considerably. I sent Annie off to Agra for a day's sight-seeing while I got on with the shopping, and doing the inevitable sums. I did some furious haggling over embroidered bags and hangings with the Gujarati ladies on Janpath Lane and bought some super things from Fabindia. My friend Jasleen Dhamija who has a lifetime of activity and research in textiles and craft gave me excellent advice and arranged a couple of meetings.

I had received a polite reply to my letter from Central Cottage Industries Emporium in New Delhi and on arrival at the store, we were taken to meet Mr Durgesh Shankar who was then the Managing Director of the corporation. He handed us over to Mr Saini and Mr Lashkari from the Export Department from whom we received gentle and efficient help. The staff at Cottage are sometimes criticised for a certain lack of interest—call that sheer boredom— but this shopping expedition was different. I was even invited to write an article about 'Cottage' for their House Journal and *Gone for Shopping*, the same title as this essay, was published a few months later. The title is the message often given by household helpers on the phone when a friend is out. 'Hello Madam, no Madam has gone for shopping.' Textiles have always been a great strength of Cottage so shopping for *From Sari to Sarong* was a breeze. I bought *mashru* and *kalamkari* by the metre, *zariwork* velvet purses and sequin-dotted crewel-embroidered tablecloths, ikat and *bandhani* dupattas, embroidered cushion covers, quilted bags, blockprint indigo bedcovers and brocade stoles.

In a spot of personal shopping I bought a copy of *Crafts of India and Cottage Industries* written by Mr Shankar which traced Cottage's 50 year history as well as giving a comprehensive view of the richness of India's crafts. I was delighted to discover that the day which Cottage recognises as its birthday is also mine, 1st November.

In 1969 I had arrived in Delhi with Jane Sheaffe, another Australian student who like me had been staying with a family in Mysore after our first passage to India. How we ever knew where to go is now a bit of a mystery in pre-Lonely Planet days but somehow we found our way to the YMCA International Hostel in Jaisingh Road. After a couple of weeks on third class trains it was luxuriously clean, warm and comfortable. Here we discovered that tickets for folk-dance performances, concerts, polo and above all the Republic Day Parade and Beating of the Retreat could be purchased at the Cottage Industries Emporium a few minutes' walk away on Janpath. What an Aladdin's Cave it was and every time I revisited the old shop, located in a former World War II Barracks Building, I felt that same frisson of excitement. Part of its charm was the curious layout where it was easy to get lost while discovering a new section at the end of a little staircase never seen before. It was a higgledy piggledy arrangement and I can almost hear the creaking of the wooden floors. It was a huge relief not to have to haggle over prices and having worked out the rather complicated payment and delivery protocol, it is possible to shop for hours unhindered by parcels.

My purchases on that first visit were small and insignificant but exciting beyond measure for someone on her first trip abroad. Silk head-scarves similar to those worn by the Queen were terribly smart at home at the time and I returned with many. For my grandmother I bought a white Kashmir shawl with pretty blue embroidery which she gave back to me before she died. Living in Peshawar twenty years later a shawl merchant in the Sadar Bazaar thought it very beautiful. I braved the predatory Kashmiris in the little fur salon and bought fur bonnets for my sister and myself which we wore skiing. A little papier maché box decorated with iris was a prize but the thrills were not just limited to merchandise. The first cheese pakoras I ever ate were in the little Bankura café, sitting on a wrought iron chair and laughing over a copy of Laxman's cartoons which I had just bought for my father in the adjacent book department.

Some of those purchases have been cannibalised into other forms over the years—the royal head-scarves for instance became linings for smart little evening bags I had made in Laos. But several of the acquisitions from my next visit to Cottage in 1977 are still treasures. With the two little children, aged 4 and 5, we had arrived in India just before Christmas 1976. Emily, the four-year-old, was in a state of distress as her favourite toy, a pink rabbit called Rattly Bun, had become mixed up in the bedclothes in a pre-dawn departure from our hotel in Rangoon and was never seen again. It was such luck then that we found a replacement in Cottage. It was red, not pink and lapin couchant rather than rampant, but he was loved from the moment she saw him. Jamie chose a rolling drum like that of Siva Nataraja which survives somewhere with other family musical instruments. Em had *ghunghru* and bangles by the mile, Jamie loved his beautiful wooden toy soldiers and elephants and we found colourful clothes for both of them. During that week in Delhi my husband and I gave each other a precious solo afternoon. While I took the children to the zoo, he had a wonderful wander but on my child-free afternoon I headed straight for Cottage. A beautifully smocked silk chiffon dress, a miniature painting of a courtly couple playing with fireworks, a little pietra dura marble plate and a book on Amrita Sher-Gil were my purchases. The book is now so rare that an academic from Sydney University once urged me to donate it to his Library. I've since met Amrita Sher Gil's nephew, Vivan Sundaram, also an artist. His interesting work often revolves around his aunt and one such installation was once on display in an Asian portraits exhibition at our National Portrait Gallery. In a happy continuity I bought a book on his work at Cottage some years ago.

I rarely drink Coca Cola at home but in India it just seems to hit the spot. While waiting for a friend on the first NGA shopping expedition on a hot April day where the temperature was in the low 40's, a Coke in the Emporium café was a perfect choice. Somehow the chalky feeling on my teeth from the first welcome mouthful is a very Indian sensation for me, ridiculous though that may sound. I should have had a cheese pakora too for old time's sake.

In 1992 on arrival at my favourite shop I was shocked to find the old rambling rabbit warren shut and barred. The anticipation of entering the magic palace, past the huge brass chests full of the promise of treasure was dashed. That is until I discovered that on that very day the new magic palace was to open, further down Janpath and on the other side of the road. What a piece of timing that was. Some things don't change. There are goods in the shop even now which might have been there in 1968 or even in 1952. The charming Bankura horse logo remains and the devious little staircases of the old shop have been replicated by the many levels of the new premises. The payment and despatch system is the same but the big old clanking cash registers have now been replaced with modern computers. This year returning from the Kumbh Mela, I had the whole of the next day in which to enjoy New Delhi but my friend, Christiane, had only a whirlwind few hours in which to tick off a long shopping list. As shawls were a major item, I thought Cottage was the place to go and as usual this was a very good choice. They may not be the ultimately best price but the range and quality is remarkable and we both emerged with parcels and smiles.

A very interesting response to my 2003 email had come from Anokhi in Jaipur. I had known their shops and happily worn their stylish clothes for years. Yes, they would be very happy for us to come and shop but also wondered if we could help them. Then came a thoughtfully constructed wide-reaching series of questions about establishing a museum. The email came from Rachel Bracken-Singh whom I would meet for the first time when Annie & I arrived in Jaipur. The questions were in connection with the Anokhi Museum of Hand Printing, a project already underway. I went around the National Gallery canvassing specialists in such aspects as lighting, storage, membership, textile conservation, programs for school children and events. My boss, Ron Ramsey, who had encouraged me to volunteer for the shopping job in the first place, was head of both Exhibitions and Education & Public Programs and was able to address many of the questions. Rachel & her husband Pritam, kindly invited Annie & me to dinner out at Anokhi Farm with Pramod Kumar KG, the consultant implementing the Museum project. It was my introduction to what was going to lead to one of the most interesting episodes in my life.

Anokhi, which means unique, is a company started more than forty years ago by Faith & John Singh, parents of Pritam. Faith was born in India but left as a very small child at the time of Independence with her father, the Anglican Bishop of Nagpur, medical missionary mother and four older siblings. She returned to India as a young woman and fell in love not only with India but with John, who despite his name, bestowed upon him by an English nanny, is a Rajput and connected to the Royal Family of Jaipur. As a married couple with three small children, they established a private retail business which revived the ancient craft of hand block printing for which Jaipur and other places in the state of Rajasthan had been famous for centuries. By the mid-20th century the craft was languishing. Faith, with her fine eye, recognised its beauty and the skills required to maintain standards, and with John, she successfully built up the business which ensured the revival of one of India's great traditions. With help from her family in England, fashion parades were held, Anokhi clothes were sold by Liberty in London and were an instant success. Some of the gorgeously flamboyant early designs, reminiscent of the Ballets Russes, are now to be seen in the Anokhi Museum at Amber.

The first shop in Jaipur was located in C-Scheme in the city, among sprawling post-Independence bungalows and Government office blocks. It was slightly difficult to find and cycle rickshaw drivers in the earliest days used to say 'oh no, it's closed today', if they either couldn't be bothered taking you there or wanted to steer you instead to their 'friend's shop'. Here it flourished for years—a slightly unusual but friendly lay-out in a space which had grown like Topsy. In its last years at that location it accommodated a café, badly needed in Jaipur, in the narrow side garden. One of Pritam's many successful schemes included growing organic vegetables at the farm at Jagatpura, and safely delicious rocket was available in a salad or a sandwich of excellent home-made bread while sipping the best cup of coffee in India. The café has gone onto another incarnation in the new third floor shop on Prithviraj Road and it is one place in which when I am leading a tour group, I can happily urge tour participants to eat salad greens. The new shop doesn't have the quaint character of the old, but who needs quaint? It is light and airy, there is tons of space and many of the long-term staff members remain—Jabbar whom I've known since the early 1990s who does a brilliant job of despatching parcels all over the world, Sonali at the desk and helpful Sunaina who is always full of smiles. I love going there.

Rachel came to Anokhi as an intern on a ten week design placement in 1993, a new graduate in fashion design from Central Saint Martin's in London on a short placement. The ten weeks turned into six months until her visa expired. This blossomed into a total commitment to the company in more ways than one, with marriage to Pritam and now three beautiful daughters. Somehow between balancing her life as wife and mother and being Director of the Anokhi Museum, she works full-time which in India is six days a week, designing both fabric and garments for at least twelve collections per year. As well as traditional Indian *saris, churidars* and *shalwar kamiz*, the collections include dresses, trousers, skirts and accessories plus quilts, curtains and table linen in the homewares line. The shop at the Anokhi Museum carries some different and specialised stock which relates to exhibitions. When for the 2007 Jaipur Festival, we linked felt production at nearby Tonk with a travelling exhibition of Inuit felt embroideries displayed at the Museum, Rachel came up with beautiful felt toys and highly desirable fairy wands.

The creation of the Anokhi Museum of Hand Printing was the initiative of Rachel and Pritam. It is located in a superbly restored *haveli*, a mansion or ancestral house, in the town of Amber below the great yellow fort palace, tucked in against the encircling palace wall near the Kheri Gate. John Singh had purchased the Chanwar Palkiwalon ki Haveli in a sadly dilapidated state. In 1989 a three year renovation project began to restore it to its original beauty. And what a beauty it is—like a gorgeous pink sugar cake with domes and projecting balconies, cusped archways, niches and panels picked out in white, staircases inside and out, surprising little elevated courtyards and a soaring atrium. The restoration involved skilled local builders and craftsmen who used local materials and traditional construction methods. The result was so splendid that it won a UNESCO award for Cultural Conservation in 2000 and the Museum Project, dedicated to hand-block printing began in 2003.

The process of printing can be viewed through all its many stages and in the demonstration area skilled resident craftsmen show how wood-blocks are cut and then how cloth is printed. The archive comprises a large collection of textiles, tools and supporting images and continues to expand. Research continues into regional techniques and exhibits include displays of natural dyes, *dabu* mud-resist and *varak* silver and gold printing. Excellent publications support the research.

The Inuit felt embroidery exhibition *Baker Lake Tapestries* at the 2007 Jaipur Festival on which I worked for six months, came to us from the Canadian High Commission through my dear friend David McKinnon, the then Trade Commissioner. I knew not only from the NGA but also from having worked at Canberra's Nolan Gallery, that a loans agreement was something we really needed to have. I contacted Travelling Exhibitions at the NGA who kindly sent me a copy of their document which we tweaked for use at Jaipur. Another thing I was keen to pursue was condition reporting and thank goodness we did this. Rachel and I unpacked the many long cardboard tubes in a spare room in her house at Anokhi Farm and wow, did we ever find some insect damage. Fortunately their depredations did not actually detract from any of the hangings. It was old damage and we found no insect corpses, but we marked all our findings on the forms that we had devised and sent these back to the Canadians in Delhi. The curator, Judith Varney Burch, was horrified but we were thoroughly delighted that we had had the foresight to have done this and would not be held responsible by a future vigilant host of the collection. It was a good lesson learned. Judith and her daughter came Jaipur for the opening of the show and Judith gave an interesting lecture in the series of lunchtime talks I had organised for the art strand of the festival.

Many Anokhi block-print designs are traditional, others are adapted and some are brand new. Cotton of different weights is the fabric used most frequently but silks and a blend of silk and cotton called *chanderi* is light and cool for the summer while heavier wool and *tussar* silk are used in cosy quilted jackets, waistcoats and coats for the winter. Indian colour combinations have always been unique and exciting but somehow Rachel gives them a further lease of life and they look new all over again—red and yellow, olive and burgundy, lilac and tan, mint green and black—pairings not everyone is brave enough to put together themselves. The embroidery for which Rajasthan and other areas of India is famous, adorns some garments and Rachel seeks fresh inspiration from British embroidery experts who develop new designs. There is always a look of Indian heritage. Some of the embroidery, block-printing and dyeing is outsourced to village-based craftspeople. This supports rural craft-based livelihoods and allows the practitioners to work in their own homes. I have an old skirt and top embroidered in Barmer, far to the west of Rajasthan. They were part of an order given almost as a grant in aid to help women during a bad drought. When it eventually surprisingly rained the stitching was abandoned in favour of farm-work which rather held up the Anokhi production.

Back at Jagatpura, on the outskirts of Jaipur, the people-friendly factory is a state of the art work unit. There are over eight hundred staff members performing every production task. There are more than 200 sewing machines, a dry cleaning plant, quality control and a packaging unit. My friend Jennie Cameron and I started an import business in 2004 and our visits there were focused on the buyers' room with its racks of clothes. I was exactly the size of the sample garments and some days I would try on scores of different outfits which started to blur by the end of the session. But that was quite a way down the track.

On the 2003 trip Annie and I spent quite a long time in the Anokhi godowns choosing dozens of little cloth-covered notebooks, bags and cloth. We loved staying at the slightly eccentric Narayan Niwas Hotel. A turbaned waiter sashayed into the breakfast room each morning singing falsetto which made us giggle. He would then say 'No Complaints', plonk down our omelettes and waft out again. It was incredibly hot and if we arrived back in time, we cooled off in the pool in the grounds. Ron Ramsey had sweetly given me some American dollars and said we should go and have a drink somewhere smart. This we did one evening on the lawns of the Rambagh Hotel and it was perfect.

We went out to Sanganer for block-print table-cloths and cushion covers. We bought dozens of pairs of beautiful Rajasthani puppets, fending off the aggressive vendors on M I Road whenever we were there. Jaipur is the jewellery capital of India and we bought strings of semi-precious stones, ear-rings and bracelets. We roamed the bazaars for *bandhani dupattas*, traditional enamel jewellery, silk-covered bangles, tiny quilted children's waistcoats and bags and bags of *gota*, the gorgeous foil ribbon which is important in decoration of women's clothing in Rajasthan. At Badi Chaupal, the *chowk* or intersection of roads in the middle of the old walled city where crossing the road is a hair-raising experience, I found a marvellous *gota* shop. Mr Chainsukh Nandlal Jain, the proprietor, was a charming older gentleman with a big slow smile, seated by a low wooden desk on the white sheeted floor of his busy little shop. Customers sit on the edge of this area, feet on the footpath, but if invited into the shop itself, sandals are left out on the foot-path. I subsequently met him many times. Sometimes he would send out for a refreshing *nimbu pani* and we talked about this and that. I was very sad to learn from his son last year that he had died.

Eventually we found our way down to the line of shops just inside the Jorawar Singh Gate on the road to Amber. Many of the shops are run by members of an extended Sindhi family, immigrants to India from Pakistan decades after Partition. I discovered them first in 2000 and since 2003 I've done masses of business there. Sometimes the chaos is beyond description and I wonder exactly why I persist. But it all seems to turn out in the end. Kishan Kumar Maheshwari and his son Kishor run one business which is called variously Jaisalmer Arts & Crafts or Saurashtra. It has undergone a few changes in the years I've known it but until they move into a flash new building nearby which they say will incorporate a textile museum, each episode in the shop's evolution lapses into the same recognisable bedlam as the last. When the shop is open textiles, umbrellas and miscellaneous items hang on the shop-front, fading in the sunlight and not looking at all inviting, in fact they give the shop a pretty bad look. There are always lots of shop assistants but none of these boys are permitted to give prices. If there are tourists brought there by their guides within earshot and I have happened to ask the price then the voice is lowered or it's given behind a hand or else they pretend to ignore the question and ask if I'd like a cup of chai. I do know that I definitely do get excellent bargains. Everyone is always frightfully pleased to see me, even more so if I'm on a National Gallery errand, but it can be very, very arduous.*

Last summer while buying for the shop attached to a beautiful exhibition of Indian paintings called *Divine Worlds*, Kishor who really wishes he had been allowed to pursue his promising career as a cricketer, was distracted. It was June and terribly hot—the temperature was in the high 40's. I think he chooses his sales assistants as much for their cricketing prowess as their retailing expertise because they all seemed to be team members of Kishor's side playing in a competition. I timed my visits to the shop to suit them and their match fixtures—it usually takes three or four trips to really nail down the order, see it packed and pay. Each time Kishor was either breathlessly just back, yelling down the phone that he was on his way, or in his whites just about to go to the next match and dreamy-eyed thinking of cricket heaven.

Just before this consignment was to arrive in Canberra there was a big flurry of phone calls and emails and much consternation. Our goods were held up at Customs but not Australian Customs, the hiccough was on the Indian side. I always do everything absolutely by the rule but at the other end things are more flexible. There had obviously been a little misunderstanding over the creative interpretation of values. How could hundreds of kilos of merchandise have only cost such a small amount of money? This was the problem and I was asked to do a bit of juggling in their favour from my own bank account to help them out. I refused with visions of being dragged before Senate Estimates and shaming all my friends in the Gallery. Of course they were being dramatic. They extracted themselves from their panic and the merchandise was so successful we had to re-order. When despatching the re-order I think he was in the midst of another cricket nirvana because some of our gorgeous big embroidered garden umbrellas went to America and we received <u>a few things we</u> didn't want at all. As usual, it all worked out.

* The new shop has opened but the old continues. A kind of order prevails at the new and so far I have encountered no mice.

On one occasion when I was giving final confirmation to an order, Kishor was completely incommunicado with no mobile contact at an India Premier League match where the Rajasthan Royals were playing at the Jaipur stadium. A couple of months after organising a study tour for a group of twenty Volunteer Guides from the National Gallery, I was back in the shop on a mission but I also had something to investigate. One of the guides had sent home a parcel of purchases from Saurashtra and additionally, two books bought elsewhere. One was an illustrated volume of the Kama Sutra she had bought for her husband, the other was a copy of *The Kama Sutra for Women* given by the author, art historian and curator Alka Pande, to the NGA Guides Library. The parcel arrived but minus the books so I wanted to find out where they were. Kishan is a little deaf and tends to shout. While on the telephone to the freight forwarders, who turned out to be the thieving magpies, he shouted at me, good-naturedly I hasten to add, 'What is the title?' 'The Kama Sutra' I shouted back 'and the Kama Sutra for Women'. It was very funny and the boys were all snickering behind their hands. The books were suddenly found and sent off to the rightful owner.

Sometimes in the shop—quite often really—I've felt like screaming but there's no point at all and to lose my cool would cause everyone to lose face and make the situation worse. They are very benevolent people and do much good amongst their community, each winter for instance giving blankets to poor people. Whilst Sindhis are known and thus criticised for their business acumen and enterprise, they care less about caste than most Hindu communities, they are warm and amusing and it's always a delight to see them, even in that frightful mess!

Annie and I had a truly peculiar driver, hired in Delhi, on that 2003 trip. His car was pretty dilapidated and I don't recall that it was air conditioned—surely it was, it was like an oven outside. I do know that somehow a box of chocolates I was taking to a friend in Delhi which had been carefully shuttled from fridge to fridge in our hotels, ended up on the car floor and melted completely. We had to buy the driver sheets of plastic and rope to tie over our bags and purchases on the roof rack. Had we known all the dramas that lay ahead in Delhi with the dastardly freight forwarders there, we would have sent everything off from Saurashtra who turned out to be utterly brilliant and coped marvellously with a re-order I had to make when the stock sold faster than hot cakes. The only mistake turned out to be a hundred miles of pale pink baby bootee ribbon bought because I had failed to identify the ribbon I wanted as *gota*.

They were our last port of call before we set off in our hot laden car for Delhi. We had enough time to stop at the Amber Fort eleven kilometres from Jaipur on the road to Delhi. In those days before the highway by-pass the road ran along the valley beneath the fort ramparts with a brilliant view of the yellow fort palace nestling into the ridge behind it, walls and watch-towers running over the heights on either side of the road. We bought an entry ticket and ran the gamut of the *mahouts* who take tourists up the hill on their elephants. The heat was intense and we somewhat reluctantly climbed aboard an elephant, we were the only visitors. The poor animal slowly plodded off and then started to swing her trunk from side to side, spraying us with water. We felt a little alarmed as her pace became slower and slower but I said something which made Annie laugh uproariously. Into her open mouth landed a great dollop of elephant spit! That was so extremely unpleasant but it made us almost hysterical. But not for long as the poor animal started to lurch. The Amber *mahouts* are very cheeky and ours didn't want to stop but we insisted at a point where we could scramble off on a low'ish part of the wall. If she had fallen we didn't want to end up underneath her. Annie meanwhile had spat out the contents of her mouth.

Meeting Pramod KG and hearing about the Anokhi Museum project from him and Rachel was fascinating. Pramod comes from Kerala and after a couple of years in the corporate sector of Mumbai he realised he had to follow his passion for arts and culture. He has become an entrepreneur, museologist and is one of the best people in India to ask about anything in the arts whether it be books, textiles, photography or painting. He worked with Rajeev Sethi who is seen as being at the top of India's creative and aesthetic tree, but went out on his own as a freelance consultant and it was in this role that he came to be running the Anokhi Museum project. He was then engaged as the Director of the Jaipur International Heritage Festival in 2005 and 2006, introducing the Literature component in 2006.

After Jaipur Pramod joined the Alkazi Foundation in New Delhi for four years. He worked with Ebrahim Alkazi to bring his entire collection, over 90,000 works, of 19th and 20th century Indian photographs to New Delhi. He arranged spectacular exhibitions from the collection focused on Lucknow, Vijayanagara and New Delhi. Next came another interesting photography project, to be the consultant curator at the City Palace Museum in Udaipur where he found incredible treasure. When I led a tour there in 2010 we were lucky to have Pramod speak to us about the collection in the newly opened gallery, arranged with his usual flair and attention to detail. It was at this stage that Pramod knew it was time for him to set up his own consultancy and as a result Eka was born. It is one of the few, if not the sole cataloguing and archiving company in India today. Their expertise is to catalogue and archive collections both in India and abroad, to create galleries and art spaces, to curate and facilitate dialogue between museums all over the world. One brilliant exhibition I saw in Delhi in early 2011 at the Indira Gandhi National Centre for the Arts was an exhibition of photographs by Lala Deen Dayal from the IGNCA collection, jointly curated by Pramod and Dr Jyotindra Jain.

Somehow I stayed vaguely in touch with Pramod and saw him a few times when I returned to Jaipur buying for both Hyles & Cameron and the National Gallery. I was in far closer contact with Rachel and Pritam and I had yet to meet Faith & John who were usually away when I visited. The idea of working on the Jaipur Festival became very interesting and an extremely generous gift from my mother at just the right time meant I could retire from my job at the National Gallery. It really was a wrench as I love the place and I had really enjoyed working as Director Ron Radford's assistant for his first year in Canberra in 2005. But the possibility of being able to live and work in India, something I'd always wanted to do, with the wherewithal to do it just could not be ignored. It was a matter of *carpe diem* and I thought that working with Pramod would be an education in itself.

The Festival was part of Jaipur Virasat Foundation's activities—*virasat* means 'heritage' and the foundation had been started by Faith & John. A citizen's initiative and a charitable trust since 2002, JVF's strategy for development linked with UNESCO charters and aimed at the conservation of heritage, both tangible and intangible, and the preservation of cultural diversity in Rajasthan. It works with and for traditional artists and is dedicated to preserving heritage in any form whether music, poetry, textiles, painting and sculpture, craft, architecture or the environment. With a cross-cultural base, the foundation sought to promote income and livelihood generation through its many events, advocacy forums and networks. Faith and John had flung themselves into the Foundation having relinquished their role in the everyday running of Anokhi which is now in the hands of Pritam and Rachel. Their energy and vision is extraordinary and Rajasthan has much for which to thank them. The Foundation has had its ups and downs especially in connection with sponsorship and funding. There is now a spectacular music festival, close to John's heart, held annually at Jodhpur and in Jaipur the original arts festival has changed into the acclaimed Jaipur Literature Festival.

I attended the 2006 Jaipur Festival as an observer and on Rachel's invitation, stayed at Anokhi Farm. There at last I met Faith who would become my boss in six months' time. By then I had retired from the National Gallery and wound up other commitments. It was arranged that I would come to work as a volunteer for JVF the following July—as Faith would say I had 'organised the grandchildren' and here I was. I think the grandchildren with their perfect parents would have managed without me anyhow, but it was a nice thing for Faith to say. The 2006 festival was absolutely stunning and to stay at Anokhi Farm was the icing on the cake. The only disappointment was that Pramod had decided to end working for JVF but he generously gave me excellent advice.

My great friend Louise Goldsmith, who was living in Delhi at the time, came with me and we spent fascinating days with Faith's sister, Brigid. Biddy had been recently widowed and was visibly overcome with sadness from time to time but was wonderful company and the three 'older women' had a lovely time together. Apart from having dinner there in 2003, this was my real introduction to the oasis at Jagatpura which John and Faith had established. With the help of an Israeli irrigation expert they had established a small forest where there previously had been no trees at all. The forest had become a haven for birds who had no fear of anything within the farm walls. Peacocks strutted about and flapped onto walls and roofs, guardian owls were seen in trees at night, kingfishers and parrots abounded and there were nature trails named for famous ornithologists. When I spent two months living there later that year I took long walks before breakfast every morning—up through the garden, across the road, around the polo ground three times and back. It was a precious hour of the day when the world was waking up but still dewy-fresh and quiet.

At the time of the festival there was neither the time nor the need for pre-breakfast walks. So much was happening and breakfast then, and as I have found again in the last few years, is not something to be missed. With writers such as William Dalrymple and Brigid Keenan, performers like Paban Das Baul, Mimlu Sen and Krupa, academic Som Batabyal, film-maker Robert Golden and his wife Tina Lee, one of the founders of Opera Circus, composer Nigel Osborne, sculptor Christian Lapie, the conversation is always fascinating and the coffee very good. The festival has attracted a certain amount of rather unwelcome publicity in the last couple of years and sometimes the chat around the breakfast table revealed guarded information about developments.

I met Brigid Keenan through writing her a fan letter. My daughter had given a copy of her book *Diplomatic Baggage: The Adventures of a Trailing Spouse* to my daughter-in-law who is an incredibly supportive trailing spouse. Amanda had sent the book back to me from Hong Kong where the family was living, saying she had loved it, that I must read it as it was full of people I knew. I was busy at the time and the book sat unread on one of the permanent towering piles beside my bed. I was going up to stay with the Hong Kong family a month or so later so decided to read it on the plane and return the book that way. I half expected Amanda's 'people I knew' to be *types* rather than real people, but there were Faith & John, William Dalrymple and others in India but more amazingly Wilma Hoyte my friend and GP in Trinidad and Ross Burns, who led a small group of friends in a memorable trip around Syria. The discoveries were fun but the book was so hysterically funny that I was laughing quite uncontrollably on the plane, always a little embarrassing. I wrote by snail mail to Brigid via her publisher and not so long afterwards she replied by email. And then we met at the 2009 Jaipur Literature Festival and became immediate friends.

Part of the basis for our friendship were shopping expeditions in Jaipur. We decided to leave the literature one afternoon to find various things on Brigid's list. At our first stop the poor woman tripped over a dreadful little solid wooden stool and went sprawling. She had a nasty wound on her shin and the shop assistants rushed out to the closest pharmacy, returning with two band-aids! They had some Dettol so we bathed the poor leg and applied the plasters. From there we went straight to the Anokhi Café for a restorative coffee which gave her strength to carry on to the bazaar, to chaotic Saurashtra and then to M I Road to look for a ruby.

On other Jaipur Literature Festival shopping sorties we were accompanied by Brigid's husband Alan, the ever patient AW in the book. After searching unsuccessfully for a special kind of hair-pin, we took authors Hanan al-Shayk and Karima Khalil to Saurashtra which in that particuar incarnation was at a low ebb of messiness and I thought they would hate it. But they loved it and ordered coats and jackets. It's good if companions enjoy everything but are not too greedy. I have known some very serious shoppers who had perfected the hoovering technique which is quite awful and cramps the style of others. It is also very nice to be in the company of someone who finds the perfect treasure when I have been 'just looking thank you'. These days I don't need things for myself so the Gallery purchasing is a great indulgence as I can visit shops whose wares I love but don't need. Stainless steel shops are marvellous but once you have bought one tiffin carrier or a wonderful shiny bucket you don't need another. Tiffin boxes, tumblers, spoons and lovely little tin-lined copper *katoris* were on my list last June so I could shop vicariously.

The first time I visited Chettinad, an interesting region in the southern state of Tamil Nadu, I discovered an unusual cache of old Burmese lacquer-ware. I spotted it first in a small shop on the main road with other strange odds and ends, English stoneware crocks and a selection of enamel basins, ladles, lidded billy-cans and containers of many sizes. That seemed utilitarian and rather dull, but the lacquer was gorgeous. It was either shiny black or dark rich orange, some decorated with European-looking flowers or bands of small leafy designs. Some had Burmese writing, some had additional roughly painted English initials on the outside and some even had the original paper labels still stuck on. It was mysterious as well as seductive and I bought a few pieces and a beautiful big colourful cloth fan with a leather handle.

Jennie Cameron and I were doing a terrific trip around Tamil Nadu and we had stayed at the oasis of The Bangala, one of India's most charming hotels. It is located in an old house, nearly 100 years old, owned by a Chettiar family. It was a sort of private family sporting club with a popular tennis court but by the 1950s the family, now based in Madras, used it less and less and over the years the state of the buildings had deteriorated. Mrs Meenakshi Meyappan, now a family matriarch, decided to take charge and turned it into a heritage hotel which opened in 1999. She is devoted to the preservation of Chettiar culture and its superb cuisine in particular is something all guests can sample—it is sensational. Chettinad chicken has a place on the menus of many Indian restaurants but just the thought of Meenakshi's quail makes my mouth water. (In 2014 *The Bangala Table* was published so some of Meenakshi's secrets are now available for all.)

The town of Karaikudi is dotted with imposing baroque mansions, some slowly descending into dilapidation but others beautifully maintained. They give an unworldly atmosphere to the town and elsewhere in the region—pillars, impressive doorways and staircases, castellated roof-lines, huge rampant lions on gateways, a painted clock on one, murals on another. Some are unoccupied and others are inhabited only by care-takers. This is because, like Meenakshi's family, many owners spend their time now in Madras or overseas. Chettiar or Chetty is a title used by various merchant classes in South India, particularly in the state of Tamil Nadu. Some groups count themselves as members of the Vaishya or merchant class but others belong to what are termed OBC or Other Backward Classes. Generally speaking they are a very wealthy community. Many astute Chettiar men tried their luck in Burma, Malaya, Ceylon, Singapore and other parts of South-East Asia. They had traded in salt for centuries and from the early 19th century they became bankers for European traders. There is a Chetty Street in Singapore and the community's history there is well documented in the Asian Civilisations Museum.

Marriages are the greatest celebration in a Chettiar family. Marriage meant a dowry and for wealthy Chettiars these dowries were huge and conspicuous. This was the source of my lovely Burmese lacquer. Family members in banking and trading houses in Malaysia sent back the German and Czech enamel and the English stoneware crocks which were popular for storing pickles. Huge quantities of pillows, mats and mattresses, tons of stainless steel and brass were of Indian origin and Chettiars based in Burma sent the lacquer. Meenakshi is one of the authors of a very weighty book, *The Chettiar Heritage,* in which there are photographs of storerooms crammed with dowry articles. It is a matter for speculation just how much of it was ever used but some, to my advantage, has trickled out to antique shops. The small shop that I had spied on my first visit has closed but now there is a whole street of shops where days can be spent rummaging around in dusty rooms.

I bought a few pictures of gods on one sortie. Some are adorned copies of Raja Ravi Varma (1848–1906) oleographs which I adore. I have one showing Goddess Lakshmi with a lustrating elephant. Silk flowers in bright colours sparkle in the sky like fireworks, the goddess wears a jewelled crown and a hot pink sari decorated with sequins and tinsel and she stands on a pale pink silk lotus. Another shows the birth of Lord Brahma from the lotus flower emanating from Lord Vishnu's navel, another which I gave as a wedding present to some young friends is an image of the marriage of the Maharaja of Mysore. Most pictures were undoubtedly decorated in studios but in South Indian households, young women would make these gorgeous creations as an act of devotion. Hundreds of thousands hung in the shrine rooms of homes all over the country.

After seeing a huge exhibition of these pictures arranged by Maneka Gandhi in New Delhi from the collection of her grandfather, Sir C.P. Ramaswamy Aiyar, to raise money for her animal welfare organisation, I was dying to try it myself. I started with some reproductions of Raja Ravi Varma paintings which I had bought at the Baroda Palace—Lakshmi, Saraswati, Shantanu and Ganga and a modest maiden sitting by a river. I went on to post-cards from the National Gallery of Modern Art in New Delhi and a poster I bought on the street near VT in Mumbai of India's cricket captain, Sourav Ganguly, looking balletic in full swing at the crease. It was such fun to find the right pieces of silk, beads and tiny pieces of jewellery, tinsel, thread and braid and then sew them on carefully. When I ran out of Indian images I started on ones closer to home, post-cards and reproductions from Gallery magazines. I have dressed the Jiawei Shen portrait of Princess Mary of Denmark located in the National Portrait Gallery of Australia; a handmaiden at the 'Arrival of the Queen of Sheba at the court of King Solomon', a detail from the huge painting by Poynter in the Art Gallery of New South Wales; two versions of the 'Naked Solicitor' by Lucien Freud and John Brack's portrait of 'Barry Humphries in the character of Mrs Everage'. Some were shown and sold at a small exhibition at Alphaville Gallery in Melbourne. Krishna Hutheesing, Prime Minister Nehru's sister, painted by P.T. Reddy in 1942, Stephanie Alexander as Kitchen Goddess from a photograph in Australia's National Portrait Gallery and several more mainstream goddesses adorn my home.

Other great caches of old Burmese lacquer from Chettiar dowries can be found in the big antique clearing houses in Jodhpur. The first time I visited Jodhpur these big warehouses were yet to spring up but on return journeys I have had a great time delving into the endless rooms of several big godowns on the road close to the great Umaid Bhavan Palace. It's very dirty work but there are treasures waiting to be found and I have bought quite a bit of Burmese lacquer. The last time there I found a wonderful Shekhawati hero painted on glass, he and his horse greatly enhanced with gold paint as they gallop from right to left. I had to carry it very, very carefully for weeks. I'd had something of a very bad fright with another glass painting bought a few years earlier. By a terrific contemporary artist from Bombay, Shrilekha Sikander, my picture was one of a series of portraits of Indian women heroes, painted on glass. I chose Jhansi ki Rani, a particular hero of mine, and I thought I had wrapped her up very soundly. When it came to extracting her at the Sydney airport for Customs to examine the wooden frame, the image appeared to be shattered. There were no borers in the frame but what of the glass? When I got home I was astounded to find that what had broken was another layer of glass over the glass painting which miraculously was still intact.

I love wandering in bazaars anywhere and those in Rajasthan are often very interesting where you the production of goods may be observed, not just the finished product—felt carpets in Tonk, brass vessels in the old city of Jaipur, silver rattles in Alwar and Fatehpur, fine Kota Doria saris at Kaithun and Kota. I have been with friends who have bought bicycle seat covers for their grandsons and handkerchiefs to cover their heads before entering a *dargah* to hear *qawwali* music. As well as swooping on treasures being created in tiny shops, kitchens preparing huge quantities of tempting sweets or savoury *namkeen* are very hard to ignore. There is rarely pressure to buy, generally the artisans in less visited towns are just happy someone is taking an interest in their work.

There is nothing like the atmosphere of the narrow winding streets, the sounds of a clanking hammer or the clack of the loom but, now and then, particularly if one's spirits need elevation, there is the reward of brilliant Khan Market in New Delhi. My great friend, Victoria Walker when she saw it the first time, having been told it was the Double Bay of Delhi, thought her informants must be raving mad. All that mess, power lines criss-crossing the internal lane which is usually littered with building rubble. Chaos in the car-park at the back and the subsequent removal of what used to be a pretty little garden. It is quite a rabbit warren and the stairs which reach shops on upper floors would never pass safety regulations in Australia, narrow, twisting and instant concussion for unwitting tall people. It didn't take her long to be seduced by its charms and every time I visited we would head off for a dose of the shops.

Established in 1951, many people think it was named in honour of Khan Abdul Ghaffar Khan, the great Freedom Fighter, popularly known as the Frontier Gandhi. Greatly saddened at the idea and then the reality of Partition, he felt he had to stay in his homeland which was to become part of Pakistan. He died while we were living in Peshawar and some of my workmates from the Afghanaid Office journeyed to Jalalabad just across the border in Afghanistan to attend his funeral. A Pashtun political and spiritual leader, his memory was nevertheless deeply respected in India. I would be glad to believe that the market was named for him but it is actually for his brother, Khan Abdul Jabbar Khan, in thanks for the great efforts he made helping the market's first traders to migrate to India safely during the partition.

The market was built in the early 1940s to serve the needs of British forces who were living in hurriedly constructed barracks at the nearby Lodi Estate. After independence it was often called 'The Refugee Market' as many of the original shops were allocated to immigrants, displaced at the time of Partition in 1947, some from the North-West Frontier Province, others from the Punjab. Most of the refugees who came to Delhi came from urban areas of West Pakistan with former occupations in trade and commerce. They were hard-working and ambitious and took over sections of the city and are the main reason post-independence Delhi became such a big retail city.

In the original Khan Market there were 154 shops and 74 flats on the first floor of the double-storey U-shaped complex. Until the 1980s many shopkeepers lived in these flats and as late as 2006 when I had to make a quick visit to Delhi for work, I spent a night in a tiny apartment attached to the Anokhi shop. Now there is scarcely a flat left as space in upper storeys has been converted into smart little shops. The real estate boom has seen Khan Market become one of the costliest retail locations in India and in 2010 it was ranked the world's 21st most expensive retail high street in a Cushman & Wakefield survey. High street doesn't really describe it at all but it's probably my favourite shopping centre in all the world. So much so that when I lead tours to Delhi I prefer to stay in the comfortable old Ambassador Hotel, located right next door so the shoppers have no need to do battle with taxi drivers. When by myself or with just a couple of friends, the pleasant Lutyens Bungalow in Prithviraj Road is my lodging of choice, a serene walk across the Lodi Gardens to the merchandise of desire.

Wonderful Anokhi is there where I've done plenty of damage to the credit card on my own behalf but not so much for the Gallery whose Anokhi purchases were mostly made in Jaipur where they can be shipped home easily. There are some other good clothing shops, great jewellery, shoes which have improved out of sight over the last ten years, hand-bags, Indian film and music on DVD and CD, stationery and all kinds of tempting homewares at Fabindia and Good Earth. Cutlery, a coffee plunger and a few more necessities for my flat in Jaipur came from Shyam di Hatti, I always buy soap and tulsi tea at Fabindia and flowers for Delhi friends at one of the florists where they are wrapped in cellophane and tied with ribbon and can be delivered to the door.

Once while buying little boxes of Kashmiri saffron at one of the grocers, I spied a marvellous poster, an advertisement for Ching's Sweet Devil Chilli Sauce, stuck on the side of the shop's freezer. 'Tantalising' it says in the corner of a depiction of the Mona Lisa. Her enigmatic smile has been manipulated. Her lips are parted to reveal sharp little teeth and two protruding fangs, warning enough for consumers of the sauce to be on guard for heat. I asked the shopkeeper if I might have it, showing him my Mona Lisa watch and half-explaining a bit of a passion I have for the lady's image. Without a second's hesitation he ripped it off the freezer and it's been stuck on the inside of my pantry door ever since, making me smile every time I see her. She is featured on the cover of my book about the pineapple and the original, a Saigon artist's augmented image of her, graces my laundry. She is holding what looks more like a hand grenade with leaves than a real pineapple.

My brother gave me our father's old watch to be repaired at Khan Market and once I bought some good sunglasses. I've photocopied documents at one of the print-shops, had masses of film developed, bought prints of photos taken at the terrific CanAssist Ball, acquired an umbrella for monsoon rain, changed money, topped up my sim card and had my shoes heeled by a cobbler who sits under a tree. I have bought power point adaptors and an electronic mosquito zapper shaped like a tennis racquet. With Victoria I've visited the pet supply shops and her dogs have very smart little tartan winter coats bought there which ward off the winter cold, even now in Canada. At the toy shop I once bought bags of balls to give to a boy's home in Old Delhi and I've called my family from an ISD booth. I've had some good lunches and endured palpitations when the ATM's have either told me I have zilch funds (untrue!) or been loath to regurgitate my card (worse!). I haven't bought overpriced papier maché and other Indian souvenirs, but it is quite exciting to buy antihistamine or paracetamol at the pharmacy for miles less than home and new smart prescription spectacles are another bargain.

The bookshops are often first port of call. The late dear Mr K.D. Singh used to be here at The Book Shop but later concentrated his energies in his Jorbagh Market shop where I used to visit him. I bought beautiful stationery from him for our daughter's wedding invitations and enough to send out again when she called it off! Full Circle Bookshop is good and has the advantage of the Café Turtle, a great place to start reading a new book over a delicious iced coffee. Some favour Faqir Chand & Sons Book Store and I did go there a few times while the old gentleman was still alive. But through thick and thin the book shop of choice for me has been Bahri Sons. The thin was the certain reluctance to pay me for copies sold of my pineapple book but after all, that was reason for the unintended start to my Indian shopping career. The problem was thankfully sorted without me and because there was never a confrontation, we could ignored the unfortunate incident and start again. They did also pull the plug on a second commissioned pineapple book after it had reached the design stage which was pretty disappointing, but there you go! Maybe it's a sign I've become a little Indianised—I wouldn't dream of going back to someone here who had done all that to me.

The staff at the shop are terrific and they are very reliable at despatching parcels, patiently listed and weighed in the back of the shop. In the past sea mail was available on payment of a pittance. It took forever and a day but eventually it would arrive. The sea voyage is no longer available but because we pay such exorbitant prices for books in Australia, even airmail postage on top of the price of the book makes purchase here worthwhile. The books arrive in better shape too having flown rather than swum all the way. I sometimes buy twelve copies of a particular title for my book group in Canberra. Once I had seen a good book at a South Indian airport but failed to write down the title. By the time I got to Delhi I had forgotten not only the title but the author. At Bahris I told marvellous Mithilesh that it was a book by a woman about her writer mother and I thought it had a short title. He thought for a moment and said 'It's *Diddi*.' And so it was—by Ira Pande and what a great read. The book group loved it and I could tell this to Ira at a Jaipur Literature Festival.

The parcels packed by Dhanpal come in a box, covered in calico sewn up and sealed with sealing wax. Paper registration forms are pasted on with sender's and receiver's names written in several places in indelible ink. The whole thing is so lovely it is impossible to throw out. I've laundered several pieces, minus the paper, and put them in the general useful drawer. We all know that as long as the memory serves, the contents of these miscellaneous caches generally find a miraculous second life. The calico was so nice on the last book parcel I think I probably had Christmas puddings in mind but it came in for an unexpected use.

My daughter asked if could make a rather strange hat for my grandson, Maitland, to wear in the school production of *Just Macbeth* by Andy Griffiths. It's a terrific play commissioned by the Bell Shakespeare Company in 2005, to help introduce children to the works of Shakespeare and the pleasures of live theatre. The play was revised to become the seventh book in Griffiths' *Just!* Series—

that series included *Just Annoying, Just Disgusting* and *Just Shocking*. It blends the characters from the series with the characters and story of *Macbeth* and is suitable for ages 7 to 107. Bell Shakespeare's website says it's a 'really silly version of Shakespeare's great big gory tragedy ... and when we say really silly we mean really, really silly as it's performed by six funny but tragic actors and a garden gnome and has witches and Wizz Fizz and ghosts and girl germs and ...' Bell promises that 'this hilarious and irreverent take on one of Shakespeare's most popular plays will have the whole family in stitches.' And it does. Andy Griffiths really appeals to children because he is rude, rude, rude and writes books titled *What Body Part is that?, Once upon a Slime, The Bad Book, The Day my bum went Psycho*, and even *Zombie Bums from Uranus*!

With Emily and her boys, I heard Griffiths speak at the National Library one Saturday morning to hundreds of adoring children. *Just Macbeth* starts in Mum's kitchen where the kids are using her brand-new food processor to make a potent brew. Drinking it results in them being spirited back to 11th century Scotland. Andy becomes Macbeth, Lisa is Lady Macbeth and Danny is Banquo. Much of the Scottish play left intact and the introduction of modern elements is clever and very funny.

John Bell adores the film *Shakespeare Wallah*, the famous Merchant Ivory Productions film made in 1965. Ruth Prawer Jhabvala, loved by Israel Merchant and James Ivory, wrote the story and screenplay based loosely on the real-life story of Geoffrey Kendal and his family theatre troupe of English actors. They performed Shakespeare in towns across post-colonial India, aging thespians and aspiring young names performing the classics while modern India inclined more and more towards Bollywood. Sometimes they performed in palaces, sometimes in schools, the very idea of the company is fascinating and the film is enchanting. Geoffrey Kendal, whose real name was Bragg, and his wife Laura Lidell, were the parents of Jennifer and Felicity Kendal both actors in the company although Felicity was rather young at the time. She however, played a part in the film. Jennifer married the handsome Indian actor, Shashi Kapoor, also in the film and together they made a huge contribution to both film and theatre in India.

Maitland had a couple of parts in *Just Macbeth,* a Scottish henchman and a small speaking part as a servant. One very noble school mother has made dozens of kilts for Macbeth's henchmen. My daughter with humorous ingenuity has made two splendid sporrans from small purses and fake fur for the henchman part, one for the son of the noble kilt-maker. She soaked an Arab dish-dash in turmeric and tea for a week to get the right colour for the servant's costume. Emily doesn't sew so I made half a dozen monks robes for the chorus—grandson Harry was included in that—as well as Maitland's servant's hat. The image provided by the director was an unusual cross between a Phrygian cap and deerstalker with flaps down and I had thought I would make it from a couple of old damask table napkins that had been in my mother's trousseau. But in a search for something else in the great box of fabric tricks, I found the neatly folded Bahri Sons cloth. Perfect. My grandson has quite a large head but I was able to cut the hat and lining and still avoid too much of the indelible ink. The only bit visible is on the inside lining and says Regd. Parcel Airmail. Marvellous really and perhaps I should have left it on the outside. And he loves it! He even arrived here wearing it for an afternoon with Grandma. He's an unusual boy! I've sent a photo of him in costume to Bahrisons. Who knows they might even start to stock Andy Griffiths books.

The shop and the family make an interesting story and a few years ago on the eve of Balraj Bahri's 75th birthday and the 50th anniversary of the shop his son, Anuj, who under the eye of his venerable father runs the shop and now the publishing house, brought out a nice little book *Bahrisons: Chronicle of a Bookshop.* The history of the Khan Market and that of Bahrisons is entwined, Bahri's were allocated a shop when few were left, only two years after the market was established. The family who had managed to stay united after the upheaval of Partition, had scarcely heard of this new market. In the words of Balraj Bahri Malhotra, 'we did not guess at the time that this scheme to benefit refugees, this Khan Market, would one day become such a success.'

The shopping exercise is never-ending really. When we lived in

Peshawar we had to buy furniture for an unfurnished rental house and that was a terrific exercise. We knew the city was famous for furniture and as our flat at home was furnished with only a few odd sticks, so we came with pictures from magazines to have copies made. The dining chairs were copied from an old Italian piece available at great cost in a Sydney antique shop. The Peshawar chairs turned out rather more solid than the Italian prototype but were tested for comfort by the proprietor of the New Victoria Furniture House. He was a big jolly man who found them to be very comfortable indeed. He liked the design so much that he asked if they might put it in their pattern book. Yes, of course, we agreed. Then he said they would like to call it the *Mrs Claudia* and they would make a label for it. I imagined that a label would have been perhaps be a rectangle of sorts that would go on the inside of the chairs. But no, when we went to inspect the finished order—table, sideboard, desk, bed, and some other chairs Mr New Victoria was almost wringing his hands. 'Oh Madam,' he said 'this is very problem. This one label was taking one man three days to do. So we have made but one.' We could see why. The 'label' was two rows of inlaid brass lettering which ran around the outside of the back of the seat. It should say 'Designed by Mrs Claudia, Manufactured by New Victoria Furniture House, Grand Trunk Road, Peshawar Cantt. NWFP, Pak''. But the best part of it is that *Designed* has been misspelled and it says *Desinged*. It's my family heirloom.

After the success of the *Sari to Sarong* exhibition shop, a friend with a shrewd eye, asked me if I would think of going into business, importing lovely things from India and further afield. She said her husband would do the books which was something of a relief. I thought about it and as I had just had a most unexpected legacy from a dear old lady, I had the wherewithal to join on an equal basis. So my dear friend, Jennie Cameron, and I set up our business 'Hyles & Cameron: Textiles to Treasure'. I said to Jen the she definitely had to come to India and see for herself and we set off in 2004 for a great look-see. At the outset we tried to sell beautiful pieces of fine textiles as well as garments, accessories and homewares but the clothing side of things fairly quickly took over from the textile treasures. I introduced Jennie to all my contacts and she greatly appreciated the beauties of Punjabi *phulkari*, Gujarati *torans* and Bengali *kantha*. From time to time we also stocked gorgeous things from Indonesia, Laos, Thailand and Burma after visits that I had made to these countries, in some of which I had also lived. We had great fun for five years at home-sales and doing the rounds of fairs run by charities in Sydney, Melbourne, Canberra and country areas and we had a lot of laughs along the way. I decided that was about enough for me but Jen has successfully continued by herself with Barry's assistance.

People often say 'oh I really hate shopping' and I do believe them. But it's something I love—even the supermarket. After living in wild places where there are none, it is the height of delight to come home and roam the aisles of Colesworths. Yes, I'm often 'gone for shopping'.

Juti shop in Jaipur, Rajasthan

With Ranji & Anuj Malhotra and all the staff of Bahrisons Book Store, Khan Market, New Delhi

Krishna! Krishna!

Each Indian shopping expedition has been fun in its own way and all have been successful but the most interesting journeys have been to the two Krishna pilgrimage towns of Vrindavan and Nathdwara in search of wonderful religious paraphernalia. There have been two such spiritual shopping trips, in 2009 and 2012, and I have visited both towns at other times.

Lord Krishna has long been known in the west and even more since the 1966 foundation in New York of the International Society for Krishna Consciousness (ISKCON) or as it is colloquially known, the Hare Krishna movement. All over the world exotically clad people have danced and chanted their way through city streets, looking like happiness personified but at the same time sometimes quite cold and pale. Outside India most of the distinctive acolytes are Caucasian—men in dhotis with shaved heads banging drums, women in saris tinkling cymbals, all to quote Mr Fielding in *A Passage to India*, in shades of 'pinko-grey', oblivious to their surroundings, intent on spreading their message. It is different in some ways from the practice of other Krishna-worshipping sects but its basis is in Hindu scriptures such as the Bhagavad Gita and the aim is to dedicate thoughts and deeds towards pleasing the Supreme Lord. By chanting their *mantra*, the sixteen word *mahamantra* popularised by the bhakti saint Chaitanya Mahaprabhu in the early 16th century, they are transported to the highest platform of spiritual consciousness. It may seem odd to be starting this story of Krishna with the Hare Krishnas but there you go, I'm setting the scene.

In Vikram Seth's remarkable novel *A Suitable Boy*, Dipankar, the likeable flute-playing economist ascetic, is asked by a *guru* to which divine form or power he is most attracted—Rama, Krishna, Shiva, Shakti or Om itself? Dipankar replies 'Om is too abstract for me; Shakti too mysterious, Shiva is too fierce; and Rama too righteous. Krishna is the one for me.' Despite some admiration, his problem with Rama, was his treatment of Sita, his consort, and his attraction to worldly glory. 'He had a sad life,' says the *guru*. 'Also his life was one from beginning to end—at least in his character,' said Dipankar, 'but Krishna had so many different stages, even if at the end he suffered defeat.' Sanaki Baba, the *guru*, still coughing from the incense says 'Everyone has tragedy but Krishna had joy.''

There are two important things in that extract—the fact that Krishna had so many stages in his life and that he had joy, both significant points in understanding the popularity of the Hindu god who is one of the most easily recognised of all the hundreds of thousands of gods in the pantheon. Lord Ganesha, the elephant-headed god, must be the *most* recognisable of all and although he is the son of Lord Shiva, he is worshipped by Vaishnavites and indeed also by Buddhists.

Krishna is the eighth avatar or incarnation of Lord Vishnu, the Preserver in the Hindu Trinity. Preceded by Matsya the fish; Kurma the tortoise; Varaha the boar; Narasimha the man-lion; Vamana the dwarf; Rama with the Axe known as Parasurama and Rama the Prince of Ayodhya. Krishna is followed by the Buddha as ninth avatar and Kalkin, the tenth who is yet to come. He may not have Ganesha's distinctive elephant head, but his identity comes from his beauty and his blue or black skin. Shiva and Rama are shown as blue-skinned, but *the* Blue God whether it is Nijinsky dancing in the Ballets Russes or whether a more Indian depiction seems most likely to be Krishna.

The corpus of Krishna stories is enormous. As Vikram Seth's character said he 'had so many stages' but in the interests of popular merchandise, on the shopping trips I concentrated on the earlier phases of his life. Krishna was born in perhaps 3228 BCE at Mathura, a town in the region of Vraj situated on the banks of the Yamuna River between Delhi and Agra, ruled at the time by the wicked King Kamsa. The King's aunt or cousin was Devaki, Krishna's mother, who was married to Vasudeva. A prophecy was made that Kamsa would be killed by Devaki's eighth son so he set out to destroy all her children. Babies were swapped before and after birth to delude the king in his determination to remove his potential assassin. The story of the murder of male children in the kingdom sounds similar to the slaughter of the Holy Innocents by King Herod following the birth of Christ. Somehow the new-born Krishna and his elder brother, Balarama, were spirited out of the palace during a torrential storm and taken across the Yamuna to a village called Gokul. Here the boys were given to a cowherd, Nanda, and his wife, Yashoda, who became their loving foster parents.

As a child Krishna was mischievous and played many childish pranks. He is often shown as a plump crawling infant, holding a pat of butter in his hand which he has stolen from Yashoda's churn. Later this butterball will change to a laddoo, the Indian sweet of which both Krishna and Ganesh were very fond. In his infant form, so appealing to mothers in particular, he is widely worshipped in both domestic shrines and temples all over India. The child god element of the Krishna legend is said to be the latest part of the legend to have been assimilated. This could have been inspired or assisted by tales from Christian merchants or Nestorian missionaries on the west coast of India in the early middle ages. Whatever the origin, this infant form of the god with his intimate relationship with the devotee has become so popular.

The child Krishna enchanted everyone in Gokul but the evil King Kamsa reappeared and in the guise of several demons, attempted to kill the boy. Nanda moved his little family to the safety of idyllic Vrindavan. This town is just ten kilometres from Mathura and the whole region of Vraj where all the exploits of the child and adolescent Krishna took place, is not very large. Vrindavan is famous for less bloodthirsty events than the destruction of devils but stories tell Krishna killed them in playful manner, adding pleasure to the lives of his playmates. One frisky despatch was splitting the giant crane Bakasura in half by pushing his huge beak in opposite directions!

Although he performed such heroic acts, Krishna in his pastoral and erotic aspect in Vrindavan and in Vraj in general, is not Krishna the hero-god which is actually the earliest chapter in the traditional legend. Krishna, son of Devaki is mentioned in the Upanishads, the ancient scriptures of the later Vedic period (1000–700 BCE), described as a beautiful youth of glowing complexion, the colour of rain clouds. Many tales of heroes were fused within the story of Krishna. Famously he was the friend and mentor of the Pandava brothers, the heroes of the Mahabharata. As Arjuna's charioteer, Krishna preached the great sermon of the Bhagavad Gita on the eve of the battle of Kurukshetra which is the centre of the great epic, the Mahabharata.

The youthful Krishna eventually slew King Kamsa but after successfully seizing the kingdom of Mathura, he was forced to leave. With his followers he journeyed all the way to Dwarka on the edge of the Arabian Sea in modern-day Gujarat state. It is one of the oldest cities in India, located at the *sangam* or confluence of the Gomati River and the sea, and considered by Hindus to be one of the holiest of places. Here he made as his chief queen Rukmini, daughter of the King of Vidarbha. He had 16,000 others who gave him 180,000 sons so his life must have been fairly busy.

After destroying wicked kings and demons all over India and seeing the Pandavas safely back into power after victory over the Kauravas, he returned to Dwarka. If he had hoped for a little time to relax this was not to be. The local Yadava chiefs began brawling, the city descended into uproar and for all his divine power, Krishna could not subdue the fighting. His son Pradyumna was killed and so was his faithful brother Balarama. Sorrowing in a forest, Krishna is mistaken for a deer by a hunter. An arrow pierces his heel, like Achilles the only vulnerable part of his body. He dies and the doomed city of Dwarka is engulfed by the sea. This potted history of the life of Krishna covers a large area of India but my interest is concentrated on Vraj with a logical and interesting offshoot to Nathdwara.

In Vrindavan the adolescent Krishna had many dalliances with *gopis,* the cowgirls or milkmaids. Much Indian art is focused on the theory of *rasa* or sentiment and *shringara rasa,* the erotic sentiment, is reflected with passion yet great sensitivity in the stories of Krishna and his favourite *gopi,* Radha. It is symbolic of the love of God for the human soul.

Krishna may have been originally a fertility god from Peninsula India, whose cult was carried north by nomadic herdsmen. It is not unusual that as a cowherd, Krishna like those earlier nomadic herdsmen, when the cattle are peacefully grazing, would while away the hours in the pasture by playing hypnotic melodies on his flute, charming both cow and milkmaid. He is more often than not depicted with his flute to his lips. Its sound represents the voice of God, calling man to leave aside earthly desires and turn to the joys of the divine.

Everything depicted in art about Krishna in Vraj is benign and lovely and Krishna is the embodiment of seductive beauty. The handsome youth and his beautiful *gopi* companions live in the idyllic paradise of Vrindavan and all inhabitants of this world of rural bliss, human and animal, are quite perfect, especially the cows. In paintings their flanks are often decorated with auspicious *sindur* handprints, pretty tassles hang from their gilded and painted horns, their fetlocks and shoulders are sometimes hennaed, their necks are garlanded and hung with bells, and peacock feathers perch as top-knots on their beautiful heads. Their eyes are soft and doe-like and their mouths are almost smiling. It is impossible not to be enchanted by them both in paintings and in reality in Vrindavan. I have often risen early and walked along the *ghats* as the dawn mists wreathe the fine old buildings and the bridge of boats, where laden horse-drawn carts and tractors rattle across the river which later in the day will reflect the peaceful blue sky. Cows are on the move and they know where there is the possibility of finding something delicious to eat. They nose around piles of marigold garlands and other religious rubbish that daily pollutes the river and its banks. Some trot purposefully off to the green fields in their minds' eyes, some just meditate as the sun's first rays warm their backs, other young ones congregate in gangs on corners looking for their best chance.

One splendid art-form glorifying Lord Krishna is the *pichhwai*, painted cloth hangings which are part of the worship of Lord Shrinathji, a *swarup* or form of Lord Krishna. In this form he is worshipped by a sect called the Pushti Marg or Path of Grace, founded by Vallabhacharya, a scholar-mystic who lived at the turn of the 16th century. Far from advocating asceticism as the path to enlightenment, as practised by other sects, Vallabhacharya felt that such withdrawal led to self-centredness. He saw that the way to achieving the ultimate spiritual goal was through personal devotion to Krishna and a constant remembrance of him through daily worship and observance of special festivals throughout the year through *sewa* or devotional service. The main temple of the Pushti Marg is at Nathdwara, literally the Portal of the Lord, located 48 km from Udaipur in the southern region of Rajasthan.

The word *pichhwai* comes from the word *peechhe* meaning behind—the hangings being placed behind the lord. They are not a mere backdrop but interact with and alter the meaning of each viewing. When they were first made it is hard to know. The earliest dated works belong to around the first quarter of the 19th century, but they could have been created much earlier. It is a highly distinctive art form and the practice of placing a textile behind the deity in a temple or shrine is unique to the Pushti Marg.

When Krishna was a boy the people of Vraj worshipped Indra, the great Vedic war-god who also controlled the weather. Those who lived near Mount Govardhan, not far from Vrindavan, believed it was Indra who bestowed the rains on their land. Krishna, aware of the environment and known as the saviour of nature, persuaded them to realise that the rains were really due to the mountain and its forest. Disguised as a mountain spirit, he ate the offerings which had been left for Indra. The enraged Indra created a huge storm. Torrential rains lasting seven days threatened the lives of the villagers who begged Krishna for help. He, then a child of 9 or 10, some sources say perhaps only 7, effortlessly picked up the mountain and held it aloft as a sheltering umbrella to shield the populace. He is often depicted in this attitude in miniature paintings and folk art and in a particularly stylised form, this is how he is shown in *pichhwais*. Lord Shrinathji, as he is known to members of the Pushti Marg, is not quite how many would describe as the epitome of youthful male beauty. He is a squat dark stone sculpture, almost 1½ metres tall and resides in the Nathdwara temple.

When first discovered, only the upraised arm in the attitude that symbolises refuge, was visible and this was worshipped as a snake. Even then it was perceived to have power and a sense of divinity.

Appearing in a dream to Vallabhacharya who was in South India at the time, Krishna told him to go immediately to the summit of Mount Govardhan to uncover the complete image, a form of himself, the Supreme Being. It was installed there in a shrine in 1492 and later moved to another shrine at nearby Gokul. In 1699, fearing destruction by the zealot Mughul Emperor Aurangzeb who had ordered the wholesale destruction of temples and images, devotees loaded the image onto a bullock-cart and set off in a south-westerly direction. In a way they were re-enacting the flight of baby Krishna from his birthplace in Mathura. Their destination was to be Udaipur but some 50 km short of the city, the cart's wheels stopped and were impossible to budge, a sign taken to mean that the god wished to stay and here he has been ever since.

The great Nathdwara temple is a sprawling complex of linked structures built in the manner of a Rajasthani palace. It is a *haveli* or mansion, a comfortable home for Krishna. Although it represents his foster-home with Nanda and Yashoda in Vraj, it is far from the reality of that humble dwelling. Aerial views of the temple, painted in Nathdwara on both paper and cloth, were a popular purchase for pilgrims though not used in any kind of religious ceremony. These renderings show a maze of courtyards and chambers, alcoves, ramps and stairs, gardens and shrines, alleys, terraces, roofs and spires and white walls adorned with paintings of tigers or elephants flanking gateways. Lord Shrinathji himself can be glimpsed with other *swarups*, priests, cows and processions marking the festival of Annakut. The microcosmic world of the worshipper is enticing.

The temple is located at the top of a low rise in the town of Nathdwara. The road leading up to its gates is lined with small shops selling paintings of Lord Shrinathji. Here and in some of the side streets on Krishna shopping trips I bought tiny images of the god to wear as pendant or brooch and stout cardboard cut-outs set on wooden feet of cows, worshippers, *gopis* and musicians. Archways span the street and an old twisted tree has somehow managed to hold onto life amidst the buildings, casting a patch of welcome shade. Nothing can be carried into the temple so shoes, cameras and bags are surrendered at a cloak-room before entering the shrine.

Every day in the temple the god is worshipped at eight *darshans* or formal viewings. He is cared for as a living being and the *darshans* are the daily punctuations of his life. The first marks the awakening of the drowsy child, next he is dressed before he leads the cows to the pasture. Later comes the midday meal, he is reawakened after a three-hour afternoon nap, then comes the afternoon meal. Twilight marks his return from the fields and finally in the evening the child is put to sleep. At each of these times, worshippers flood into the building and when the doors of the sanctum sanctorum are opened, they pray and sing and above all gaze at the deity. They lock eyes with him. His staring upturned and elongated eyes, dagger-like in shape, blackest pools in the whitest white, compel a return gaze and this locking of eyes is how connection is made with the god. His dress is dependent on the season or the festival. His turban will be a particular shape, ornamented by peacock feathers or a jewelled *sarpanch*, his clothes will be suitable for the heat of summer or the chillier temperatures of winter months, his jewellery and garlands are sumptuous.

I have had *darshan* at the temple four times but I still rely on pictures of *pichhwais* and other images of the god to really know what he looks like. The experience is overwhelming and I find it difficult to retain. On my last visit I lined up in the general section with other women worshippers rather than be channelled into the so-called VIP queue. This VIP privilege requires payment which allows a siphoning into the crowded shrine from a side entrance closer to the front, slightly ahead of most of the other worshippers. A very sweet teenager took charge of me as we entered and literally pulled me along in her wake, it was quite a scramble. Thank goodness for segregation as I have never, ever been in such a sardine situation and it was far preferable to be amongst women. I focused on the fact that I was upright and having no trouble breathing but it was quite impossible to move. Being taller than most of the women in the crowd, I had a wonderful view, but the pious devotion and the atmosphere is so extraordinary, it is difficult to describe the scene. It's clear I will have to go again with my wits more about me. I do know that the backdrop for the image was not a painted *pichhwai*.

As we watched, the white cloth was adorned by one of the priests, drawing shapes in regular spaces in vermilion powder, more like a tick than a V. Then he threw spaced puffs of the powder at the cloth before hurling great pelting handfuls into the cheering crowd. It was amazing. As we left the hall, splattered with powder, in a slower, more orderly manner than our entry, my sweet little friend said 'Now we will line up and go in again.' But I said 'No, I'm too old!'

The National Gallery has a wonderful collection of *pichhwais* and also some interesting *manoraths*, donor portraits which incorporate photography and painting, blurring the mediums in a manner that echoes the ability of Hinduism to absorb and accommodate external influences, changing them into something that is truly Indian. An example of this enveloping capacity is the identity of the God Vayu who is the god of the air and part of the Vaishnavite pantheon. He dates not from ancient Vedic times but appears after the dawn of the Christian era and the arrival of Christianity in India and seems to be a version of the Holy Ghost. In the Gallery's *manoraths*, donors have been photographed in a Nathdwara studio and the photographs subsequently collaged onto a painting which usually incorporates a *pichhwai* in the background. Are these people meant to be posing in front of the *pichhwai* or have they indeed become part of it? Or is it just a representation of them worshipping at the shrine?

At the end of my six months work for the Jaipur Virasat Foundation I had five days in which to write my final report, pack up my funny old flat and get myself to Delhi to meet a group of twenty voluntary guides from the Australian National Gallery. I had organised a study tour for them which focused on aspects of the Indian art in the Gallery's collection. As well as Delhi we travelled to Vrindavan, Agra, Jaipur, Udaipur, Varanasi and Chennai. The Udaipur stop was in order to visit Nathdwara, the temple and studios of a number of famous *pichhwai* painters. My friend Desmond Lazaro, took charge of this part of the tour, starting in his Delhi studio where he explained the rudiments of the painting technique. A British artist and academic, he spent eleven years as a craftsman in a traditional studio in Jaipur. He studied the elaborate detail, the often laborious methods and the philosophy and faith which underlie the creation of these beautiful creations.

In Jaipur we visited an upper room close to Badi Chaupal, walls and ceilings painted superbly by Desmond's teacher and his assistants. From this sublime elevation he led us down the hill to the lower part of the city close to the Amer Road. Rhythmic hammering sounded through the winter air. It came from small cell-like workshops where men with hammers pounded gold and silver leaf under small leather pillows, constantly turning the packet and miraculously not crushing their fingers. In a nearby dark little workshop we saw an ancient, dangerous-looking machine turn a small lump of gold into a long narrow ribbon which would eventually be applied as paint on a *pichhwai*.

The colours of traditional *pichhwais* come from pigments from several sources—minerals such as lapis lazuli, malachite or conch shell; earth surface deposits such as red and yellow ochres; organic origins from plants, animals or insects such as indigo or red lac, metals such as gold and silver and some pigments made through chemical processes e.g. vermilion or lead white. Nathdwara *pichhwais* are famous for a distinctive green and a rose or lotus pink called *kamal ka rang*. The lotus is not the source itself, the perfect pink pigment is extracted from the small fruits of the plant Mallotus Phillippinensus, a member of the spurge family. Greens which are used a great deal, come from several sources but one, *mungiya*, is a mixture of *neel* or indigo and *pyori* or *goguli*, the yellow. Artists often mix their paints in pearly sea-shells which add a further magical element to the process.

How can someone with blue skin be so compelling? Cobalt blue is a colour that appeals to many people and it is said to have an ecstatic effect on the psyche. Regina Spekter, a Russian singer who lives in New York, sings of blue as the most human colour—'blue lips, blue veins, blue the colour of our planet from far, far away.' Krishna's blueness which represents the sky, changes from school to school, from region to region, from one place of worship to another. In Nathdwara it is important to paint the god as close as possible to the colour of the actual sculptured image, the darkness of his skin suggesting the black clouds of the great storm sent down by Indra onto Mount Govardhan. The blues used in *pichhwais* are an indigo base mixed with red lac and other elements. Tradition says that Krishna should be painted with blue skin and yellow *dhoti*—in the gorgeous Poussin colour combination. As Shrinathji, he appears in some festival *pichhwais* in glorious yellow clothing, a four-pointed *chakdajama* and pyjamas rather than a *dhoti* and behind him hangs a deep blue cloth, enhancing his dark skin. If *neel* or indigo is the colour of Krishna and *goguli* or yellow is the colour of Radha, the distinctive Nathdwara green then is a mixture of the two colours and the resulting green, the true colour of nature, symbolizes the union of Radha and Krishna.

Goguli, the yellow is even further loaded with symbolism. The term in Hindi, means that which the cow brings or the gift of the cow, a symbol of Krishna. As late as the latter half of the 19th century, this Indian Yellow, a wonderful deep shade, came to colour men in London such as Messrs Winsor and Newton, direct from Calcutta in little nuggets of unpleasant smell. The pigment, called *piuri,* came from the town of Monghyr, on the banks of the Ganges in the modern state of Bihar. It was made from the urine of cows fed on a diet of mango leaves. The poor cows apparently looked unhealthy and did not live long. The process has been completely forgotten, entirely erased from Monghyr's living memory. Victoria Finlay, the author of the fascinating book *Colour* went there in pursuit of Indian Yellow. The people thought she was crazy, especially when she had to resort to mime to demonstrate the process.

A similar colour to this Indian yellow was considered a very fashionable shade in the early 19th century and it was known as Turner's Patent Yellow. It is not the mango variety but was developed by James Turner based on lead and is a brilliant sparkly yellow. The South Drawing Room in Sir John Soane's Museum in London is decorated with Turner's Patent, rarely found and no longer made. The room is very yellow indeed with the walls, draperies and upholstery matching perfectly with touches of red on the swagged curtains.

There are about 300 painters active in and around Nathdwara

today. Some are absolute masters while others produce repetitive, unappealing work. Desmond took us in small groups to visit four artists in the town. We walked down narrow lanes lined by tall houses painted lavender, mint green and white. Some artists worked on large works in studios, others in small apartments on the upper floors of old buildings concentrated on small works, details from conventional *pichhwais*.

Several princely dynasties in Rajasthan were devotees of Lord Shrinathji and *pichhwais* were painted in both Kota and Kishangarh with stylistic differences to those created in Nathdwara. The artist is immersed totally as a *bhakta* or devotee and conventions can be forgotten, ignored or slightly changed. I have found this when twice, a couple of years apart, in some form of incipient religious dementia I had forgotten the symbolism of something of which I had read, one of many small details included in most *pichhwais*. Both times, different artists didn't know the answer and so therefore it really shouldn't matter a scrap, it just needs to be there. An artist might like the shape and balance that something small gives the painting as a whole and the convention becomes a habit. I remember in Laos, a weaver friend of mind used to sigh and shrug when asked 'And what does this *mean*?' in a deeply serious way by a well-meaning visitor. 'Nothing,' she would answer 'I just like the design.'

On another journey to Udaipur I went to the studio of Raja Ram Sharma, a master painter of *pichhwais*. Later I bought a small work by him of six stately cows, their noses splendidly in the air, spurning all but Krishna. I lived in the Australian countryside for more than thirty years where the bellowing of bulls was often the noisiest sound of the day. I didn't ever have anything much to do with our cattle at close quarters but I saw them every day, enjoying their placid beauty, amused at the antics of sprightly young ones and sorrowful when the death of a calf would leave his mother confused and sad, or when a poor mother in difficulties calving would have to be despatched. Humans are fortunate to be able to speak, it's too sorrowful to hear to the wretched mooing of some poor beast in trouble. At least we can shriek or swear or call upon someone to help. Perhaps my years as farmer's wife has made me more likely to be charmed by Indian cows. They certainly abound in my home in pictorial form. In a *pichhwai* I bought in Udaipur a few years ago there are no fewer than 110. My friend Robyn Beeche used to enjoy sleeping in my spare bedroom where Krishna keeps watch over visitors. Lord Shrinathji is not the version of Krishna to which she was devoted, but he is Krishna nevertheless and in my *pichhwai* he appears as Gokulachandramaji which was closer to her deity.

This *pichhwai* is a popular one—*gayon wali pichhwai* or *pichhwai* of cows and celebrates a festival in November which commemorates the day when Krishna became a fully-fledged cowherd. It more than likely comes from Ahmedabad in Gujarat where many *Pushti Margis* reside and it may have been hung in a household shrine. Krishna is shown in the form of the moon of Gokul. The vibrant colour of many *pichhwais* is absent. Here everything is silvery—silver block-printed border, silver cows and Krishna who is playing his flute is dressed in silvery moonlight clothes. His torso is bare but his four pointed *chakdarjama* and *suthan* are silver as is his large peacock feather cockade. His jewellery however is gold—armbands, bangles and ear-pieces and also his flute. His beautiful pink lotus *mala* is the same pink as the lotus platform on which he stands and the background is a rich burgundy shade. I nearly gave myself heart attacks when I mounted it on some *mashru* of a perfect matching colour. I had to iron it and turn it inside out and straighten corners and I knew if my friends in the Textile Conservation Department at the Gallery could see me they would fall down in a dead faint. What I was doing would *not* have met their approval. Fortunately they didn't have to witness my efforts and thankfully it all worked out beautifully.

Mashru is another fascinating Indian textile tradition. I've seen it woven in Patan, the town known for the production of the far more famous and very expensive *patola* cloth. The word *mashru* is Arabic for 'permitted' and the cloth was made for devout Muslims not permitted to wear silk next to their skin. The cloth has a silk warp and cotton weft and in a satin weave, the cotton ends up on the wrong side which will be next to the skin. Much was made for export to Arab countries and the cloth was woven in several silk towns in India. Now a couple of weavers in Patan are among the very few who still produce it. The cloth comes in beautiful colours, sometimes with tiny subtle dots, more often with simple stripes, sometimes incorporating a line of ikat or a simple spotted motif. Rajasthani women in some regions wear backless *mashru* blouses with their wide colourful skirts.

On one of the NGA Krishna searches I found my way back to a small shop, the Ganesh Art Emporium, near Jagdish Chowk in Udaipur. Years before I had bought a painting of Lord Ganesha from Madhu Kant Mundra, the talented, award-winning artist who owns the shop. Madhu has exhibited as far away as Japan and was one of the earliest miniature painters in Udaipur to combine modern and original ideas with traditional techniques. Udaipur is full of shops, large and small, selling miniature paintings but few have much originality, the artists preferring to run off repetitive copy after copy of works from the past.

At that stage in Madhu's career he delighted in painting the elephant-headed god in a variety of whimsical poses. Lord Ganesh's vehicle is the rat and in one painting he is seen, sitting in a *jarokha*, resplendent in crown and garlands tossing *ladoos*, his favourite sweets, to happy-looking grey rats scampering on the ground below him. In another he is the bridegroom, leading his bride around the sacred fire. In my work, he is balancing on a tight-rope, one foot on a hoop, his small rat vehicle held aloft on a garland while four other ratty friends hold a safety net inscribed with the sacred syllable, 'Om', beneath the scaffold lest the god falls.

One story about Lord Ganesh recounts a spectacular fall. After a substantial evening meal he felt in need of a ride to aid his digestion. He is always shown with a bulging stomach and one of his names is Lambodara which means 'of the full belly'. He jumped astride his rat but while riding along in the moonlight, his path was suddenly blocked by an enormous snake. The rat took fright, plunged off the path into the jungle, unseating his rider who was flung to the ground with such terrific force that his belly burst open. Out rolled all the *ladoos* that he had recently eaten. He gathered them up and stuffed them back into his paunch. The offending serpent was used to bind up the tear and is clearly visible in most paintings or sculptures of the God. No sooner had this bit of extemporaneous surgery been completed than the night sky was rent by sounds of uncontrollable laughter, the moon, highly amused at all he had witnessed. This was insult added to injury for poor Lord Ganesh and in a fury he broke off one of his tusks and hurled it at the moon which since that time has been regularly deprived of some of its light.

Apart from this display of temperament, Lord Ganesh is usually of calm and gentle disposition and a tower of common sense and amiability. This and a certain comic air due to his appearance is another reason for being one of the best-loved of Hindu deities. He is endowed with the intelligence of man and the sagacity and strength of the elephant. There is another more serious and worthy version of the reason for his broken tusk. Having no writing implement, he broke off the tusk in order to use it as a pen to write down the words of the sage Vyasa as he composed the great Indian epic, the Mahabharata. It is probably the longest single poem in the world with 90,000 stanzas usually of 32 syllables. Lord Ganesh is the patron of grammarians and is particularly interested in educational and literary activities. Indian books will very often start with the words '*Shri Ganeshaya namah*', an auspicious formula which means 'reverence to Lord Ganesh'. He is known as Vinayaka, the remover of obstacles, so students will pray to him before they sit exams, travellers before setting out on journeys and businessmen before starting new ventures. The auspicious place for a Ganesh image is at the entry, whether at a temple or by a front door. He is a powerful ally and images of him have sold very well indeed in the Gallery's exhibition shops.

Madhu's shop at Jagdish Chowk is tiny but a short distance away, down a steep hill lined with the typical white houses of Udaipur, is his home, workshop and godown. He manufactures artwork in a big way. Charming little paintings of gods and heroes backed and framed with tin are churned out in scores. Mass production to be sure, but in truth all are hand-painted even if to a template. Madhu told me he once commissioned 5,000 works for an export order from a good miniature painter at a good price of 500 rupees each. The artist was delighted at first but after taking three days to complete the first, he realised he had fifty years work ahead of him and cancelled the deal. Mass production to be sure, but in truth all are hand-painted even if to a template.

In the same way as a century before in Calcutta, Kalighat artists tossed off copy after copy of quickly produced sketches, Madhu and his assistants paint images of Lord Shinathji in many sizes. They are rough but their naivety is appealing. I bought a good number and he agreed to include in the parcel all the purchases I had made in the Nathdwara bazaar. Then I asked him if he had any *pichhwais* and he showed me what he had. None were particularly old but they were in good condition and were quite a varied collection and my heart started to pound in the same way as it does when I've seen a painting at an exhibition and wonder if I will get to the keeper of the red dots before anyone else.

One was for the festival of Annakut, or the Mountain of Food which takes place in November, the day after Diwali, the Indian festival of light, and recalls the raising of Mount Govardhan by Krishna. It is also a harvest festival and the mountain of food is literally a huge mountain of rice in the central foreground below the feet of Lord Shrinathji and seven other *swarups*. It is also a re-enactment of the historic *mahotsava* or grand festival held in 1822 when all the seven *swarups* with their presiding priests gathered in Nathdwara from far-flung parts of India. Lord Shrinathji is dressed in in *chakdarwagha*, a coat with four pointed ends at the hem, *suthan* or pyjamas and a turban. His turban is crowned with a *gokarna mukta*, a diadem in the shape of cow ears holding a cockade of peacock feathers. As well he is splendidly covered in necklaces and garlands that fall to his feet.

The mountain of rice which symbolises Mount Govardhan is topped by a sweet cake representing the head of the great god Vishnu and four other cakes represent his weapons. The feast of *chappan bhoga* or 56 offerings is laid out in rows behind the rice and ladies with their heads covered sit on the floor below the *goswamis* or priests who flank the whole formal scene, waving fly-whisks and performing *aarti* or worship with lights. Madhu showed me a photograph taken of his own family's celebration of Annakut from the year before which was a contemporary jerk back to reality. The outer border of the *pichhwai* is floral and inside that, small depictions in a border enclosing the top and sides of the cloth, are miniatures showing the god in raiment particular to other festivals. These celebrations take place in the Nathdwara temple but in sections beneath the main image of the shrine, friezes tell other stories of Krishna. We are transported to idyllic Vrindavan, first with a narrow frieze of his beloved cows which at the time of Annakut are decorated with handprints and peacock plumes. Next in a wider band is an image of the Festival of Daan Lila or Extracting the Toll. Here Krishna and his brother Balarama demand a toll of milk and curd from the Vrindavan *gopis*. Below them gently flows the beautiful Yamuna River.

These images are so full of life and vitality they repay long study. The NGA has some brilliant examples. One is a map of Vraj where many of Krishna's exploits may be traced. Another, painted at Kota, a princely state located in between Vrindavan and Udaipur, is almost 3 metres square. Blue Krishna clad in a dance skirt, plays his flute while more than 100 gopis stand on either side, totally entranced. It is hard for any onlooker not enter a similar state.

The Yamuna appears at the bottom of many of the paintings, always blue, lotus-dotted and inhabited by fish, turtles and waterfowl. Two works that I bought are called Kamal Vana or Jal Vihara, displayed for the festival of Gangadashmi in the hottest month of June when both Vrindavan and Nathdwara are baking in temperatures in the 40s. This form of *pichhwai* show refreshingly cool images of the calm waters of the Yamuna, covered with pink-tipped lotus flowers and dotted with waterfowl. In some, devoted pairs of ducks and herons bill and coo and schools of fish dart beneath the surface. Insects hover over the lotus and the pollination of the flowers by the bees is a metaphor for Krishna, the divine lover. His name means black or dark and the dark bees buzz around the lotus as Krishna buzzed about the *gopis*. The underlying sensuality is indisputable. Had the god been present in this painting, he would be dressed for the summer in a light muslin half-dhoti or sarong.

In some *pichhwais* the Yamuna takes a very important place in the narrative of Krishna's life. In particular is the depiction of Chirharan Lila, a celebration of the story of the stealing, literally abduction, of the milkmaid's clothes. The *gopis* who are all deeply in love with Krishna, decide to take a dip in the Yamuna, more of a swim than a quick holy dip. Unusually they remove their clothes and enter the water, splashing and swimming, enjoying the waters. Suddenly they hear the sound of their beloved's flute and looking up they see him high in the branches of a *kadamba* tree with their clothes festooned around him. Having already stolen their hearts, now he has taken their clothing as well. Indian women would not normally dream of bathing naked in a stream. They enter the water wearing their clothes and somehow after their dip, manage to change into dry clothes without any loss of modesty. Krishna up in his tree ignores the *gopis*' entreaties to return their clothes and says that by bathing naked in a religious observance they have committed a serious transgression. Poor things, they were not really involved in anything spiritual, just feeling the heat at the end of a warm autumn day. But in order to save themselves he requires them to bare their very souls and so doing, they are instantly clothed with spiritual garments, gaining entry into the *raaslila,* the circular dance of Krishna's divine play. The interpretation of this story is that the god has taken and then restored the outer corporeal layers of the body which camouflage the soul.

An old *kadamba* tree still lives, growing close to the ashram where Robyn Beeche lived at Vrindavan and is usually decorated with colourful saris in remembrance of things past. It is not the only tree claimed to be Lord Krishna's arboreal hideout. There is also confusion over the true identity of the *kadamba* as there are two related varieties of the tree. In modern paintings the wrong one is usually shown probably because the yellow flowers are brighter and showier. This variety is native to the moist forests of north-eastern India and would not tolerate the hot, dry summers of Vrindavan. Their flowers are similar, clusters of tiny little fragrant budlike blooms which appear in fluffy pom poms. The true variety is known locally more often as *kaim*. Its flowers are a paler yellow than those of the other variety and are famous for providing excellent bee-forage which is significant. Krishna likened to a bee, becomes drunk with the nectar of flowers and Radha is likened to the flower-bed. In one story he turns himself into a bee to fly close to his beloved and is roundly admonished for it.

The word Vrindavan means the forest of Vrinda and the area was famous for its groves and forests, most of which have been cleared for farming. Some sacred groves connected with events in the life of Krishna have disappeared completely and others are under threat. The town of Vrindavan has grown and stretches far away from the river to include condominiums and housing estates on the outskirts near the Delhi-Agra road. Developers do not let a tree or two stand in their way and there are few to be seen in the once forested area. *Kadamba* wood is suitable for turning and carving and I bought pretty wooden jewellery for the Krishna shop. Some showed images of peacocks which are always associated with Krishna.

A most unpleasant feature of Vrindavan today is the colossal population of monkeys. They are everywhere—sitting on parapets, scampering up light poles, ranging along walls, squabbling in temple forecourts. Wearing spectacles while walking around the town is a perilous act as a monkey scout will come from nowhere and remove them. I have had to lead short-sighted people around the narrow streets, temporarily unable to see for fear of losing their specs. It certainly affects their enjoyment of what is usually a one and only visit to the town and its temples and much of the atmosphere is lost. Some temples are infested by the mean-faced little creatures. They also snatch cameras or anything they perceive as food and you don't argue with them. They try to enter houses and one who found its way into Robyn's apartment stole her spectacles. The Tulsi Garden or Seva Kunj where the *gopis* used to dance, is monkey paradise and there are so many there it's almost too dangerous to enter.

The *gopis'* circular dance is celebrated at the Sharad Purnima Festival at the autumn full moon. In many *Raaslila* paintings Krishna is shown to have miraculously manifested himself eight times to dance in the circle in between two *gopis* so each has the joyous fulfilment of dancing with the god. They are possessed by him and the culmination is when he presents himself in the centre of the circle. My *Raaslila pichhwai* is rich with gold paint and shows one Krishna dancing in the centre with his beloved Radha. The other *gopis* whirl in their circle, hennaed hands upraised. Gods look down from the sky in their celestial chariots and the Yamuna flows gently below. I purchased a second Sharad Purnima *pichhwai*, last year in Udaipur. It shows Shrinathji, dressed ready for the dance, his sashes flicking, electricity in the air. He is flanked by *gopis*, beautifully dressed in their best, waiting to dance with their Lord. The god is dressed in a dancing skirt and pyjamas, a jewelled crown studded with jewels, garlanded and bejewelled, the back of the stele is cased in a dazzling white cloth for the occasion. It is very seductive. This one has gone into the NGA collection as well as another fascinating form of Indian painted cloth which also made my heart pound when I saw it—a *phad* painting, about 5 metres long, which tells the story of a Rajasthani folk hero, Pabuji—but that's another story.

On my last day in Udaipur I set out for Madhu's shop to finalise payment and organise freight. On the walk from Rang Niwas, my delightful old hotel on Lake Palace Road, I noticed a great deal of action at a temple. Across the road in an empty shop-house, a *pichhwai* of the *Raasila* had been hung, Krishna and the *gopis* swirling around in their circular dance. A group of ten men were singing and happily waved as I walked past. Torrential rain had cooled the town but as the sun came out again, the humidity rose and it became terribly hot. There was a power outage so generators had roared into action outside some of the shops. As Madhu and I completed the paperwork in the semi-gloom, suddenly there was an enormous explosion. I rushed to the door to have a look and saw a man with an enormous weapon with a trumpet-like muzzle at least 4 inches in diameter. Heavens, it did make a noise which was taken up by a brass band, its members marching along in perky red, gold and navy uniforms, some coiled inside their shiny instruments, playing the loud, cacophonous music that accompanies weddings and other Indian festivities. The band had a cart loaded with loud speakers and then boys started to let off deafening double bungers. It was all happening just feet away as we were trying to find a friend's telephone number.

The noise started to fade as the band moved on, disappearing down the hill, followed by a procession. A large group of women walked past, their heads covered in *odhnis* of brightest pink, red, orange and yellow, some with offerings of sprouted grass poking from vessels atop their veils. They were followed by carts drawn by camels carrying gangs of happy children. Garlanded paintings of gods were propped on the carts, first Lord Ganesha and then Lord Shrinathji. The combination seemed a very good omen and I was happy to get onto the train that night and be conveyed through the darkness back to Jaipur.

The first time I visited Vrindavan was in 2001 for Janmashtami which is Lord Krishna's birthday, his 5229th. Jasleen Dhamija had organised her cook as guide and companion to take my friend Jan Connolly and me to the festival. It was quite an ecumenical day as we first attended morning service at St Martin's church in the Delhi Cantonment, an extraordinary building designed by Arthur Shoosmith, one of the architectural assistants to Lutyens, the creator of New Delhi. It is a splendid building, massive and brooding. Begun in 1929, the church resembles a great fortress and has been compared to war memorials and even Battersea Power Station which is contemporaneous. Constructed of three and half million thin red bricks and almost windowless, Gavin Stamp the architectural historian considers it one of the great buildings of the 20th century. At the time of our visit I was writing a paper comparing it to a church of similar age in Canberra—St Paul's at Manuka. By extension there was comparison between New Delhi and Canberra and their designers Sir Edwin Lutyens and Walter Burley Griffin.

The contrast between St Martin's and the temples we visited in Vrindavan in the afternoon was immense. We parked our car some distance from the edge of the town and walked down a road crowded with devotees. The headquarters of ISKCON and its temple is close to the entry to the town so we stopped here first. People thronged the white marble forecourt of the *mandir* where the images of Radha and Krishna were smothered with garlands, fruit and flowers. We wandered around the little town, entering temples here and there and eventually found the *ashram* where Jasleen had told us we must go before continuing to the Shri Radharaman Temple. It was a beautiful old temple, crowded with people listening to a performance of music. The display of devotion, even though exuberant, was somehow more dignified than that at ISKCON and there were few foreigners. I had no idea where we were, we had followed Chotilal like obedient sheep along high walled narrow lanes. We were there for *darshan* and it was a great end to a fascinating day.

I had been back to Vrindavan with the National Gallery guides in 2007 but when I returned in 2009 to stay for the first time, it was quite startling to have complete recall when I entered the gates of Robyn's ashram—it was sight of the lattice on the ground floor really. When in the evening we went to the temple, I just knew this was where I had been eight years before. That mightn't seem particularly profound, but we had visited several temples and in a day of temple-going they can blur. When I arrived home after that very happy stay I looked up the old photos and most uncannily but in a way that is not surprising in magical India, I found that I had even taken a photo of the back of Robyn's head. I didn't know her at the time, we met at the Art Gallery of New South Wales some years later. It was Krishna's mystical spell.

On this first stay at the ashram I came on from the Jaipur Literature Festival on Republic Day, passing through towns on roads quiet for the holiday where school children were lined up for celebrations under the flag in school compounds. It seemed very auspicious. Robyn was a brilliant help with the shopping and showed me corners of the town I wouldn't have found alone. The bazaars are full of little shops dealing in merchandise for pilgrims and devotees. Many are called after one of Krishna's 108 names which are based on his attributes—Gopala or Govinda both mean Protector of Cows, Manmohan or All-pleasing Lord, Keshava the long-haired one, Nanda Lal means beloved of Nanda. Other shops might be called after a saint such as Chaitanya or after Radha, Yashoda or other members of Krishna's family. Stationers sell cards with images of Krishna, cloth shops sell scarves, shawls, shirts and rosary bags with printed or embroidered images of the god or texts from scriptures, *mukut wallahs* sell robes, crowns and jewellery to fit any size of deity and hypnotic pairs of eyes to place last on a newly made image of the god. Ironmongers sell every kind of brass and copper vessel used in worship, silversmiths have fine images of the god or tiny toys to amuse the holy child. Grocers sell food, hardware shops sell plastic buckets and life goes on as in any Indian town.

I was entranced with the tiny garments created to clothe the deity. Devotees will change his clothes daily and he has special warm things for the winter, light ones for the summer. It was winter and some wonderful furry dresses were on sale, the magenta ones really caught my eye. Peacocks are very dear to Krishna and at the advent of the monsoon season with its brooding black clouds, lightning and thunderstorms, the peacock starts his extraordinary courtship dance to attract the peahens, very much like Krishna dancing with the milkmaids. Beautiful Nathdwara *pichhwais* portray the peacock's dance and in Vrindavan I bought little feather dresses and feather cockades for his crowns. Of course, along with any other dangerous item, they were declared and spent time in the National Gallery freezer to kill any possible infestation of nasty creatures.

Robyn took me to meet a very famous *zari wallah* or embroiderer, Ashok Ladiwal. His workshop was behind an unassuming doorway in a back street where in the semi darkness caused by a power blackout, we looked at his superb embroideries. I remembered seeing his work in *The Golden Eye,* a wonderful exhibition at the Cooper Hewitt Museum, the Smithsonian's National Museum of Design in New York in 1985. That exhibition was an 'international tribute to the artisans of India' where designers from many parts of the world worked with Indian craftsmen on exciting and beautiful creations.

Ashok's family have been embroidery artisans for five generations. Much of the work done in his studio is the creation of clothes for images of Krishna and other cloths associated with worship. Orders come from all over the world where diasporic

Indian communities worship Krishna but when I visited, the global financial crisis was having a very bad effect on his business. Since then trade has picked up and he has again collaborated with fashion designers who recognise the rare quality of his work. I bought pieces which have since entered the NGA collection. The colour combinations are irresistible, the stitching superb and images are sometimes playful as well as pretty, depicting cows, peacocks, fish and flowers.

Robyn Beeche was archivist, official photographer and wonderful all-round administrative person at the Gambhira Ashram which was her base from 1985. She was instrumental in 1997 in establishing an NGO in India, Friends of Vrindavan (FoV), which is dedicated to sustainable development and preservation of the heritage town, environmental and sociological issues. FoV collects and sorts rubbish, much of it discarded by pilgrims to the town. Recycling turns organic matter into marketable compost, so good it has a waiting list of customers. FoV which now has 40 staff members, conducts tree-planting programs and environmental education for children. It trains low caste people for jobs that will help elevate their status, and delivers HIV–AIDS education. In 2009 Robyn galvanised many into action to fight the construction of a large bridge outside the 16th century walls of her ashram. Plans for the bridge had bypassed due process and heritage consultation and paid no attention to the disastrous affects it would have on the Yamuna River. Thanks largely to Robyn's work, construction ceased.

Holi is India's spring festival of colours and Robyn's photographs of Holi are famous world-wide. Celebrated all over India and wherever there are communities of Indians, it is at its wildest and most colourful in the towns of Vraj. She photographed it every year and fantastic images of it are included in *A Life Exposed*, the excellent documentary made on her life by Lesley Branagan. You can't buy Holi but Robyn, in her typical efficient and generous way had been able to start a cottage industry for the wives of low-caste sweepers making recycled paper products. I bought notebooks for the Gallery with vivid splashy covers which encapsulated Holi. Plastic bags are also recycled into beautiful baskets and placemats.

On one visit to Vrindavan a most marvellous *sewa* (service to the gods) was taking place at the Shri Radharaman Temple. It was an annual celebration of worship when every day for three weeks gorgeous *phul bangalas* or flower houses are created in the sanctum sanctorum, surrounding the deities of Radha and Krishna. On my first night all was a white and green. The following night the colours were white and a subtle pink, and warmed by the glorious silver and gold printed rich saffron curtains behind the flowery bowers. The silver throne and gateways which usually frame the gods were hidden but the beautiful ephemeral creations last only one day. By the morning *darshan*, everything has been taken down and the golden curtains alone frame the silver doors which open to reveal the gods on their silver thrones.

We went to see the start of a new creation early in the morning. In a work-room half a dozen men were making the panels that help form the flowery structure of the houses. Sections of the pale cream-coloured inner part of banana trunks were quickly and unerringly cut into strips and geometric shapes, petals and leaves for lotus *mandalas* set centrally within squares, arched borders encompassing birds in sinuous scrolls. They were anchored with millions of pins to wooden frames spiked with nails around which the jasmine strings would be wound. The banana strips had a pretty pearly lustre and in the finished scene they shone against highlights of dark green amid the paleness. Miles of strung garlands of jasmine formed scalloped borders of the pavilion roof sheltering Shri Krishna and Radha on the first night and their clothing each day toned perfectly with their ephemeral flower homes. Strings of jasmine intertwined with green leaves snaked up miniature columns and the roof-lines looked like the *bangaldar* roofs of a Rajasthani palace or even the exterior of the temple *haveli* itself, with fanlights and niches and the suggestion of *chhatri*, projecting balcony and *jarokha*. Above the triple arch edifice of the pink construction, there was even a rectangular hanging *punkah* to cool the gods in the hot summer weather. Everything was framed by the old cusped triple stone archways of the temple itself which gave a solidity to the otherwise fragile creation. 'Frail as summer's flowers we flourish.'

Special music and dance performances were scheduled for many nights in the temple. On my first night it was superb Shubha Mudgal, the well-known singer of Hindustani classical music and a Krishna devotee. Her voice soared through the old temple and thrilled the congregation, further heightening their emotions. The next night several worshippers spontaneously rose and danced to the music performed by local artists. It was devout and joyous and a truly wonderful spectacle.

I've yet to go to Dwarka but as I'm rather keen on confluences, perhaps I had better plan a future Krishna trip. Robyn's depth of knowledge about Vrindavan, its history and current incarnation is manifest but I don't think she's been to Dwarka either. We have been to his birthplace and important sites connected with his early life so I'm sure we should see him through to the end. It could be the start rather than the finish of another Krishna adventure.

I wrote this before Robyn's death but I think will leave it as it is and go to Dwarka one day with her in my heart.

Udaipur, Rajasthan, India. Lotus ponds (kamal vana) of the Yamuna; shrine hanging (pichhavai) c.1995. Pigment on cotton, 192.5 x 147.8 cm. National Gallery of Australia, Canberra. Gift of Claudia Hyles through the Australian Government's Cultural Gifts Program, 2010

Phul bangala at Radharaman Temple, Vrindavan, Uttar Pradesh

Bibliography

Achaya, K.T. *Indian Food: A Historical Companion.* Oxford University Press. Oxford. 1994

Allen, Charles. *Kipling's Kingdom.* Michael Joseph Ltd. London. 1987

Bahri, Anuj & Smith, Debbi. *Bahrisons: chronicles of a bookshop. From the narrations of Balraj Malhotra.* India Research Press. New Delhi. 2004

Bannerman, Helen. *Little Black Sambo; Little Black Quingo; Little Black Quasha*

Bidwell, Shelford. *Swords for Hire: European mercenaries in eighteenth century India.* John Murray. London. 1971

Braley, Bernard. *Hymnwriters 1.* Stainer & Bell. London. 1987

Burton, David. *The Raj at Table.* Rupa & Co. New Delhi. 1995

Collier, Richard. *The Sound of Fury: an account of the Indian Mutiny.* Collins. London. 1963.

Crafti, Stephen. *Robyn Beeche: Visage to Vraj.* Images Publishing Group, Mulgrave. 2009

Dalrymple, William. *The Last Mughul: The fall of a dynasty, Delhi 1857.* Penguin Viking. New Delhi 2006

Davies, Philip. *Splendours of the Raj: British architecture in India 1660–1947.* Dass Media. New Delhi. 1985

Dharia, Namita. *Kumbh Mela. Preliminary Report from the Field. November 2012*

Desai, Kiran. *The Inheritance of Loss.* Penguin Books. London. 2006

Ghose, Baskar. *The Teller of Tales.* Penguin Books. New Delhi. 2012

Godden, Jon & Rumer. *Two under the Indian sun.* Pan Books Ltd. London. 1966

Gour, Neelum Saran Gour. Ed. *Allahabad: Where the rivers meet.* Marg Publications. Mumbai. 2009

Gross, John (ed). *The Age of Kipling: the man, his work, and his world.* Simon & Schuster. New York. 1972

Hankin, Nigel. H*anklyn-Janklin.* India Research Press. New Delhi. 2003

Heber, Reginald. *Narrative of a Journey through the Upper Provinces of India from Calcutta to Bombay, 1824–25 (with notes upon Ceylon). An account of a journey to Madras and the Southern Provinces, 1826 and letters written in*

India. 3 Vols. John Murray. 1828 Reprint General Books, Memphis. 2010

Herbert, Eugenia W. *Flora's Empire: British Gardens in India*. Penguin Books India. New Delhi. 2011

Hicks, Pamela. *Daughter of Empire: Life as a Mountbatten*. Weidenfeld & Nicolson. London. 2012

Hobart-Hampden, Mrs Hélène. *Louisa*. Chatterbox 1923

Hosain, Attia and Pasricha, Sita. *Cooking the Indian Way*. Su Books Pty Ltd. Melbourne. 1969

Hussein, Aamer with Habibubullah, Shama. *Attia Hosain: Distant Traveller—new & selected fiction*. Women Unlimited. New Delhi. 2013

Joshi, M.C. *Dig*. Archaeological Survey of India. New Delhi. 2006

Jaffer, Amin. *Made for Maharajas: A Design Diary of Princely India*. Roli & Janaassen BV. New Delhi. 2007

Jasimuddin. *Nakshi Kanthar Math* or *The field of the embroidered quilt*. Translated by E.M. Milford. Hasna Jasimuddin Moudud. Dhaka. 1986

Kincaid, Dennis. *British Social Life in India, 1608–1937*. Readers Union. Newton Abbot. 1974

Krishen, Pradip. *Trees of Delhi: A field guide*. DK. India. 2006

Krishen, Pradip. *The small Plant Guide to Rao Jodha Desert Rock Park*. Mehrangarh Museum Trust. Jodhpur. 2011

Krishna, Kalyan and Talwar, Kay. *In Adoration of Krishna: Pichhwais of Shrinathji. Tapi Collection*. Garden Silk Mills Limited. Mumbai. 2007

Lazaro, Desmond Peter. *Materials, Methods & symbolism in the Pichhvai Painting tradition of Rajasthan*. Mapin Publishing. Ahmedabad. 2005

Lloyd, Michael and Desmond, Michael. *European and American Paintings and Sculptures 1870–1970 in the Australian National Gallery*. The Australian National Gallery. Canberra. 1992

Lord, John. *The Maharajas*. Hutchinson & Co (Publishers) Ltd. London. 1973 Hasna Jasimuddin Moudud. Dhaka. 1986

Masani, Minoo. *Our India—1953*. Oxford University Press. Bombay. 1953

Mehrotra, Arvind Krishna. *Partial Recall: Essays on Literature and Literary History*. Permanent Black. Ranikhet. 2012

Mehta, Ved. *Portrait of India*. Penguin Books. Baltimore. 1973

Milgate, Wesley. *Songs of the People of God*. Collins Liturgical Publications. London. 1982

Miller, Sam. *Delhi: Adventures in a Megacity*. Viking Penguin India. New Delhi. 2008

Morris, Paula. *Rangatira.* Penguin Books (NZ). Auckland. 2011

Moynihan, Elizabeth B. (Ed.). *The Moonlight Garden: new discoveries at the Taj Mahal.* Arthur M. Sackler Gallery, Smithsonian Institution. Washington DC. 2000

Mutiah, S.; Menakshi Meyappan, Visalakshi Ramaswamy. *The Chettiar Heritage.* Chennai. 2000

Naqvi, S.A.A. *Humayun's Tomb & adjacent monuments.* Archaeological Survey of India. New Delhi. 2002

Niggl, Reto. *Eckart Muthesius. The Maharaja's Palace in Indore. Architecture and Interior 1930.* Translated by Claudia Lupri. Arnoldsche. Stuttgart. 1996

Norman, Mrs Edward (collector) *A Selection of jam and preserve recipes from old country houses throughout the English Counties.* The Aldridge Print Group, London

Roy, Arundhati. *The God of Small Things.* Flamingo, London. 1997

Sherwood, Mrs Mary Martha. *Little Henry and his bearer.* 1814

Tillotson, Giles. *Jaipur Nama: Tales from the Pink City.* Penguin Books India. New Delhi. 2006

Tillotson, Giles. *Nagaur: A garden palace in Rajasthan.* Mehrangarh Museum Trust. Jodhpur. 2010

Titley, Norah & Wood, Frances. *Oriental Gardens.* The British Library. London. 1991

Tully, Mark. *No Full Stops in India.* Penguin Books. London. 1991

Tyabji, Surayya. *Mirch Masala: One Hundred Indian Recipes.* Sangam Books. Bombay. 1975

White, Stephen. *Building in the Garden. The Architecture of Joseph Allen Stein in India and California.* Oxford University Press—Oxford India Paperbacks. New Delhi. 1998

Wilkinson, Theon. *Two Monsoons.* Duckworth. London. 1976

Winchester, Simon & Rupert. *Simon Winchester's Calcutta.* Lonely Planet Publications. Footscray. 2004

Zaman, Niaz. *The art of Kantha Embroidery.* University Press Limited. Dhaka. 1993

About the Author

Photograph by Gaye Paterson

Claudia Hyles grew up in Sydney where she was born in 1947. She has lived in Canberra since 1970 with years posted in Papua New Guinea, Great Britain, Trinidad & Tobago, Pakistan, Laos, Thailand, Kenya, Vietnam and India. Her first visit to India was in 1968 as a university student, something from which she has never recovered – in the nicest way possible. She has found many ways to return, leading tour groups, purchasing for art gallery shops, attending festivals, working for six months for the Jaipur Virasat Foundation and for sheer unadulterated pleasure. She has written many articles and several books on food, art and life and has been a book reviewer since last century. She treasures her link with the National Gallery of Australia where she has worked as volunteer and staffer since 1983. Her children, their partners and her grandchildren fill her with joy.